"On the centenary of Mend
there can be no finer testam(
his own words. The presem cu...... thoroughness and skill, making available the fullest translation of Bellis s memoirs into English to date. Those who only know this martyr to bigotry from the Bernard Malamud novel will have a revelatory experience when they read Beilis's own gripping and heart-rending account of his sufferings."

– Professor Richard S. Levy, University of Illinois at Chicago, editor of *Antisemitism: A Historical Encyclopedia of Prejudice and Persecution*

"Aside from the expert editing, the most important new feature in this edition is the essay 'Pulitzer Plagiarism: What Bernard Malamud's *The Fixer* Owes to the Memoir of Mendel Beilis.' The extent to which Malamud lifted lengthy passages from Beilis's account of his imprisonment is much too great to be justified by artistic freedom. But one can understand Malamud's temptation: Beilis's description has great power, in part because of its simplicity, its graphic details. This modern Job, an ordinary Jew hit by a lightning bolt of bad fortune, asks 'Why me?' His neighbors asked the same, since 'our Mendel,' they all affirmed, was such a likeable sort — with supportive friendships, bizarre as it seems, that included members of the anti-Semitic Black Hundreds and the Orthodox priest of the area. The Beilis Affair, now largely forgotten, gripped Czarist Russia perhaps even more potently than the Dreyfus Affair had gripped France. Readers, ordinary and scholarly, will find Beilis's story fascinating, and in many regards surprising."

– Professor Albert S. Lindemann, University of California, Santa Barbara, author of *The Jew Accused: Three Anti-Semitic Affairs*

BLOOD LIBEL

The Life and Memory of Mendel Beilis

Edited by Jay Beilis,
Jeremy Simcha Garber,
and Mark S. Stein

Includes:

- A short history of the Beilis case

- The 1925 memoir of Mendel Beilis, *The Story of My Sufferings* (first complete English translation)

- 1930 letter of Chief Rabbi Abraham Isaac Kook to Beilis's American readers

- The essay "Pulitzer Plagiarism: What Bernard Malamud's *The Fixer* Owes to the Memoir of Mendel Beilis"

- Afterword by Jay Beilis

Beilis Publishing   Chicago, IL

TO THE MEMORY OF MENDEL BEILIS

CONTENTS

—

PREFACE AND ACKNOWLEDGMENTS

The year 2011 marks the 100th anniversary of the arrest of Mendel Beilis in Czarist Russia on the false accusation that he ritually murdered a Christian child. The year 2013 will mark the 100th anniversary of Beilis's famous trial and his acquittal. It is a fitting time to republish Beilis's memoir, *The Story of My Sufferings*, which forms the heart of this book.

Beilis's memoir was first published in 1925 in Yiddish. An English edition was published in 1926, with translation by Harrison Goldberg. A second Yiddish edition was published in 1931. All three editions are of course now out of print.

Our edition is based on Harrison Goldberg's elegant translation for the 1926 English edition. We have gone back to the original Yiddish in many places to correct errors made by Goldberg, or to achieve greater clarity. However, we have not undertaken a completely new translation. A summary of the changes we have made to the 1926 English edition can be found in Appendix A.

We do present here, for the first time in English, some parts of Beilis's Yiddish-language memoir that were not included in the 1926 English edition. These include the last chapter, titled "In America," and a 1930 letter from Rabbi Abraham Isaac Kook, Ashkenazi Chief Rabbi of Palestine under the British Mandate, which was published in the 1931 Yiddish edition.

Another English edition of Beilis's memoir was published in 1992 under the title *Scapegoat On Trial*. That edition, which is also now out of print, omits the last three chapters of the memoir and appears to have been prepared with no reference to the original Yiddish version. We discuss the 1992 English edition in Appendix B.

Acknowledgments

At the end of the 1925 Yiddish edition, Beilis offered his thanks to those who had helped with the publication of his memoir. His acknowledgment reads as follows (translation by Jeremy Simcha Garber):

> At the close of my historical account, *The Story of My Sufferings*, I would like to express my heartfelt gratitude to my friends Dr. Y. Miller and Dr. Arnold Margolin (the latter formerly of Kiev and now residing in New York). They took a deep interest in my situation throughout the entire affair, and above all in recent years. They have now helped me to publish my book, making it possible for the Jewish world to learn of all I endured.
> My deepest thanks and best wishes to them both.
>
> Their truly devoted friend,
> Mendel Beilis

Margolin was Beilis's first lawyer. He was unable to represent Beilis at trial because he became himself a witness in the case. Margolin's account of the Beilis case is contained in his own book, *The Jews of Eastern Europe*, published in 1926.

It seems fitting to include here, as well, some of the thanks that Beilis gave to those who helped him to overcome the blood libel. Beilis expressed great appreciation for all the Jewish and Gentile lawyers who represented him. His most effusive thanks, however, went to his Gentile defenders who took up his cause outside the courtroom. In Chapter 26 of his memoir, he remarked:

For the first time during the trial, I became fully aware of the remarkable work performed by Messrs. Brazul-Brushkovsky [a journalist] and Krasovsky [a detective]; of their heroic efforts to uncover the highly-protected murderer. While in prison, I had only a vague idea of their energy and the results achieved by them in my behalf. I had already received some information about Mr. Margolin. I had never imagined, however, that "real" Russians, non-Jews such as Messrs. Yablonovsky [a journalist], Brushkovsky and Krasovsky, would actually sacrifice their safety and positions, all in the interest of truth. Never will I, or my family, forget, to the last day of our lives, these wonderful and enlightened men.

To similar effect is an interview Beilis gave to the *Jewish Daily Bulletin* shortly before his death in 1934. Beilis was asked: "Could Mr. Beilis give one outstanding impression of the trial in Kiev?" He responded:

> Yes. The Russian Gentiles, who sacrificed themselves for me. There was real heroism, real sacrifice. They knew that by defending me their careers would be ruined, even their very lives would not be safe. But they persisted because they knew I was innocent.

In addition to the memoir of Mendel Beilis, this book contains a short introduction to the Beilis case, a short chapter on Beilis's life in America, and an essay, titled "Pulitzer Plagiarism," about the relationship between Beilis's memoir and Bernard Malamud's Pulitzer Prize-winning novel *The Fixer*. A much shorter version of the essay "Pulitzer Plagiarism" was previously published in *Cardozo Law Review de novo*, the online companion to *Cardozo Law Review*. We thank this journal for permission to republish.

For assistance with translation from the Yiddish, we thank Miriam Stein. For assistance with translation from the Russian, we thank Vitaly

Lipkansky. For consultation on aspects of the Beilis case, we thank Edmund Levin, whose book on the case is scheduled to be published in 2013. For assistance with photographs, we thank Benjamin Shechter. Errors are our own.

Much of this book was prepared while one of the editors (Mark Stein) was an Academic Fellow at Harvard Law School, Petrie-Flom Center for Health Law Policy, Biotechnology, and Bioethics. We acknowledge with thanks the financial support of the Petrie-Flom Center.

INTRODUCTION

One of the great trials of the twentieth century was the 1913 blood-libel trial of Mendel Beilis in Czarist Russia. Beilis, a Jew, was arrested in 1911 by the Czarist secret police in Kiev and accused of ritually murdering a Christian boy to use his blood in baking matzah for Passover. Beilis was jailed for over two years, under horrible conditions, while awaiting trial. He heroically resisted all pressure to implicate himself or other Jews. In 1913, after a dramatic trial that riveted the Jewish people and much of the rest of the world, Beilis was acquitted by an all-Christian jury.

After his release, Beilis moved to Palestine, and then to New York. In 1925, he published a memoir in Yiddish.[1] In 1926, Beilis published an English translation of his memoir, titled *The Story of My Sufferings*, with translation by Harrison Goldberg.[2]

Beilis died in 1934. According to a report in the *New York Times*, his funeral was attended by over four thousand people.[3] The *New York Times* article notes that Beilis's fellow Jews "always believed that his conduct... saved his countrymen from a pogrom."[4] A history of the Eldridge Street Synagogue, where Beilis's funeral was held, describes the scene at his funeral as follows: "The crowd could not be contained in the sanctuary. As many as a dozen policemen failed to establish order in the streets."[5]

In this book, we present a new English edition of Beilis's thrilling memoir, *The Story of My Sufferings*.[6] We then consider the relationship between Beilis's memoir and Bernard Malamud's Pulitzer Prize-winning novel *The Fixer*.[7] It is widely known that *The Fixer* is based on Beilis's life.[8] Not widely known, however, is that in writing *The Fixer*, Malamud plagiarized extensively from Beilis's memoir.

A Short History of the Beilis Case

The evil legend that Jews ritually murder Christian children to make Passover matzah – the blood libel – dates back to the Middle Ages.[9] Many Jews have lost their lives as a result of blood-libel accusations over the centuries.

Ritual murder and the eating of human blood are of course completely contrary to the practices of every Jewish religious group. Traditional Judaism forbids even the eating of animal blood.[10] There is no credible evidence that any Jew has ever murdered a non-Jew to make Passover matzah, and a number of supposed occurrences have been conclusively disproved. In one case, in 1529, the supposed child victim was even found alive – but not before thirty Jews were tortured into confessing to his murder and burned at the stake.[11]

The Beilis case was unusual in that the blood libel was sponsored by a national government.[12] In February, 1911, a large number of deputies in the Russian *Duma* (lower house of parliament) had supported a measure to lift legal restrictions on Jews and allow them to live anywhere in Russia.[13] The prosecution of Beilis was widely seen as a response by autocratic Russia to this liberal challenge.[14] The reactionary Russian Justice Minister, Ivan Shcheglovitov, became the leader of a conspiracy to turn the murder of a Christian child into a blood libel against the Jews.[15] The prosecution of Beilis was endorsed by Czar Nicholas II himself, who was a vicious anti-Semite.[16]

When arrested in 1911, Beilis was the on-site supervisor of a large Jewish-owned brick factory in Kiev known as the Zaitsev brickworks. He lived in a modest house on the grounds with his wife and five children.[17]

—

2

He was a traditional yet transitional Jew, celebrating the Jewish Sabbath on Friday night,[18] but supervising the factory on Saturday.[19] His eldest son attended a Russian *gymnasium* (college preparatory school), while his younger children received a traditional Jewish education at a *cheder* (traditional Jewish grade school).[20]

The district in which Beilis lived was outside the "Pale of Settlement" – Jews were generally forbidden to live there. It was possible to receive a special dispensation to live outside the Pale, however, and Beilis's employer had obtained such a dispensation for him.[21]

On Sunday, March 20, 1911,[22] the body of a thirteen-year-old boy, Andrei (Andryusha) Yushchinsky, was discovered in a cave near the Zaitsev brickworks.[23] Yushchinsky had disappeared eight days earlier, on Saturday, March 12, after going to visit his friend Zhenya Cheberyak.[24] An autopsy showed that Yushchinsky had been stabbed forty-seven times.[25] He had been killed about four hours after eating breakfast, which would put the time of death at around 10:00 a.m., if, as all later agreed, he had died on the day he disappeared.[26]

At Yushchinsky's funeral, mourners encountered leaflets claiming that Jews had killed him to use his blood to make Passover matzah. The leaflets had been distributed by a member of the Black Hundreds, a powerful right-wing anti-Semitic movement. The leaflets urged Orthodox Christians to "beat up the Yids… until there is not a single Yid left in Russia."[27]

Many honest police and court officials in Kiev attempted to resist the blood libel in the Yushchinsky case; they attempted to conduct a proper investigation into the murder. Initially, the police suspected Yushchinsky's mother and stepfather. Yushchinsky's father had disappeared while serving in the army during the Russo-Japanese war.[28] There was a rumor that Yushchinsky's father had left him a trust fund, possibly providing a motive for murder. But the rumor of a trust fund proved false, and Yushchinsky's family had strong alibis.[29]

After investigating and exonerating Yushchinsky's family, police detectives in Kiev concluded that the perpetrators of the crime were a gang of criminals associated with Vera Cheberyak, the mother of the playmate Yushchinsky had been with on the day he disappeared. Cheberyak's apartment was a base of operations for the gang, and she fenced stolen property for them. The cave in which Yushchinsky's body was discovered was about equidistant between Cheberyak's apartment and the brickworks where Beilis worked.[30]

A considerable amount of evidence linked the Cheberyak gang to the murder. At Beilis's trial, two sisters testified that a part of a pillowcase found with Yushchinsky's body had the same design as a set of pillowcases in Cheberyak's apartment. One of the sisters, a seamstress, had been asked by Cheberyak to sew a new set of four pillowcases, and she noticed that one pillowcase of the old set was missing.[31]

Cheberyak's downstairs neighbor, who was not friendly to Cheberyak, testified that on a morning in early March, 1911, between 10:00 and 11:00, she heard the cries of a child from Cheberyak's apartment, which were cut off. She then heard people carrying a burden. The neighbor stated: "I immediately understood that they were carrying whoever had been crying out."[32]

When the police searched Cheberyak's apartment after the murder, one of the detectives attempted to question Cheberyak's son Zhenya, who had been with Yushchinsky on the day he died. However, according to the detective, Cheberyak made threatening gestures to her son, and he did not say anything.[33]

Three members of the Cheberyak gang in particular were suspected of involvement in the murder. One, while being questioned by

—

4

officials about the murder, attempted to escape through a fourth-story window and fell to his death.[34]   Another reportedly confessed his involvement to investigators working on behalf of Beilis's defense,[35] though he denied he had done so at trial.[36]

Also the object of some suspicion, but probably not involved in the murder, was Cheberyak's blind young lover. She had blinded him in a fit of jealous rage by throwing acid in his face, but they still maintained a relationship.[37]   (Cheberyak's husband was a timid civil servant who worked at night and did not try to interfere in his wife's activities.)[38]

Kiev officials had two theories as to why members of the Cheberyak gang killed Yushchinsky, both of which might have been true. The Cheberyak gang had benefited greatly from the 1905 pogrom against the Jews in Kiev, with its attendant looting; the gang had acquired a large amount of stolen property.[39] One theorized motive for the murder was that the gang was attempting to foment another pogrom.[40]   Shortly after Yushchinsky's body was discovered, anonymous letters were mailed to Yushchinsky's mother, the police, the coroner, and others, alleging that Yushchinsky had been ritually murdered by Jews. The letters delivered to Yushchinsky's mother and the coroner were mailed before the coroner had completed his autopsy. These letters reportedly showed a close familiarity with the number of wounds on Yushchinsky's body. The author Maurice Samuel, whose book *Blood Accusation* is to date the most comprehensive account of the Beilis case, suggests that the anonymous letters must have been sent by a person connected with the murder, as some of Yushchinsky's wounds were barely visible.[41]

The second theory as to why the Cheberyak gang killed Yushchinsky is that they were silencing a possible informant. Though it was well known in the neighborhood that Cheberyak's apartment was a den of thieves, her apartment had never been raided by the police until

March 10, 1911, two days before Yushchinsky's disappearance.[42] There was a rumor, which the police never managed to track down to its source, that Yushchinsky and his friend Zhenya Cheberyak had quarreled on the day of Yushchinsky's disappearance, with Zhenya Cheberyak threatening to tell Yushchinsky's mother that Yushchinsky was playing hooky from school, and Yushchinsky threatening to tell police that there were stolen goods in Zhenya's mother's apartment.[43]

The first police detective in charge of the Yushchinsky murder investigation, Mishchuk, was fired after he concluded that the Cheberyak gang was responsible for the murder. The government also prosecuted and jailed Mishchuk on trumped-up charges.[44] The second police detective in charge of the investigation was Nikolai Krasovsky, who had a reputation as a sort of Russian Sherlock Holmes.[45] Krasovsky pretended to cooperate with the Black Hundreds in making out a case of ritual murder,[46] but he too tried to conduct a proper investigation. With the aid of the honest prosecutor, Brandorf, and the honest investigating magistrate, Fenenko, Krasovsky actually had Vera Cheberyak arrested, on June 9, 1911.[47]

However, the anti-Semitic Black Hundreds and their allies in the Kiev and national governments prevented the prosecution of members of the Cheberyak gang. The prosecutor of the Kiev appellate court, Chaplinsky, was part of the blood-libel conspiracy, and he worked to thwart the efforts of the honest officials in Kiev. After five weeks in jail, Vera Cheberyak was released.[48] Soon thereafter, on July 22, 1911, Beilis was arrested for the murder of Yushchinsky.[49] Beilis was the logical target of the blood libel, as he was the only Jew who lived in the neighborhood where Yushchinsky's body was found.

Having selected Beilis as a scapegoat, the government also disposed of the honest local officials who stood in the way of the blood libel. After a few months, prosecutor Brandorf was fired. Detective

—
6

Krasovsky was transferred and, a few months later, was also fired. Fenenko, the investigating magistrate, could not so easily be disposed of, but he was eventually taken off the case as well.[50]

After he was fired by the government, Krasovsky reentered the case as a private investigator, pursuing his theory that the murder was committed by the Cheberyak gang. The government then prosecuted Krasovsky on a trumped-up charge: it alleged that he had embezzled sixteen kopeks (eight cents) from a prisoner nine years previously.[51] Krasovsky went to trial and was acquitted, then resumed his investigation, uncovering valuable information.[52] At Beilis's trial, Krasovsky testified that he was convinced the murder was committed by Cheberyak's gang.[53] Fenenko, the investigating magistrate initially in charge of the case, likewise testified that he was convinced the murder was committed in Cheberyak's apartment.[54]

Beilis was arrested for the Yushchinsky murder on July 22, 1911. He then remained in prison, awaiting trial, for over two years. The initial indictment against Beilis accused him of murdering Andryusha Yushchinsky, but did not specifically allege ritual murder. The government later drew up a second indictment against Beilis, specifically alleging ritual murder. Of the five-member board of judges that was required to approve the second indictment, two members resigned rather than sign the indictment. The other three judges approved the indictment on the ground that Beilis had been in prison so long that he must finally be indicted and tried.[55]

Beilis was finally brought to trial on September 25, 1913. The government's case against him, exceedingly weak from the beginning, became even weaker at the trial, as witnesses who had given pretrial statements implicating Beilis, under pressure from the government, repudiated those statements.[56] The major witness who initially implicated

Beilis was Shakhovsky, a lamplighter. Shakhovsky evidently bore a grudge against Beilis because Beilis had threatened to have him arrested for stealing wood from the brick factory.[57] At trial, however, Shakhovsky recanted; he testified that a police investigator had plied him with vodka to get him to incriminate Beilis.[58]

The government's contention at the trial was that the murdered child Andryusha Yushchinsky, along with his friend Zhenya Cheberyak and other children, was playing in the yard of the Zaitsev brickworks on Saturday morning, March 12, 1911. There was a large machine in the yard, a clay mixer, on which children often played until they were shooed away by a janitor.[59] The government claimed that Beilis abducted Yushchinsky that morning, in broad daylight, in sight of the other children. The factory yard was full of people on that day, as bricks were being hauled away.[60]

At trial, the only witnesses who tied Beilis to the crime were from the Cheberyak family: Vera Cheberyak, her husband, and her daughter Lyudmilla. Cheberyak's son Zhenya and another daughter, Valya, had died before trial.[61] Apparently, they died of dysentery, though an agent of the Justice Minister speculated, in a confidential report, that "it is possible that the mother herself poisoned them, a matter which competent persons consider more than likely."[62]

Vera Cheberyak and her husband testified that Zhenya had told them, before he died, that he, Yushchinsky, and other children had gone to play on the clay mixer, and that Yushchinsky had been abducted by Beilis.[63] Cheberyak's daughter Lyudmilla testified that she had been present and that she had actually witnessed these events.[64] One absurdity of this story is that none of the Cheberyaks had mentioned it when Vera Cheberyak herself was jailed under suspicion of murdering Yushchinsky.[65] The story also was contradicted by a girl, Dunya, who Lyudmilla

—

Cheberyak testified was in the group that played on the clay mixer. Dunya testified that "[i]t never happened."[66]

Beilis had a strong alibi that resulted, ironically, from his incomplete devotion to Jewish religious practices. On the Saturday morning when he was supposed to have abducted Yushchinsky, Beilis was working in one of the buildings of the brickworks, in full view of co-workers.[67] Receipt slips for the shipment of bricks, countersigned by Beilis, were produced in evidence.[68] At trial, one of the prosecuting attorneys had to argue, in summation, that Beilis could have excused himself for a few minutes, abducted Yushchinsky, and then returned to his duties.[69]

Beilis was also fortunate in that his good reputation made it difficult for the government to fabricate evidence against him. Beilis was very well-liked by his co-workers and neighbors, and even by anti-Semites who knew him.[70] As Professor Albert Lindemann puts it,

> Mendel Beilis was a modest person, but he seems to have been one of the most respected, even beloved men in his neighborhood. That neighborhood, it should be noted, was composed entirely of Gentiles, since Beilis and his family, benefiting from special privileges, did not live in the Jewish districts of the city. The prosecution was repeatedly frustrated in its efforts to get hostile testimony against Beilis. Time and again, those who knew him had only praise for 'our Mendel.'[71]

Under the Czarist procedure governing criminal trials, the victim of a crime could participate in a criminal trial in order to receive an award of compensation from the accused. Yushchinsky's mother was represented at Beilis's trial by two anti-Semitic lawyers, one of whom was a *Duma* representative.[72] However, Yushchinsky's mother had not asked for this representation, and her testimony was not helpful to the prosecution. As to

—

9

who may have killed her son, she testified: "I cannot suspect anyone."[73]

Despite the feebleness of the government's case against Beilis, the outcome of the trial was not a foregone conclusion. The government had packed the jury, and seven of the twelve jurors were members of a Black Hundreds organization.[74] The presiding judge, who had sometimes been fair in presiding over testimony, gave a charge to the jury, just before it retired, that was extraordinarily prejudicial to Beilis.[75]

The reading of the verdict was a moment of high drama. The jury was required to answer two questions, one as to whether the crime was committed in the manner charged, and the second as to whether Beilis committed the crime. The first question was as follows:

> Has it been proved that on March 12, 1911, in one of the buildings of the Zaitsev brick factory... Andrey Yushchinsky was gagged, and wounds inflicted on him... and that when he had lost five glasses of blood, other wounds were inflicted on him... and that these wounds totaling forty-seven caused Yushchinsky agonizing pain and led to almost total loss of blood and to his death?[76]

To this question, the jury foreman answered: "Yes, it has been proved."[77] At this point, Beilis was certain that he would be found guilty of the crime. But then, the second question:

> Is the accused, Mendel Teviev Beilis, guilty of having entered into collusion with others, who have not been discovered in the investigation, in a premeditated plan prompted by religious fanaticism to murder the boy Andrey Yushchinsky, and did the accused in order to carry out his intentions, seize Yushchinsky... and drag him off to one of the buildings of the brick factory?[78]

To this question, the foreman answered: "No. Not guilty."[79]

While some sources (including the 1926 English translation of Beilis's memoir) report that the verdict of "not guilty" was unanimous, it is now widely accepted that the verdict was evenly divided, at six to six, resulting in an acquittal.[80] According to Oskar Gruzenberg, one of Beilis's lawyers, the vote to convict was initially seven to five, which would have led to a verdict of "guilty" under Russian law at the time. However, "when the foreman began taking the final vote, one peasant rose to his feet, prayed to the icon, and said resolutely, 'I don't want to have this sin on my soul – he's not guilty.'"[81]

Despite the enigmatic character of the verdict, it was for the most part perceived as a repudiation of the blood libel. Indeed, the trial of Mendel Beilis proved to be the last of its kind; the blood libel has persisted, but no government has since used it to attempt judicial murder.[82]

As a result of his trial and acquittal, Beilis became an enormous hero and celebrity. He could have made a great deal of money capitalizing on his fame, but he refused to do so.[83] He and his family moved to Palestine, even though, as he later wrote, "the word Palestine conjured up a waste and barren land."[84] Beilis actually came to love life in Palestine, but he could not make a living there, so he moved with his family to New York in the early 1920's.[85] Interviewed in December, 1933, six months before his death, Beilis stated: "I still long for Palestine."[86]

The Story of My Sufferings is a memoir, not a transcript. There are inevitably some inaccuracies, and some events are not presented in the order they occurred. On the whole, however, Beilis's account matches up surprisingly well with other accounts, including newspaper reports and books about the case that contain English translations of excerpts from the trial transcript.[87] Beilis's memoir presents an essentially true picture of historical events as well as a vivid recreation of his own experience.

A Note on Dates: Throughout this volume, all dates of events occurring in Czarist Russia are given under the old Russian calendar.[88]

11

THE STORY OF MY SUFFERINGS

by Mendel Beilis

Translated by Harrison Goldberg and Jeremy Simcha Garber

PUBLISHERS' NOTE [from the 1926 edition]

The publishers of Mendel Beilis's memoirs were confronted with a double opportunity. The first was of national concern for the Jewish people. It was not only Mendel Beilis who was indicted but the Jewish people; it was not Beilis alone who was acquitted of the terrible charge of ritual murder, but his entire race. It is thus important to preserve this notorious incident in the history of Jewish life in the Diaspora in the form of a book, to record the fate which almost befell every Russian Jew, as also the sufferings which fell to the share of Mendel Beilis, scapegoat for a people.

The second purpose of this publication is to ensure in some slight measure the continued existence of the martyr. Mendel Beilis could very easily have benefited financially from the tale of his own experiences and that of his people. He refused, however. He regarded those experiences as too holy for commercialization.

This volume – the publishers believe – will give the Jewish people the opportunity to repay in slight measure the onerous duties which Beilis undertook for the Jewish people, to show him a portion of the honor befitting a martyr for his people.

The publishers herewith wish to express their thanks to Herman Bernstein and Arnold D. Margolin, attorney for Mr. Beilis, both of whom gave of themselves freely in counsel and effort to ensure the publication of this volume.

THE PUBLISHERS

—

13

Chapter 1: Work and Peace

When Czar Nicholas II ascended the throne of Russia, it was a time of much hope for the Jewish people. Stories were afloat that Nicholas was friendly to the Jews, and that this had led him to quarrel with his father, Czar Alexander III. There was even a rumor that Nicholas intended to marry a Jewish girl. Relief and sympathy were the least that the Jews expected. Here would be a ruler of justice and clemency.

History gave the lie to these hopes. What actual happiness the Jews found under the reign of Nicholas II is known only too well to the world. It was my lot, however, to feel, more than anyone else, the weight of his sovereign arm. Why I should have been particularly selected for my role is one of the secrets of Providence.

It was about a year after I had returned from my period of military service, that I married and settled down in Mezhigorye, a town about eight miles from Kiev. I secured work at a brick-kiln which belonged to my wife's uncle, and lived a quiet and uneventful existence.

Some time later I received a letter from a cousin of mine, in which he offered me the superintendentship of a brick-kiln about to be erected. The well-known sugar-king Zaitsev had a hospital for the poor in Kiev, of which my cousin was superintendent. In order to establish a perpetual endowment for the hospital, Zaitsev decided to build a brick-kiln, the profits of which would maintain the hospital. My cousin himself, being entirely unacquainted with brick manufacturing, thought of me. Kiev meant only better opportunities for me, and I therefore accepted the position.

The factory, of which I was now the overseer, was situated on the borderline of two city districts, the Plossky and the Lukianovsky. The Jews had the right to reside in the Plossky district. Zaitsev's hospital and my cousin's residence were located within that boundary. The factory itself was "outside the Pale," and Jews were forbidden to live there. It was due only to Zaitsev's influence that I was permitted to live on this "sacred" territory. Since he was a merchant of what was known as the "first guild," the Russian law permitted him to have a Jewish employee. In the population of ten thousand that lived in the vicinity of the factory, I was the only Jew. I found no difficulty, however, even though there were about five hundred Christians employed within the factory.

My personal contacts with people in the locality were limited. My work was restricted to the office, where I supervised the selling and the shipping. I never experienced any unpleasantness with the Christians of the neighborhood, with the exception of a period in 1905, during the Revolution, when a torrent of pogroms swept over every Jewish city and town. When I was endangered, the local Orthodox priest came to my rescue; he commanded that I be guarded because I was the only Jew in the district.

The priest's protection during the pogroms was a reward for favors I had done him. It had been decided to build a school for a local orphanage, of which the priest was a director. He came to me and requested that I sell him the bricks at cheaper rates. I took the matter up with Zaitsev, and finally secured the bricks at a very low rate.

There was another thing for which the priest felt indebted to me. Some distance away from our factory was one owned by a Christian, Shevchenko. To ride to the district cemetery, one had to pass through the grounds of both factories. When I first came to the town, the priest asked me for permission to allow the various funeral processions to trespass on the factory grounds. I consented. When Shevchenko was asked for the same, he refused. The priest often used to hold it up before the Christians: "You see, the Christian did not give permission, but the Jew did."

And thus I lived about fifteen years in our house on the factory grounds. I was profiting by the privileges to be obtained in a large city. One of my boys was attending a governmental *gymnasium* (college preparatory school) in Kiev; the younger ones were going to a *cheder* (Jewish religious school). It was quite a distance from the factory to the city of Kiev, it is true. But what more could one ask? I thanked the Lord for what I had, and was satisfied with my secure and respectable position.

Everything pointed to a peaceful future. It seemed that I had the right to expect to end my days in contentment. Who could have known that the "demon of destruction" was dancing behind me, jeering at all my hopes and plans?

Then came 1911, and plunged me into a swirl of misfortune – misfortune which I shall never forget, and which broke my life for all time.

Chapter 2: The Murder of the Boy Yushchinsky

Though fourteen years have passed, the old scenes stand out with remarkable vividness, as if they had been etched on my brain. It was on the 20th of March. Everything was as usual. The dawn had not yet broken when I got up and went to the office.

The window which I faced while at my desk overlooked the street. As I looked through the window on that cold, dark morning, I saw people hurrying somewhere, all in one direction. It was the usual thing to see individual workers coming to the factory at that time, or occasional passers-by. But now there were large groups of people, walking rapidly, coming from various streets. I went out to discover the cause of the commotion, and was told by one of the crowd that the body of a murdered child had been found in the vicinity.

In a few hours the papers carried the news that in the Lukianovsky district, within a half mile of the factory, the body of a murdered boy, Andryusha Yushchinsky, had been found. The body had first been discovered in a cave, where the murdered boy, covered with wounds, had apparently been deposited.

That evening, one of my Christian neighbors came to visit me. He was a member of the "Double-Headed Eagle," a powerful Black Hundreds organization. He told me that he read in the newspaper of his organization that the murder of Yushchinsky was not of the usual kind; that the child had been murdered by Jews for purposes of "ritual." The newspaper, which went by the name of the organization, was a "patriotic" one; it was devoted to the "saving of Russia from the Jews."

At the time of Yushchinsky's burial, three days after his discovery, handbills were already being circulated, calling upon Christians to exterminate the Jews, charging the Jews with having slain Yushchinsky "for the Jewish Passover." Vengeance was to be taken for the boy's blood.

This was the first attempt to direct the attention away from the real culprits, and to start the religious pot boiling in order to divert correct suspicions.

The ordinary people, however – those who were not concerned with great plans for the salvation of Russia – were saying that the murder had been committed by a certain Vera Cheberyak or by Yushchinsky's mother.

Suspicion had at once attached to Yushchinsky's mother because she had not betrayed any anxiety when her boy first disappeared, or since. Yushchinsky disappeared on the 12th and was found on the 20th. How could one explain the fact that his mother had not at once notified the police, nor shown any apparent interest in his finding, nor evidenced any grief? The neighbors were not slow to comment on these facts. As time went on, further suspicions were awakened.

Andryusha Yushchinsky's father, who had been killed in the Russo-Japanese war, had supposedly left his son five hundred rubles, which the bank held in trust for the boy, and which he could not get until he became of age. In the meanwhile, Andryusha's mother had found a fiancé for herself, who was dissatisfied with the prospect of not receiving any of the five hundred rubles. This caused people to suspect Yushchinsky's mother of complicity in the murder.

The Cheberyak woman (in fact, the true culprit) was suspected on other grounds. First of all, it was known that Andryusha and her own boy, Zhenya, were schoolmates of the same age – thirteen years – and that Andryusha would often stay over night at the Cheberyak house. Also, hundreds of people came to see Yushchinsky's body and none of them recognized him; the boy's face was swollen out of recognition. Vera Cheberyak recognized him at once, which fact aroused suspicion.

Vera Cheberyak was well known around the Lukianovsky district. Her husband, who was a clerk at the telegraph office, was seldom at home, even at night. She was known to have dealings with a gang of thieves. These were not ordinary breakers of the law, however. They used to dress royally; some even appearing in officers' uniforms. In this gang were her brother, Singayevsky, and two other friends, Latyshev and Rudzinsky. They would do the stealing and she would sell the loot. The neighbors were fully aware of her nefarious activities, but no one dared to interfere.

Cheberyak lived in a house belonging to a Christian by the name of Zakharchenko, who lived close to our factory, and who was himself a member of the Black Hundreds. Zakharchenko often used to confide in me how happy he would be to get rid of Cheberyak. He was afraid, however, to start trouble. He told me several times, after the murder, that he felt certain that it had taken place in Cheberyak's house, in that den of crime.

Vera Cheberyak was in fact arrested for Yushchinsky's murder. Three days after her arrest, the Moscow police arrested three suspicious young men, and as they were found to be residents of Kiev, they were sent to that city. Upon examination it was found that they had left Kiev on March the 12ᵗʰ, that is, on the day of Yushchinsky's disappearance, and that on the same day they had been in Vera's house, where they had spent some time. As a matter of fact, these were actually the three leaders of her gang, Singayevsky, Latyshev and Rudzinsky.

When policemen from the Lukianovsky station were brought down to identify the apprehended trio, the police were terribly frightened. For in the arrested men they recognized the gentlemen whom they had often seen parading in officers' uniform, and to whom they had so often extended the officers' salute, believing them to be genuine officers. The police had known that these gentlemen used to visit Cheberyak's house, but they had never doubted their honesty.

Upon the arrest of these three, the "Double-Headed Eagle" came out with loud indignation. "What a public scandal! Is it possible that the Jews who have murdered Yushchinsky should be allowed to get off scot-free, while such innocent persons are to be imprisoned? Let the child be taken out of its grave; and let the world see how the body has been stabbed by the Jews."

The uproar of the Black Hundreds had its effect. The boy's body was disinterred, and the notorious Professor Sikorsky declared that it was no usual murder; that it had been committed for "religious purposes," which "could be seen" from the stabs, and their number, "thirteen."

In the beginning, it all seemed ludicrous. Every one by this time was certain that the crime had been the work of Cheberyak's gang, and there were sufficient proofs for that, and here were people who came with fantastic tales of "thirteen stabs" and "religious purposes." However, it proved to be no joke. The Black Hundreds worked out a devilish plan against the Jews, and since the pogromists had powerful influence at the time, they proceeded energetically to realize their plan.

Chapter 3: My Arrest

The case of Yushchinsky's murder was taken over by Investigating Magistrate Fenenko. The investigating magistrate began to visit our neighborhood frequently. He would measure the distances from the cave where Yushchinsky's body had been found: to the factory, to Cheberyak's house. He investigated in this manner for several months. The pogromists' newspapers continued at their work of whitewashing the gang of thieves and throwing accusations at the Jewish people.

Of a sudden, Russian detectives began to visit our factory. They asked my children whether they had known the Yushchinsky boy, and whether they used to play with him. One of the detectives occupied the house opposite ours, and watched wherever I went and whatever I did. I was informed that the detectives, seeing that the investigation was not going well, began to give sweets to the Christian children of the neighborhood in order to make them say that Andryusha used to visit us, and that my children played with him.

After a while, one of the detectives, Polishchuk, began to visit me rather frequently. He once told me that there was a "feeling" that the crime had been committed on the factory premises, and furthermore that it must have been my work.

On the morning following Polishchuk's declaration, a squad of about ten persons appeared at the factory in company with Fenenko, the investigating magistrate. Fenenko appeared to be in the best of moods, as he began asking me:

"You are the manager of this factory?"

"Yes."

"Since when?"

"For about fifteen years."

"Are there any other Jews here besides you?"

"No. I am here alone."

"You are a Jew, are you not? Where do you go to pray? Is there a synagogue here?"

"I am a Jew. There is no synagogue here; one can pray at home as well."

"Do you observe the Sabbath?"

"The factory is kept running on Saturdays, so that I cannot leave the place."

Suddenly he asked me:

"Have you a cow? Do you sell milk?"

"I have a cow," was my answer. "But I do not sell milk; we need all of it for the house."

"And when a good friend of yours, let us say, comes to you, do you sell him a glass of milk?"

"When a good friend of mine comes to me, I give him food and drink, milk also, but I never sell it."

I simply could not understand the necessity of these questions about my piety and as to whether I went to synagogue. Had the authorities become so pious that they could not tolerate my praying without the official *minyan* (ten worshippers) required by the Jewish law? And what was the purpose of all those questions about the cow and the milk?

Fenenko and his confreres seemed quite satisfied and bid me

—

23

a cordial goodbye. As they were leaving, I noticed that one of them photographed me. Evidently, they were quite earnest about their work.

Fenenko's visit to the factory occurred on Thursday, the 21st of July, 1911, on *Tisha B'Av*, a day of fasting for the Jews. On this day, the Jews bewail their great misfortune, the destruction of the Temple, and their exile from the Homeland, from Zion, from which time all their sufferings in the Exile date. Dark clouds foretold my own misfortune, but still I was totally unprepared when it came.

The next day was Friday, July the 22nd. At dawn, when everybody was still fast asleep, I heard a great commotion, as if caused by a great many horsemen. Before I had a chance to look out, I heard a loud banging on the door. I was naturally quite alarmed. What could have happened at this time of morning? In all the fifteen years that I had lived at the factory, I had never heard such noise. In the meantime, the knocking grew louder.

My first thought was that a fire had broken out at the factory. I rushed to the window, and although it was quite dark, I could recognize the well-known uniforms of the gendarmes. What could the gendarmes be doing here at night? Why all that knocking at the door? Everything turned dark before my eyes; my head swam; I nearly swooned with fright. The ceaseless knocking, however, made me realize that now was not the time for reflection, and I rushed to open the door.

In swarmed a large squad of gendarmes with Colonel Kuliabko, the notorious chief of the *Okhrana* (secret political police) at their head. After placing a guard at the door, Colonel Kuliabko approached me closely and asked with severity:

"Are you Beilis?"

"Yes."

"In the name of His Majesty, you are arrested. Get dressed," thundered his diabolical voice.

In the meantime, my wife and children awoke, and a general wail began. The children were frightened by the glittering uniforms and swords and were pulling with all their might for me to protect them. The poor things did not know that their father was helpless himself, and needed protection and help from others.

I was taken from my family. None was permitted to come near me. I was not allowed to say a word to my wife. In silence, restraining my tears, I dressed myself, and – without being allowed to reassure my children or to kiss them goodbye – I was taken away by the police.

The colonel remained in my home to conduct a search, while I was taken to the *Okhrana* headquarters. On the way, we met many of the workers going toward our factory. I felt ashamed and asked the police to walk with me on the sidewalk instead of on the street (walking on the street being the custom when police escorted arrested persons). The police refused to grant me that favor, however.

I was later informed that around the time of my arrest, Vera Cheberyak and her gang of thieves, and also Madam Yushchinsky, were released from jail as innocent and wrongly suspected persons.

Chapter 4: At the Okhrana Headquarters

It was still quiet in the *Okhrana* headquarters when we arrived there. The Russian officials did not care, as a rule, to get up too early. The desk sergeant was busy with his books, and was issuing orders to some clerks and spies. The latter looked at me with cunning and piercing eyes.

I had never imagined, in the course of my peaceful work, that I should ever be arrested and have to sit in the *Okhrana* headquarters, watched by a deputy who would not take his eyes from me for a second. But as the saying is, "There is no insurance against prison and death."

I sat there in a fever; hot and cold at the same time. I had a fierce headache. Presently I heard the stamping of horses' hooves, and later the tinkling of spurs in the hall. The door opened, and the gendarmes who had remained in my house for the search entered. Seeing that the gendarmes were along, I felt more assured.

Then tea was brought in. I was asked whether I should like something to eat, but I thanked them for their courtesy. I could not touch the tea, though my tongue was as dry as hot sand. I was thinking all the time: "What is coming next? Why am I arrested?"

Finally Kuliabko came in. He handed me a large sheet of paper, a questionnaire. I was to answer the following questions:

Who are you?

Whence do you come?

Who is your father?

What is your religion?

Do you have any relatives?

And finally there was the question: What do you know of Yushchinsky's murder?

Kuliabko left the room, telling me: "When you have filled out the questions, ring the bell, and I shall come back."

When I noticed the last question, I felt "the knife at my throat." I at last understood what had happened. I tried to find consolation in the form of the question: What did I know about the murder? If so, I was no more than a witness.

I answered all the questions. As for the murder, I stated that I knew nothing, except what people in the street were talking about it. Who had perpetrated it, and the purpose, I did not know.

I rang the bell. Kuliabko entered, looked over my replies, and said: "Is that all? Nonsense. If you do not tell me the truth, I'll send you up to the Petropavlovsky Fortress (a well known political prison in St. Petersburg)." He banged the door furiously and left the room.

About four in the afternoon, I heard the weeping of a child; it sounded like my own. I finally recognized the voice of one of my children. Out of sheer horror, I began to knock my head against the wall. I knew that my boy was very timid and nervous, being especially afraid of the police. I actually feared he might die under their hands.

While he was crying, the door opened, and Kuliabko re-entered the room.

"See, your boy is also telling lies..."

"What lies?" I asked.

"Zhenya, come in!" He brought in Cheberyak's boy, and

turning towards me, snapped:

"Zhenya says that your boy used to play with Andryusha, and your boy denies it."

Thereupon the colonel led the boy out of the room. A few minutes later, I heard footsteps in the hall. I looked through the grating and saw the deputy leading my boy, eight years old. I felt a violent tug at my heart, as I saw the deputy lock my boy in one of the cells. I expected to be held for a few hours, to be interrogated and finally released. I was innocent, and they were bound to see that a mistake had occurred. Meanwhile, all my thoughts were preoccupied with my child. Why had they brought him into this hell?

In the evening, a Christian woman came in and said, "Your child is here, but have no fear. I am looking after him. I am a mother myself; I understand your suffering and sympathize with you. Have no fears: God saves the honest men."

As night came on, I remembered that this was the first Friday night in all my life that the evening was spoiled. I thought of my usual Friday nights with the candles on the table, with the children dressed in their Sabbath best, and everybody so warm and friendly. And now? The house in disorder. My poor wife alone at the cheerless table. No light, no joy. And all of them weeping their eyes out. I almost forgot my own troubles, thinking of my unfortunate boy imprisoned and my mourning family. I rang the bell, and Kuliabko came in.

"Listen," I said to him, "I do not care what happens to me. The truth will out and I shall be liberated, but why keep my child a prisoner? You are yourself a father. My child may fall ill here, and it will be on your conscience. Can't you release my boy?"

28

He smiled at me. "Tell me the truth."

"What do you want: truth or falsehood? Even if you would insist, I could tell no lies. I am innocent."

"Nonsense, nonsense," he motioned with his hand. "I shall send you to prison, and then you will change your talk."

He went out with the usual banging of the door, and I remained alone. All along, I expected: another minute, just one minute, and I shall be freed. But when I heard the clock strike midnight, I realized that I was expected to spend the night in the place. I could not sleep. From time to time I heard the coughing of my boy, and it made my very brain reel.

Saturday morning, the Christian woman came in again and told me that she had slept in the same room with my child.

About noon, I heard somebody asking my boy: "Will you be able to get home by yourself, or shall I send a man to take you home?"

An hour later, a deputy came into my room, and told me with a smile that he had brought the boy to the street-car, but the boy refused to board it, and ran home on foot. With the boy freed, I felt happier.

On Sunday I again heard children's voices. Those were my children; they must have been brought to the *Okhrana* headquarters for questioning. I was given permission to go out into the hall for a minute to see the children and to greet them. In a moment we were separated again.

Eight long days I was kept in the *Okhrana* jail. None of the officials came to see me. This increased my anxiety. I hoped for the best, but expected the worst. If they ask me nothing, it looks as though this will continue without end. Why? Why?

In the evening of August 3rd, a deputy entered my room and told me to get ready to go to the investigating magistrate. This cheered me up. At last! Whatever happens, at least I'll find out just how things stand. I dressed quickly and two deputies escorted me to the magistrate.

During the short time I had spent in jail, I had almost forgotten what the streets looked like. I looked at the carefree passers-by and enjoyed the freedom and light as though I had never experienced them before. I was considerably weakened by my enforced seclusion, and found it rather hard to walk. I asked my guard to use the street-car.

"You are an arrested person, and you cannot travel with other people," was the abrupt decision of one of the deputies.

Some of the passers-by recognized me, and I was pointed at by others.

Chapter 5: The Inquisition

Exhausted by all the unwarranted insults to which I was subjected at the *Okhrana* headquarters, and weakened by the long march through the city under the escort of the policemen, I could hardly reach the district court. Upon our arrival, I was brought into a large hall in which there were Fenenko, the investigating magistrate; Karbovsky, the prosecutor; and Karbovsky's assistant, Loshkarev.

They looked at each other significantly, as though the outcome of the meeting was a foregone conclusion. I felt rather heavy at heart, especially when I remembered the questions put to me at the house by Fenenko. There was a mocking tone to them.

Ordinarily, the police who bring an arrested person to the investigating magistrate are supposed to remain on guard during the interrogation. They are not permitted to let the prisoner out of their sight. Here I saw something new: my guards were told to leave the hall. This increased my apprehension. It seemed as though the crafty officials were up to some trick. But I had no alternative. Hope and despair alternated in rapid succession. The former was inspired by the knowledge of my innocence; the latter was born of my acquaintance with Russian officialdom.

Soon Fenenko turned to me: "Did you know Andryusha Yushchinsky?"

"No," I replied unhesitatingly. "I work in the office of a large factory; and my daily relations are with merchants, adults and not with young children, especially children of the streets. I might possibly have seen him at one time, but one meets quite a few people on the street. I am certain that I could not have distinguished him from any other boy."

The prosecutor, Karbovsky, who had been leaning back on his chair, watching me intently, suddenly bent over the table and asked me:

"They say there are people among you Jews who are called '*tzadikim*' (holy men). When one wishes to do harm to another man, you go to the '*tzadik*' and give him a '*pidion*' (fee) and the '*tzadik*' uses the power of his word which is sufficient to bring misfortune upon other men."

The Hebrew words that he was using, "*tzadik*," "*pidion*," and the like, were written down in his notebook, and each time he wanted to use the word he would consult his notebook. I answered:

"I am sorry, but I know nothing about '*tzadikim*,' '*pidionot*,' or any other of these things. I am a man entirely devoted to my business, and I don't understand what you want of me."

"And what are you," he asked, as he again consulted his notes. "Are you a '*Hasid*' or a '*Misnaged*?'"

"I am a Jew," I answered, "and have no idea of the distinction between a '*Hasid*' and a '*Misnaged*.'"

"What do you Jews call an '*afikomen*?'"

"To these I have but the same answer."

I began to regard these men as somewhat unbalanced. What could they possibly want? What had Yushchinsky's murder to do with the *afikomen*? And furthermore, how did the difference between *Hasidim* and *Misnagdim* concern them? I could only imagine that they were poking fun at me, and at some of the Hebrew

---

32

ritual.

But unfortunately, it was no matter of jest. On the surface they were sincere. In their heart, perhaps, was the deep conviction that Vera Cheberyak had murdered the boy. Perhaps these questions were directed at me under orders from the powers above.

After the questioning, Fenenko ordered the deputies to escort me back to the *Okhrana* jail. Although my hopes were again dashed, I believed that their mistake would soon be apparent to them and they would soon send me home.

When we reached the *Okhrana* headquarters, I was led into a room where I found three "political" prisoners: two Jews and one Christian. At that period the *Okhrana* jail was particularly busy, for Czar Nicholas was about to come to Kiev, and it was necessary to rid the city of all "disloyal" elements. When my fellow-prisoners discovered who I was, they began encouraging me, telling me that I would soon be released, and not to lose hope.

Fate seemed against me, however. I felt more helpless than ever. What could I, a man with no connections, do against an organized, autocratic bureaucracy? This was not the first time that the government, through some of its agents, was attempting to instigate pogroms. But I became reassured as I realized that they had no vestige of proof against me.

A few days later, I was again summoned to the investigating magistrate. These questionings invariably excited me. On the one hand, I felt encouraged, for if they desired to question me, it was a sign that they wanted to know the truth. On the other hand, I would become frightened of the wild questions they were in the habit of putting, questions designed to confuse and entangle me, and which had no sense or relevance in themselves. My fears were heightened when I was told by some of my fellow-prisoners that the whole case smelled of "politics," that its chief purpose was to harm the Jews, to incite pogroms. The Minister of Justice himself, it seems, was interested in creating a "Jewish case" and was extending the protection of the government to the real criminals. For some strange reason I feared Fenenko the most, although I discovered later that he was the least hostile toward me.

When brought to the district court, I found Fenenko alone. Again he dismissed my guard. After being absorbed in thought for a while, he turned toward me abruptly: "Beilis, you must understand that it is not I who am accusing you; it is the prosecutor. It is he who has ordered your arrest."

"Will I be sent to prison? Will I have to wear prison clothes?"

"I do not know what is to happen to you. I only want you to know that the orders are the prosecutor's and not mine."

This message was anything but cheering to me. I was thrown into a cold fever. All was lost. I was to be sent to prison.

My terror at the prospect forced me to speak: "But may I remind you of something? This is the first time in my life that I have had to deal with an official of your rank, but I know that it is the duty of an investigating magistrate to determine the truth, to investigate it. When the investigating magistrate collects all the possible evidence, he makes out an indictment and turns it over to the prosecutor; and if the evidence is against the suspected person, the latter is imprisoned. If there is insufficient evidence, the man is set free.

"If you send me to prison now, I take it that you have found something against me. What have I done? For what crime have I been indicted?"

"Ask me no questions," was all that Fenenko would answer. "I have told you enough. It is the prosecutor who accuses you, not I."

I could tell from Fenenko's manner of speaking that there was something ulterior behind the whole incident. I was not given much time to reflect upon the matter, however, for the deputy was called in and I was taken back to the *Okhrana* headquarters.

Very shortly afterward, I was called to be transferred to the prison. I petitioned to spend the night, at least, with the Jews whose acquaintance I had made in the *Okhrana* jail, and the officials granted my request.

Chapter 6: Prison

The deputy who accompanied me to the prison permitted me to take the tram-car, but we did not go inside where the passengers were; we stood on the platform. While riding to the prison, I met some of Zaitsev's employees going to work, and a few of my acquaintances. That was all I needed to complete the picture of darkness.

During our ride, a Christian boarded the car, and upon noticing me embraced and kissed me. It was Zakharchenko, the owner of the house where the Cheberyaks lived. "Brother," he said, "don't lose spirit. I myself am a member of the Double-Headed Eagle, but I tell you that the stones of the bridge may crumble, but the truth will out."

With these words, he jumped off the car. My guard let the man go unharmed because he was then wearing the badge of the "Double Eagle," whose owners are allowed to do pretty much as they like. The deputy had been impressed by Zakharchenko's speech, and treated me with some friendliness. The bits of kindness shown me by many ordinary Russians before and during my imprisonment mitigated my bitterness towards my persecutors.

The tramcar stopped running at the station before the prison, so we had to walk the rest of the way on foot. Passing by a fruit-market, the deputy went to a stall and bought some pears, and offered them to me. I could not restrain my amazement. "I bought them for you," he said. "You are going to prison, and you won't get them there."

As soon as I entered the prison door, and the official called out my name – "Beilis" – all the other officials came on the run to see me. They all poked some fun at me, and devoured me with their eyes. Then one got up the courage to come near me; he addressed me sarcastically. "Well, here we'll feed you matzah and blood to your heart's content. Go on, change your dress!"

I was led into a small room and was given the "royal garments" – the drab prisoner's clothes. As I took off my boots, the blood rushed to my head, darkness swept over me, and I felt I was going to faint. A guard came over and took off my shoes. When I was put into the chair to have my hair cut, I was again about to faint. The same guard came over and gave me some water.

About noon I was brought into my residence, where I found about forty prisoners. The door was locked. No way out of here. One had to hope, to hope, to steel oneself, to be as strong as the grating-bars in order to survive these foul and dark quarters.

I surveyed my new home and my new friends. The walls were painted with tar. Hardly a ray of light came through the bars. The appalling smell of dirt and unwashed humanity was nauseating. The crowd of prisoners was jumping around, dancing, cutting crazy pranks. One was singing a song, the other telling smutty stories, some were wrestling and sparring. Was I condemned to this atmosphere for a lifetime, or was this part of a horrible dream?

"The prosecutor has ordered it, not I" – Fenenko's words came back to me. "It is not I that am accusing you."

I sat down in one of the remote corners, head bent on my prison-issued greatcoat, reflecting on my fate. While I was thus in deep thought, the door of the big cell was opened, and a drunken voice shouted: "Dinner."

When I had first come into the cell, I had noticed several pails on the floor, like those used in our bathhouses. When the call for dinner rang out, several prisoners rushed for the pails, of which there were four or five. There were about forty men in the room. There was no dispute about the pails, for ten people could easily eat from the same pail. But there were only three spoons. Who was to eat first?

A free-for-all began at once. The fierce scuffle lasted for some time, and after some had been injured and most everybody was tired, the spoons fell into the hands of the strongest and quickest. Peace was declared and the men sat down on the floor to eat. Each had just so many spoonfuls and then passed the spoon to the next man. At times a man would cheat on the number of spoonfuls, and would take one or two extra spoonfuls. Another scuffle would begin, with its accompaniment of the choicest and finest language to be found in the felons' dictionary.

I sat in my corner and looked with consternation upon this picture of life in prison. When the meal was over, tea was brought in, which looked more like water. Suddenly, one of the company came over to my corner and offered me a lump of sugar. He did not speak, but made signs; he was mute, apparently, and seemed to be a Jew. He drank his tea and then brought some for me in a small pitcher. Thus elapsed the first few hours in prison.

In the evening, a new prisoner was brought into our quarters, a Jew. His arrival made things brighter, for now at least I had somebody to talk to. I approached him and announced who I was. He was greatly surprised on hearing my name. Although he

---

had troubles of his own, having been arrested for setting his house on fire to collect insurance, he forgot his own difficulties and concerned himself with mine. He was a person of some influence. His cousin was a builder-contractor in Kiev, and had good connections with the government. The prisoner was therefore allowed to get food from the outside into prison, which food he shared with me. In the morning, however, my friend fell ill and was taken to the hospital.

I may say that the room in which I was lodged was not the usual prison quarters. It also belonged to the hospital, and one had to spend thirty days there before being taken into the "real prison." I was also informed that the pails from which we were eating were used as wash-pails in the laundry.

For the first two days, I was not registered on the ration-list and received no bread. On the third day, I was marked down as a regular boarder, and I began getting my bread ration, which was the only thing I could bear to eat. I could not touch the soup because of the wash-pails.

Once while we were having dinner, one of the men found a quarter of a mouse in the pail, which must have gotten there from the fine grits in the prison-stores. The man who found it exhibited it, not so much to protest against the prison administration, as to deprive the others of their appetite and get more for himself.

As the days passed, I found myself weakening. I had to begin eating. I could obtain food from home only on Sundays. I waited for Sunday with greatest impatience. I was also anxious to hear news of my family.

I shall never forget the eagerness with which I looked forward to that first Sunday. On Saturday night, I was unable to

---

sleep from impatience. My back and shoulders ached from lying down, for the floor served as a bed. I would rather have walked around, but it was forbidden. I was lying as on a rake.

At last, the day of happiness. On Sunday, a package of food was brought in to me, which was supposed to last for the whole week. When my prison comrades saw the package, they showed the greatest joy. They tore it out of my hands in an instant, and devoured its contents in no time. They tore at each other and at the package, each trying to get a larger share. As they tore at each other like dogs, I was reminded that I had to face another week of fasting. I was watched by the group, as to whether I showed any signs of displeasure. For being displeased with comrades meant a good beating. I had to put on a happy face, almost joy at their eating, and to say: "Eat heartily, boys."

That autumn was particularly cold. The window-panes were nearly all broken. At night it was freezingly cold. Things were not made any pleasanter by the wet and filthy floor and the vermin crawling all over the place. My body was all bitten and scratched.

A month passed, and I was transferred to other quarters, where there were also about forty prisoners, most of them prison-guests of long standing. At this place I found three new companions, Jews, who made much over me upon hearing of my case.

It was on a Saturday morning that I was transferred to my new quarters. Sunday morning I was again impatient. When I received my package of food, the Jews advised me how to go about it so as not to be robbed. I was to give them the package, and they would look after it; the others feared them and would not interfere. I acted accordingly, and we spent five days together eating and drinking. Then their court trial took place, and they were released. They said they would get word to my wife from me.

As long as the Jews had been with me, the Christian prisoners had not approached me. No sooner did the Jews leave than the Christians became quite familiar, and treated me rather respectfully. They knew of my case, and were amused by the questions that the officials had put to me. They all predicted it would come to nothing.

One of these men became especially friendly, and was continuously showering me with compliments. In the beginning I could not understand his excessive kindness, for he did not seem to be a person of natural kindness. It was only later that I found out his game. But the finding out cost me dearly.

Chapter 7: The Bloody "Analysis"

On the next Sunday I again received a food package. I was happy to see it – and apparently, the other prisoners were no less pleased. One of them offered to take charge of it for "safe keeping." But recognizing him as one of those who could go through a package in the twinkling of an eye, I thanked him and said that I felt I could take care of it myself.

A little later, three new men were brought in: a young Jew and two Christians. The Jew confided to me that he could not eat the food, and that he had no sugar for his tea. I offered him some *challah* (braided bread) and sugar, which he accepted with many thanks.

"What are you here for?" he wanted to know.

I wished to avoid the usual condolences and sighings, so I told him I was there for horse stealing. I asked him with what he was charged. He told me that he had had five hundred rubles, with which he had paid for some purchase. The bills were found to be counterfeit, and he was arrested.

Once, on the "promenade," one of the prisoners called to me: "Beilis." The young Jew turned around in amazement. "You are Beilis? Why didn't you tell me at first? Why did you conceal your name? I am happy to be in the same cell with you. Do not grieve – God will help you."

The time was approaching when the prisoners were to make

an "analysis" of me. At first I didn't know what that meant in the thieves' lingo. But I soon found out.

When a group of prisoners is implicated in the same case, the necessity arises for agreeing on what they are all to say at trial, so that they may not become confused. If there is a stranger in the cell, he may overhear their consultations and inform on them. He is therefore subjected to an analysis – he gets a preliminary beating. If he doesn't report that, they feel safe to speak freely in his presence.

I began to understand the reason for the friendliness of the Christian prisoners. They had assumed this attitude in order to get close to me, pick a quarrel, and perform the "analysis." It seemed, however, that not all were bent on the analysis. None wanted to be the provocateur, the bully. The peasant who was angry at my refusal to make him the guardian of my package undertook that mission. He also "had it in" for the Jews because it was a Jew who had accused him of theft. I knew that this particular prisoner was out to get me, but I was helpless.

It happened thus. I could not wear my own shoes and had to wear the prison sabots with their nails in them. From constant walking around to distract my thoughts, my feet were sorely hurt by the nails, and were bleeding. Once, having tired of walking, I sat down on a chair. The peasant came running and asked me to let him sit down on the chair. Before I could answer, he hit me so that the blood started running. All were watching me to see how I would react. Seeing the blood, they were somewhat frightened and brought me some water to wash it.

When I refused to take the water, one of them shouted: "Stab him! Do away with him. You can see: he is going to squeal."

The young Jew came over to me and begged me, "Be

———

43

reasonable. Wash the blood off. You will be transferred to another room. I shall have to remain here, and they'll take their vengeance on me. If you wash yourself, they'll become amenable. You had better do it."

I did as I was asked. I had consideration for the young man and washed myself. Whereupon all the Christians turned upon the peasant and commenced to give him a beating. "Jews," they said, "must be tested in another way."

In the morning, I was on the "promenade." With me were the peasant who had hit me and another Christian. The prison guard saw my swollen eye and asked me who had done it. Before I had time to answer, the other Christian pointed at the peasant. The guard promptly grabbed hold of the peasant's collar and conducted us to the prison office. On the way to the office, we had to pass by several guards. Each of them questioned us, and upon being told, gave a hearty blow to the peasant. The last guard we met, when informed of the culprit, got hold of the peasant and threw him down a flight of steps. I feared he would have his head broken.

In the office, he was asked by one of the officials: "Why did you hit Beilis?"

His answer was: "I asked him as a comrade to let me sit on his chair. He did not let me, so I hit him."

"Is he your comrade?" asked the official severely.

"Well, he takes our children and drinks their blood. Will he lord it over us here?"

"Have you yourself seen him kill children?" asked the official.

"No, but so I am told."

"Well, then, take this and this" – and the official gave the peasant a good beating.

Chapter 8: The Spies

I was transferred to another room, for it was impossible to remain with my peasant friend. In this room there were only twelve men, for the most part petty officials, policemen and such-like, who had committed minor offences. Among them was one Kozachenko, who was friendly to me. The others seemed to be suspicious of me.

A few days later, I was summoned into the hall by the warden, who came to ask me whether I was being treated in my new quarters as badly as in the previous ones. When I told him it was better here, he left. In my new quarters, I noticed that the guard would take letters from the prisoners to deliver them outside, and would bring replies, all for a few kopeks.

In the meantime I had no news of my family. Being friendly with Kozachenko, I told him I should like to send a note to my family. I wrote a letter and took the precaution to leave no empty space, so as not to let anybody else add to my words. In the letter, I asked about the welfare of my wife and family and wanted to know the reason for their silence and inactivity. Why were they not doing something? I was innocent, but it seemed that no one was taking any interest in me. I wrote that I did not know if I could stand further imprisonment. I also mentioned that the bearer of the letter was to be paid fifty kopeks and to be given an answer.

I gave my letter to the guard and he later brought me an answer. I read it, then carefully tore it up. A few days later, the

---

45

guard asked me whether I should like to send another letter. I told him I would not.

Kozachenko's trial was to take place shortly. He came to me once and told me: "Listen to me, Beilis. The whole world knows you are innocent. When I am released, I'll do what I can for you. I have enough information from the prisoners here who know who the real murderers are."

He went to his trial and was acquitted. He returned to prison for the night. In the morning, when he was to leave, I gave him a letter for my wife. I wrote her that the bearer would give her news of me.

This happened on Wednesday. On Friday evening, I was summoned to the prison office. I had a pang of foreboding in my heart. In the office I was met by two officials, the inspector and another one.

The inspector asked me: "You wrote letters to your family?"

At first I did not know what to say. All my suspicions fell upon Kozachenko. I decided that he must have been the one who turned the letter over to the officials in order to get into their good graces. I did not suspect the guard of treachery, the less so in view of the fact that he had brought back an answer. Therefore, I didn't want to get him into trouble. I told the inspector: "I sent a letter with Kozachenko."

In reply, he read me the two letters, including the one I had sent through the guard. It was clear that the whole thing was a trap, set by the guard from the very beginning, to get my letters in order to deliver them to the officials. I was told to go back to prison.

About two hours later, on Friday night when all good Jews were sitting down to cheerful tables and singing Sabbath songs, the

———

door of our room opened and I was told with severity: "Take your things and come with me."

I took my belongings and was brought into a small room – cold to the freezing point. I looked around: the room was empty. I implored the guard to give me at least a mattress.

"Tomorrow," was his answer. "It does not matter. You will die overnight." He locked the door.

I sat down on the cold and wet floor and trembled from cold. With unspeakable suffering, I awaited the coming of the morning. The thought of the letters would not leave my head. I feared that since the letters had fallen into the hands of the officials, they might also have arrested my wife.

In the morning I received a visit from the deputy warden. I pleaded with him to do one of two things: either order the stove to be heated so that the room would be warm, or else have me shot and put an end to my tortures.

His answer was: "I cannot do anything myself. I'll ask for instructions. Wait an hour." He returned in an hour and had me transferred to a small but warm room.

I waited for Sunday. Sunday came, no one arrived, and no package of food was received. I felt certain my poor family had also been arrested. Was it possible, however, that none was left free to take care of me?

I heard children's voices from the prison yard, and it seemed to me they were the voices of my children. I thought that they and my wife had been thrown into jail.

On Monday, the warden himself appeared. I inquired: Why had not I received anything on Sunday? Was it because of the letters?

His answer was: "For the letters, you got 'strict confinement.' Such practices are forbidden. As to the package of food, it is not our fault; something must have happened at your home. I shall find out."

I took the opportunity to ask him to have another man put into my room; a decent person, for one might go mad from lonesomeness and solitude. He promised to grant my request and departed.

An hour later, two young men were brought into my cell. Each had chains on both hands and feet. Both looked savage enough. They must have been murderers. I would gladly have foregone the pleasure of their company. I had to conceal my sentiments and put on a pleasant face, however. It could not be helped.

Another few days passed. One morning, I was given a letter from my wife. She wrote that she was not doing well, could not come herself, and was therefore sending money. I felt cheered up – thank God they were all home. But why am I imprisoned? What would they do with me? How long will my unjust, undeserved tortures last? When will there be an end to my misfortunes?

These questions oppressed my brain. I was walking around day after day as one out of his senses. I kept thinking: is there no man to take up my cause? Is there nothing being done to get me freed?

Chapter 9: The First Indictment

On a day in January, 1912, I was summoned to the district court to get my indictment. My joy was boundless. Come what might, I would at least know where I stood.

I was escorted to the district court. There I found my wife and brother, whom I had not seen for a long time. We could not talk to each other, however.

In the morning before going to court, I had received a letter from my wife and brother, telling me that I should announce in court that I had retained as my lawyers Messrs. Gruzenberg, Grigorovich-Barsky, and Margolin.

I was handed the indictment. When I realized its contents, I was stunned. I was not charged overtly with "ritual murder." I was nevertheless accused of having murdered Yushchinsky or having been accomplice to his murder with others. I was charged in accordance with the statute dealing with premeditated murder, the death of the victim having been caused by bodily tortures inflicted upon it, or the victim having been subjected before murder to cruel torment. In case of conviction, the statute called for 15-20 years *katorga* (imprisonment with hard labor).

Of course, had the investigation been carried on along the lines of an ordinary criminal case, the indictment would have been only a sort of personal frame-up, a personal libel. Since, however, the investigation and the whole case in general had been undertaken with the intention of turning it into a ritual murder case, the whole case became a frame-up on the entire Jewish people.

I was amazed at Fenenko. He told me he was not indicting me, and yet he composed the indictment. As I was later informed, he had intended at first to quash it, since there was no proof whatever against me. That is what he himself said – but the chief prosecutor in Kiev, Chaplinsky, together with the notorious Zamyslovsky and the whole band of Black Hundreds, compelled Fenenko to formulate the indictment. It should be borne in mind that Fenenko did not even intend to arrest me. All that was done by Chaplinsky.

Nevertheless, the higher authorities were far from being satisfied with the indictment. Its premises were weak at their foundation. In addition to that, the authorities actually wanted the case to have a ritual character. The prosecutor, Chaplinsky, exercised all his efforts to have it inserted into the indictment that Yushchinsky had been murdered for "religious purposes." I was told that Fenenko had been summoned several times before the Minister of Justice in St. Petersburg. Fenenko, however, would not be budged and won that particular point.

I was led back to my dark and dingy prison. About that time, I began to feel my feet swelling – they were being covered with sores. Since my shoes had no soles, the walking on the snow and ice caused me intense suffering. Hence the swelling and sores. The pain was almost unbearable. The skin burst and blood was oozing through. But I did not find much sympathy for my sufferings on the part of those around me.

One morning I asked the doctor to be brought in to examine me. I was in agony. The officials were merciful enough and sent me a surgeon's aide. The surgeon's aide looked at the sores and said that I was to be transferred to the hospital.

Later, a guard came in and shouted: "Hurry up, let's go!" I could not move, however; my feet were so swollen that I could not stand up. He did not want to listen to any reason and kept shouting, "Move on!" Finally, one of the prisoners who happened to be in the hall brought some rags and wrapped them around my knees. And in this manner, crawling on my knees over the snow and ice, I dragged myself to the prison hospital.

In the hospital I encountered another surgeon's aide, who had lived on Yurkovskaya Street, not far from our factory. When he recognized me, he became pale, and trembled from pity and amazement. He ordered at once that I be undressed and given a warm bath. I was afterwards given clean linen and put into a warm, clean bed. This produced such a beneficial effect that I slept uninterruptedly for thirty-six hours. I could not bring myself to part with the bed.

After the good rest I had, an operation was performed upon me. My friend the surgeon's aide was not present – I was operated upon by the physician. When he commenced to open the sores, the pain made me wince and scream. The doctor smiled and observed, "Well, Beilis, now you know for yourself how it feels to be cut up. You know how Andryusha felt when you were stabbing him and drawing his blood – all for the sake of your religion." You can imagine how cheerful I felt at this raillery of the doctor. He kept on cutting leisurely, and I had to bite my lips not to let myself scream.

After the operation, I was carried by two prisoners back to my bed. I lay there for three days. In all decency, I should have stayed there for a longer period of time, but the doctor was not

---

inclined to make it easy on me. I was put in my usual raiment and was sent back to prison.

I did not find my former companions in my room. Since the solitude was weighing heavily upon me, I again asked for company. A second prisoner was brought in. I feared at first that he was another of the Kozachenko band, i.e. a spy. He proved, however, to be a very honest peasant.

My new companion was an inveterate smoker – but in my room, he was forbidden to smoke. This was a great deprivation for him. After a couple of days, he therefore asked that he be transferred to his former quarters, since he could not live without smoking. The warden granted his request, and he was about to go back. However, when the guard came for him, he hesitated and said, "No, I have pity on this Jew; he is a very honest fellow. He likes my company, and I will stay with him." And so he did. He stayed with me for two weeks and was subsequently released from prison. Before the parting, he embraced me and wept. "I know," said he, "that you are suffering unjustly. Trust in God, He will help you. You will be released. The Jews are an honest people."

I was left alone, a prey to heavy thoughts that were obsessing me to the point of melancholy.

Chapter 10: The First Visit of My Lawyers

Eight months had elapsed since the ominous morning when I was first put behind the iron bars. Eight dark months had rolled away, and the end of my sufferings was not yet in view. Besides that, I did not know whether anything was being done on my behalf in the outside world. Who was planning to intercede for me, to defend me?

One dreary day, the door of my cell suddenly opened and a distinguished gentleman of Jewish appearance entered, introducing himself as Mr. Gruzenberg, one of my attorneys. Hitherto, he had been unable to see me because the indictment had not been issued. Now, however, with the indictment completed, he was able to come and visit his client as frequently as desired.

Gruzenberg's appearance made a strong impression on me. He tried to cheer me up. "Be strong. I come to you in the name of the Jewish people. You must forgive us since you are compelled to suffer for all of us. I am telling you I should consider myself happy to exchange your prisoner's clothes with you and to let you go free."

"I have one request to make, Mr. Gruzenberg," was my reply. "A man must know his situation. Tell me please, how my case stands. I shall not lose courage even if things go rather unfavorably. However, I cannot live in this state of uncertainty. Tell me the truth."

"You are right," he said, "you ought to know all, but none of us is able to gauge the situation with precision. I had a similar case with Blondes (also accused of ritual murder) in Vilna. You can't tell how the thing will turn out." I told him what Fenenko had said to me during one of my interviews with him, quoting a Russian proverb: "When the corn is milled, we will have some very fine flour."

"Well, well," said Gruzenberg, shaking his head, "we may have *muka*" (a play on words, *muka* meaning both flour and trouble). Before leaving, he cheered me up by saying that I was to be defended by the best lawyers in Russia: Zarudny, Maklakov, Grigorovich-Barsky, and others; and that I should soon be visited by each of them.

Gruzenberg's visit was a great relief for me. My faith grew stronger in my eventual release, though no false hopes were held out for me by my lawyers. I was cheered by the very fact that there were people taking my interests to heart, that I was not forgotten, and that the greatest legal lights of Russia were eager to defend me.

Mr. Grigorovich-Barsky was the next lawyer to visit me. I inquired, "Would it not be the thing to have me taken out on bail, or to appeal to the Czar himself for mercy?"

He smiled and shook his head. "Do you know that the Czar has recently visited Kiev?"

"Yes," I said, "the newly arrested prisoners told me about it. I have also heard that the chief of the *Okhrana*, Kuliabko, who had originally arrested me, came to grief over the Czar's visit since he proved unable to prevent the assassination of Prime Minister Stolypin in the Czar's very presence."

"It is so," confirmed Grigorovich-Barsky, "so now you know that the Czar was in Kiev. I was in the Government's service at the time as an assistant prosecuting attorney. I was a member of the

---

deputation selected to welcome the Czar. One of my colleagues was with me. We were present when the chief prosecutor of Kiev, Chaplinsky, was introduced to the Czar. Chaplinsky told the Czar: 'Your Majesty, I am happy to inform you that the real culprit in Yushchinsky's murder has been discovered. That is, Beilis, a *Zhid*.' Upon hearing that, the Czar bared his head and made the sign of the cross as an expression of his thanks to God. Now, I ask you, Beilis, to whom will you appeal for mercy, to the man who thanks God that a *Zhid* is suspected of the murder?"

I was nearly stunned with amazement. Mr. Barsky was silent for a while. I could hardly recover my senses from the unexpected story of Mr. Barsky about the Czar. I knew that Nicholas was not a friend of the Jews, but that he should openly exhibit so intense an interest and pleasure in the persecution of a Jew, and that before a gathering of his officials, was beyond my imagination. "I'll tell you another thing," said Mr. Grigorovich-Barsky, in that friendly and winning way he had with him. "When the Czar was in Kiev he was expected one day to visit a certain place. A great gathering was waiting for him, and the crowd made one feel quite uncomfortable, though strict order was maintained. I was there with a friend to see the procession. A certain colonel passed by and pushed a Jew, calling him '*Zhid*.'[a] I and my friend were in civilian dress at the time. The Jew, pushed by the colonel, was of fine appearance, behaved very well, and in no way deserved the insult. I turned to the colonel. 'Why were you so rude?' His answer was, 'You *Zhid* defender!' We had a heated argument and I eventually brought the

---

[a] The term *Zhid*, in Russian, is a derogatory term for "Jew." The non-derogatory Russian word for "Jew" is *Evrei* (Hebrew).

—

55

colonel before a judge, who gave him eight days in prison, well deserved for his rudeness. All these unpleasant incidents brought me to the decision to resign my position with the government. I gave up my assistant prosecutor post and became a private lawyer."

Before Grigorovich-Barsky came to me, I was given a paper to sign in which I was officially informed that Shmakov, a lawyer on Yushchinsky's side, was suing me for civil damages in the amount of seven thousand rubles. He would thus be able to take part in the trial against me as a private prosecutor. During Grigorovich-Barsky's visit I asked him who that man Shmakov was. Grigorovich-Barsky told me that Shmakov was an old man, a well-known anti-Semite, whose opinions were of little general weight. My lawyer seemed to be rather optimistic about my case. He told me that the greatest experts of Russia and her greatest scientists would be summoned for the trial, and that Shmakov would appear ridiculous before such a gathering. We parted as if we were old friends.

After this, my lawyers visited me regularly. Mr. Arnold Margolin used to be a frequent visitor. Mr. Margolin was the lawyer my wife and brother had first hired to represent me, immediately upon my arrest. He always kept in touch with my family and constantly encouraged me.

Chapter 11: A Convict with a Heart

Being lonesome, I again asked the authorities to give me a companion. My petition was granted, and a Pole, Pashlovski, was brought into my cell. He had been sentenced to *katorga* (hard labor), and was waiting to be sent to Siberia.[b] He was a very clever fellow, although he had murdered more than one man in his life.

In the evening, he was called to the prison office. I felt very uneasy about it. I knew it was a bad omen for me, since the man, already being convicted, had very little to do with the office. When he returned, he seemed to be in good humor. He came over to me nearly bursting with laughter.

"Why are you laughing?" I asked uneasily. "What happened in the office?"

The prisoner answered, "I would tell you, Beilis, but you are too nervous. If I tell you the whole story you would become excited, so it is better for you not to know."

I renewed my interrogation. "I see you are a good man since you are so mindful of my health. I thank you for that. Had you come in without laughing, I would not have known anything, but since you are my friend, you must tell me all. It is better to know the truth, even if it be unpleasant."

He thought for a while, and then with a wave of the hand, as if making up his mind, told me. "Well, if you insist, this is what

---

[b] The *katorga* system in Czarist Russia was a precursor to the Soviet *gulag*.

—

57

happened. I was brought into the office. I found quite a large gathering there. The prosecutor, the warden, they were all in a lively confab. On the table was a silver cigarette box. The prosecutor offered me a cigarette. You may imagine my amazement. Who was I and who were they? I, a convict, and they were treating me to cigarettes. Apparently they wanted me to do something for them. Well, I am nobody's fool.

"The Warden began to speak in the kindest, friendliest manner, as if the matter concerned his very life. 'You are a Christian, one of us,' he said, 'and I am certain you care for our Christians, for our blood, as much as we do ourselves.' He hesitated for a while and then continued. 'You are in the same cell with Beilis. Tell me, what does he say? Has he told you anything?'

"My answer was, 'He is bewailing his bitter misfortunes. He complains that he is suffering unjustly, and undeservedly.'

"The prosecutor joined in with a smile. 'We know that he says that; that is to be expected; but you are an intelligent man, you understand people. You ought to discern the difference between his truths and his lies. Didn't he ever slip out with a word or something?'

"I saw at once it was a crooked band I was dealing with, so I spoke up. 'Look here, gentlemen, I grew up among Jews. At the age of six, I lost my father and mother, became a total orphan. My relatives apprenticed me to a Jewish locksmith, and I learned the trade. I lived for twelve years in his house. I left it a grown man with a trade. I was able to make money and I married. I had friends among Jews and also among Jewish converts. I daresay I know all the Jewish customs, and a good deal about their religious rites. I know it from A to Z. Small wonder, since I grew up in a Jewish house as one of them. I know they would not eat an egg if there is a bloodclot in it. It is *tref* (un-kosher) with them. I have seen it a hundred times if once. I have seen them salting their meat and have asked the mistress of the house why they do it. 'Because this drives all the blood out of the meat,' she told me. They do it 'because we must eat no blood whatever.'

"'Now, when people come and tell me that the Jews use blood, human blood in particular; that Beilis has murdered a Christian child in order to have his blood, I who am a Christian and who believe in the Cross, I tell you that all these stories are a set of despicable lies.'"

"When I was through with my say, they all looked at me with murder in their eyes. They saw that they had the wrong man. The cigarette had not bought them any cooperation from me. Some of them lost their patience.

"'Well,' said the prosecutor, 'be that as it may, but does he never say anything in his sleep?' I said I never heard him talking in his sleep. They saw they couldn't get anything out of me, and ordered me back to the cell. That is why I was laughing coming into the room. I can see they have no actual proof against you, and they are looking for the 'snows of yesteryear.'"

They did not keep the fellow long with me. They saw that he was too friendly towards me. He was taken away. Since they could not make him serve their purposes, we had to part. I was left alone.

From all these incidents, the impression grew stronger with me that the government felt its case to be weak; that the indictment was feeble. It was clear that had the Black Hundreds felt their case to be stronger, they would not have resorted to the help of spies and schemes.

59

Chapter 12: New Intrigues

Rumors began to circulate in the prison that a certain journalist Brazul-Brushkovsky had written the prosecutor that he had information indicating that the murder of the boy Andryusha had been committed by Vera Cheberyak's lover. The rumors had it further that Brazul's statement, made on the grounds of Cheberyak's admissions, was not found to be sufficiently supported by evidence. Not until the spring of 1912 did the private investigators discover the right trail, and Brazul-Brushkovsky, along with former chief detective Krasovsky, came out with a new statement. The first indictment was withdrawn, and the official investigation into the murder began anew.

All this aroused new hopes in me. However, they were short-lived. In the summer a new investigating magistrate, Mashkevich, was sent down from St. Petersburg, and he thwarted any effort to charge the true criminals.

A day or two after the incident with the *katorjnik* (convict at hard labor) who refused to spy on me, I was summoned to the district court. I went there with joy. I was pleased to be able to see the outside world again and breathe the fresh air. This time my escort took me in the tram car. As ill luck would have it, the car caught fire, so that we had to go on foot. A lot of people knew that I was to be taken down to the court; some came to take a look at me, and to take my photograph. In the hall where I was brought, I found Investigating Magistrate Mashkevich and a certain professor.

"Look here, Beilis," said Mashkevich, "three hairs were found on Andryusha's trousers, so that if you do not object I would ask some of your hair to be shown to an expert."

I could scarcely look at the man, but I answered politely. "If you need it, you can take it."

"No," said the investigating magistrate, "you must do it yourself." I took the scissors from his desk, cut some hair off my head, and put them in an envelope.

Having done so, I rather regretted my course. Who knows what these tricksters might be up to? They might dye the hair. But then I thought: let them do their worst. The request for my hair was all that was wanted of me for the time being. I was immediately sent back to prison.

Three days later I was called to the prison office. My fingerprints were wanted.

"Is it done in every prisoner's case?" I inquired.

"No," I was told, "only to those whose indictment calls for *katorga* (hard labor)."

"What is this for?" was my further inquiry. I was told that an imprint of fingers was left on Andryusha's belt-buckle. My fingerprints were wanted in order to compare the two. The fingerprint obtained, I was dispatched back to the cell.

Around this time, I had a special visit from my family. My wife had previously been granted permission to see me, but "to see" was about the true extent of the favor. For we could only see each other separated by double bars, and that for no longer than five minutes. The noise and tumult in the visiting quarters was such that we could hardly hear each other. Nevertheless, her visits were a great joy to me.

One day, I was told the glad news that my wife and children would be allowed to see me in the prison office. I was immediately conducted to the office. When I entered there, none of my family was to be seen. I sat down to wait patiently. I became restless, however. I had not seen my children for a long time. How did they look? How much they had suffered – and all for what? Minutes seemed longer than years. How long was I to wait?

Six officials sat in the office, among them Investigating Magistrate Mashkevich. They were eyeing me keenly all the time I was sitting there. They were exchanging remarks between themselves.

Finally, my wife, the children, and my brother were brought in. When I saw the youngest boy, four years old, I took him in my arms and began to kiss him. A guard rushed to me and snatched the child from my arms. It was not permitted to kiss one's own child.

The child began to weep. He was frightened by the rudeness of the guard, the presence of the officials with their shiny buttons, and most of all by my prison clothes. I lost my self-control and commenced to shout with tears in my voice: "What right have you to do all this? Have you no children yourself? Don't you know a father's feelings? Are you so heartless?"

I noticed that several of the officials turned away their faces and were wiping their eyes with their handkerchiefs. I was permitted to take the child in my arms. I asked my wife how things were going with her. She answered sadly: "Even if I have enough to live on, what good is it when you are suffering so cruelly and unjustly?"

We thus spent a few minutes together, and then my family were told they must leave. I remained alone. The prosecutor

Chaplinsky came over to me, offered me a cigarette, and said in a voice of feigned compassion: "Yes, Beilis, this is how your Jewish friends are acting. When Beilis was needed, he was given money, and was a very, very good man. And now when he is no more needed he is completely forgotten by them. Your poor wife is also suffering much and must be angry with the Jews."

Chaplinsky spoke very slowly and distinctly, and simulated a tone of friendliest sympathy. His every word, however, was like a stab in my heart, and the cunning, malicious expression on his face added to my bitterness. I turned to him and asked for permission to say a few words. He encouraged me: "Certainly – you may speak."

"If an atrocious villain were found capable of murdering an innocent child, all in order to incite pogroms against the Jews, how could the Jews have a part in it? What had the Jewish people to do with it? Let me be kept in prison. I have patience. The trial will show that I am innocent."

None of them spoke to me any more. Chaplinsky turned away and was apparently far from being pleased with my words. I was let out of the office.

My imprisonment drew on, day after day, month after month. Over a year elapsed from the dark morning of my first arrest by Colonel Kuliabko, when I had been torn away from my wife and family. I kept on hoping for a long while: tomorrow I shall be free. Instead of freedom, I had to feed on hopes and expectations.

One evening, while I was sitting in my dingy cell, alone with my meditations, I heard footsteps and several voices in the hall, and a woman's voice said at my door: "It would be interesting to see this rascal."

The door opened and four persons entered. One of them was

---

in a general's uniform. The woman looked at me and said in a horrified tone: "What a terrible-looking creature. How fierce he looks."

The general came closer to me and said: "Beilis, you will soon be let free."

"On what grounds?" I asked him.

His answer was: "The tercentenary jubilee of the reign of the Romanov dynasty is soon to be celebrated. There will be a manifesto pardoning all *katorjniks* (convicts at hard labor)."

"That manifesto," said I, "will be for *katorjniks*, not for me. I need no manifesto, I need a fair trial."

"If you will be ordered to be released, you'll have to go."

"No – even if you open the doors of the prison, and threaten me with shooting, I shall not leave. I shall not go without a trial. I am strong enough to suffer all until the trial."

While I was speaking, they were all standing quiet and listening with curiosity to every word of mine. Even that finicky lady that was at first so much frightened by my appearance and thought me so cruel looking, even she approached me to have a better look at me. When I was through, the general continued in the same vein. "Listen to reason, Beilis. You know very well yourself, that you are suffering unjustly. I should probably do the same thing if I were in your place. You were a poor man and you did what you were told. If you tell us the truth you would be making a very fortunate move. You would be sent abroad and would be provided for the rest of your life; your action would supply an answer to the question that is occupying the whole world at present. However, you are persisting in hiding the truth. With your silence you think to protect the Jewish nation, and you are only ruining yourself. Why should you suffer for nothing? It is up to you but to say the word and you would be a happy man for the remainder of your life."

I could hardly keep my self-control while the man was talking. Every word of his was disgusting to me. He actually thought he was showing sympathy with my situation – according to him, I had been hired by the Jews to do my piece of dirty work and now he wanted me to tell the "truth." He came to exercise his influence with me. I saw that further conversation was useless. I could hardly stand it any longer. I gave him a short answer: "The whole world is indeed waiting for the truth. The trial will show the truth."

"Well, we shall see," muttered the general. Waving his hand as if giving me up for hopeless, he left my room with his escort.

The first year of my imprisonment had drawn to its close. My lonely prison cell was far from being comfortable – the walls were plastered with cement, and during the winter frost they always had an icy coating. The heating was insufficient. During the warmer days the lime on the walls would thaw and the walls would be dripping with moisture. The dripping from the ceiling made it almost impossible for me to sleep. I was dressed in the usual prison garb, i.e. a shirt of sack linen and a long coat of raggy cloth. I had to wear my shirts for stretches of two and three months. There was no lack of the usual vermin. In the prison itself the mortality from typhoid fever was about six or seven men per day. This was in no way surprising in view of the extraordinary filth, the disgusting food, and the unheated rooms (not infrequently during the frosts I used to find my hand frozen to the ice on the wall). All these things made a perfect breeding ground for various epidemics.

In addition to all these hardships, I was harried by constant searches instituted by the administration. The door of my cell had been locked by no less than thirteen locks – that meant that each time the door was to be opened, all thirteen locks had to be shot back. The sound of the rasping lock-springs used to set my nerves on edge. I was obsessed with the illusion that somebody behind me was hitting me repeatedly upon the head – it was one blow after another.

The searches were usually performed by a squad of five under the supervision of one of the deputy wardens. Every time they would come in, the first order for me was to undress. Often they had to unbutton me, for my fingers were awkward because of the cold. They were quite rude and at times tore off a number of buttons during the operation. Some exercised their rude sense of humor. "You liked to stab the boy Andryusha, to draw his blood. We will do the same thing to you now" – that was the standing joke. They would also look into my mouth lest I might have something hidden there. They would pull my tongue out in order to see deeper and better.

All these tortures and insults I had to undergo six times a day. It is hard to believe, but it is the truth. No protests were of any avail. Their intentions were to inflict the utmost inconvenience upon me. They wanted me to die without resorting to actual murder. They would not poison me outright, for that would create trouble. I believe they wanted to drive me to suicide.

Cases of suicide were quite frequent in the prison. Prisoners used to hang themselves to get rid of the persecution and torture. The administration must have thought that I would succumb under their pressure. A weaker vessel, in their opinion, would not be able to stand it and would take his life. In such an eventuality, the charge

---

of ritual murder would never be wiped off the Jewish nation.

My life was thus hanging on a hair. I saw once how another prisoner was shot to death in the prison hall after some altercation with one of the guards. This murder was easily explained away. The guard tore one of his sleeves and reported that he shot the prisoner in self-defense. There was no punishment, of course, for such justifiable self-defense.

On one of the walls of my cell there hung a set of prison rules. One of its clauses was to the effect that a prisoner insulting a guard or being insubordinate could be murdered on the spot, and the guard was to receive a reward in the amount of three rubles. The expression "assault" needed no special interpretation. Nor was the term "insubordination" less inclusive. If a guard ordered the prisoner to walk quicker or to stop and wait, and the guard was not instantly obeyed, it meant resistance and insubordination and the guard was justified in shooting the prisoner.

Generally speaking, the life of a prisoner is hell. A prisoner, from the very moment that the prison gates are closed behind him, is completely in the power of the administration, and his life is in constant danger.

Nevertheless, in spite of all the inconveniences that were heaped upon me, and all the dangers, they only served to strengthen my determination and to give me more courage to go through with this great trial. And while I was closely watched by the administration for some excuse or pretext for doing away with me, I was always on guard not to accommodate them in the least. In more than one case, there was actual provocation and foul play to represent my actions as insubordination and resistance. They tried often to put me in a situation where they could use their arms. But I

---

was extremely careful.

One thing I always had before me: the shameful charge of ritual murder must be wiped off the good name of the Jewish nation. It was my fate, it had to be done through me, and in order to be effected, I had to remain alive. I had to exercise every ounce of power, I had to suffer all without murmuring, but the enemies of my people would not triumph.

Chapter 13: Between Hope and Despair

The days were dragging along. When was my trial to take place? There were days when I felt that I was perilously near to insanity. On such occasions, I would look in amazement at my guard, at myself, and I would think: is all this reality? Am I the man lying here on the cold and filthy floor, among these creeping reptiles – is this the same Mendel Beilis who used to be a man of consequence, dressed like other humans and living a peaceful life with his wife and children? I experienced mental tortures of a kind hardly possible to bear or even to describe. Lack of exercise and constant worrying deprived me of sleep. If at times I managed to fall asleep, I was troubled by the wildest nightmares, which exhausted me more than the sleep refreshed. The usual kind of nightmare was that I was either led to execution, or being chased after, choked or beaten. I would awake, shuddering with fear and with the exertion of having tried to escape from my persecutors. I felt a sort of relief in finding, upon awakening, that I was still in jail – in the actual prison and not in the torture house of my dreams. The nervous strain was depriving me of all strength, and I feared I would have to succumb. I endeavored to find consolation in the thought of the speedy approach of the day of trial. The trial would come some day. The world would know the truth – the world would know me innocent and the Jewish nation unspotted by the terrible calumnies brought forth by its enemies. The Jews do not murder, nor do they draw the blood of Gentiles.

However, the day of the trial was not as yet definitely determined. The court authorities were yet uncertain about what was to be done. I was told once that the trial was to take place in March; next time it was postponed until April. There was no certainty about it. Why were they so undecided about it? Why were they so slow?

It was all very simple. Those interested in pushing the case were not satisfied with the indictment. The investigating magistrate, Fenenko, had told me himself that he did not press the charges against me, that the material gathered by the investigation concerning the murder gave him no grounds upon which to prosecute me – still less to press a charge of ritual murder.

The prosecutor, however, was more stubborn: a case against me had to be made up at all costs. A Jew was to be imprisoned in order that the Jews might remember the case for generations to come. This is why an indictment had been set up that had no foundation supporting it.

If the case was to be considered as an ordinary murder, there was a total lack of proof and evidence upon which to base an accusation against me personally. All the indications would compel the authorities to arrest Vera Cheberyak with her gang of thieves – and to press charges against them. Inasmuch as the Czar himself expressed the wish that a Jew was to be persecuted, and the higher officials naturally wished to humor him, they were thus compelled to institute a law process against a Jew, namely me. And if so, and the case had to be, so to speak, "a ritual case" – why then did they not state that fact in the indictment? Therefore, the indictment charges were not satisfactory to any of those interested in the prosecution. I was neither "meat nor fish," neither "ritual nor unritual." The Czar would not be pleased and the Jews were apparently scoring in the first set-to.

After long discussions, disputations and hair-splitting, the trial was scheduled to begin at the end of May. My lawyers, preparing for all eventualities, insisted at the court that experts and scientists be summoned for the trial. Among others, they requested the presence of Professors Kokovtsev, Tikhomirov and Troyitsky – all professors of theology or of Hebrew language in the higher academies for clergymen. They requested also that the former counsel of the Holy Synod, Prince Obolensky, and Hermann Strack of the Theological Faculty of the University of Berlin, be also summoned as experts.

One day, while sitting absorbed in thoughts of my forthcoming trial, I heard a noise in the hall that was the signal for the opening of my many door locks. I expected to see the spiteful faces of my guards coming to announce the date of my trial. The locks kept on clanging, all thirteen of them, the door was opened – and instead of the guards, Mr. Grigorovich-Barsky was ushered in. With his usual kindness and cordiality, he began to cheer me up and inquired as to my treatment at the hands of the administration.

Then he said, "Mr. Beilis, rumors are current to the effect that in spite of the indictment presented to you, the whole trial will never take place."

"Why?" I asked, perturbed as much as amazed.

"It is simple," was his answer. "There is too much proof against the real murderers. New facts have come to the notice of the public and the officials. A Russian journalist, Brazul-Brushkovsky, who has especially devoted himself to the case, has collected new material and presented it to Colonel Ivanov (of the *Okhrana*). The

---

71

evidence gathered by this journalist is so important that the investigation is likely to be reopened and there is quite a probability that your indictment will be altogether quashed. Of course, it will be a bitter pill for your persecutors, and they will put up a fight, but it looks as if they will have to give in."

The joy was so great that I began to weep. "Do not weep, Mr. Beilis," said Mr. Barsky, quite moved himself. "I understand your situation quite well. Be certain you will be eventually released. It is impossible to foretell, of course, how long they will drag it on. You can see yourself, they are trying their best to tangle up the case. But we feel very hopeful their efforts will come to naught. If not presently, then somewhat later they will have to release you." Mr. Barsky bade me farewell with cordial wishes of seeing me soon free in the midst of my family.

I was beside myself with joy. The whole case against me was falling to pieces. How about it now! The truth apparently was going to come out after all. Even the Black Hundreds were coming to realize that I was innocently thrown into the dungeon and that I ought to be released.

I experienced all the joys of the expectation of approaching liberation. I exercised my imagination in calling up the picture of the morning when the guards would come in with the announcement, "Beilis, you are free! You can go home. You are innocent."

The new developments announced by Mr. Barsky threw me into a state of impatient restlessness. Every time I heard footsteps in the hall, I felt certain that the administration was coming to announce my release. Several days passed in this manner, days of strain and impatience. Seeing that my hopes were not being realized immediately, I began to have doubts. Who knows whether the information was based on solid facts? Perhaps my lawyers simply wanted to cheer me up. Possibly the case had taken so bad a turn that they wanted to keep up my energy and strengthen me in order that I might be able to sustain the coming bitter days.

However, I did not want to believe in this pessimistic version. From Mr. Barsky's previous visits, I felt assured he was a frank and sincere man. He would not deceive me, even if it came to the worst. He would tell me the truth. And since he told me there were chances for my speedy liberation, how could I doubt his word? The more so, as we both knew how completely innocent I was.

The days were passing; weeks and months finally elapsed and there was no change in my situation. I understood that new circumstances must have arisen, but whether for the better or for the worse I did not exactly know. Above all, I was afraid of the new name of Colonel Ivanov, a colonel and a gendarme. That was not a good omen, in my opinion. The man was not likely to do anything in my favor. His duty, of course, was to please the higher officials, not to alleviate my fate.

Things became quiet for a while. No one came to visit me. I was neither brought to trial, nor was I told to go free.

Chapter 14: Once More Before the Inquisition

Rather than being put on trial, I was summoned several times for additional questioning by the new investigating magistrate. He was the notorious anti-Semite already mentioned, Mr. Mashkevich. Once, during the interrogation, he inquired, "Tell me, Beilis, had your father ever gone to see *tzadikim*?"

His question amazed me. I expected the announcement of my liberation, while he was apparently starting the interrogation all over again. What new tricks had he up his sleeve? Was not the interrogation all over? What remained was either to have me tried, or to release me.

But it was once more the same old story, with the *Hasidim* and *tzadikim*. Were not the authorities straining their point a little too far? I told him I could not well remember. If it happened, it was years ago.

"Are you a *Hasid* or a *Misnaged*?" he asked me smilingly.

"I am a Jew," was my reply, "and I don't know the difference between these two groups. We are all Jews."

"Do you know whether Zaitsev ever went to a rabbi?"

"I don't know."

"Are you not related to the family of the Baal Shem Tov?"[c]

"I have no idea of that, Mr. Magistrate."

"Do you pray with a *tallis* (prayer shawl), or without a

---

[c] Israel ben Eliezer, the eighteenth-century founder of Hasidic Judaism.

tallis?"

I had answered this question once before. Before my marriage I had prayed without a *tallis*, after my marriage with the *tallis*.

"What do you need the *tallis* for?"

"I don't know what it is for."

"Now, Beilis, tell me," the investigating magistrate's smile was becoming quite cunning. "What is it exactly that you call an *afikomen*?"

It was the same thing all over again. The same foolish questions with which the first investigating magistrate, Fenenko, had confronted me over a year ago. Besides that, I thought the new man probably wished to find out whether Fenenko had been investigating the case in the right manner, and once he had the information, he would release me. Fenenko himself had asked me those foolish questions, and didn't he finally say he had no evidence against me? I was unable to explain properly to the investigating magistrate what the *afikomen* was. In my childhood I lived in a village, then I spent several years in the military service. I did not know much about religious rites. I used to eat matzah, eat the *afikomen*, which was actually a piece of matzah. I did not know any more about it. And had I even known, it would have been difficult for me to explain.

He had some more questions. "Have you not a brother who is a rabbi or a *shochet* (Jewish ritual slaughterer)?"

"No, we have no rabbis in the family. If there were any, fifty or a hundred years ago, I am not aware of it. There might have been a rabbi or a *shochet* at that time. However, not now."

He was silent for a minute or two. He looked as if he wished

---

to remind himself of something. He looked several times at some papers before him. At last, he asked another question. "Have you any connection with Schneur Zalman Schneerson,[d] the well-known Rabbi of Liadi?"

"No," was my answer. "I have a good friend by that name. He lives in Kiev and often came to visit me, but I do not know the Schneerson family in Liadi, and I am in no way related to it."

With these and similar questions, he kept plying me for about two hours. Then he started to read from a book by a "scientist" Pranaitis, who had been endeavoring to prove with all sorts of sophistry and misquotations from the Torah and Talmud that the Jews actually use blood for their matzah, and that the blood was baked in the *afikomen*. The investigating magistrate mentioned also the names of Shmakov, Professor Sikorsky, and Golubev, who were also supposed to know all about Jewish religious rites. In short, he manifested, during the interrogation, what he must have considered as great erudition in our Torah.

His questions provoked a heart-burning anger in me. It was he who was drawing my blood with every question. However, I was helpless. I had to answer him. I was a prisoner. He had all the authority over me and could do what he liked.

The questions themselves would not have produced such a painful impression upon me had I not noticed the manner in which he treated my answers. I could see that all these questions were not put in order to clear up the case, but rather out of curiosity to hear what my answers would be. I could see from his smiles, from his

---

[d] Shneur Zalman Baruchovich, the first Lubavitcher Rebbe, founder of Habad Hasidism.

—

76

displeasure at my answers, and from some of his remarks that all these questions were superfluous. As far as he was concerned, he had it all clear, and was sure of his course. He knew, for instance, and felt quite certain, that the Jews used human blood for Passover; that the blood was put in the *afikomen*; and that all that was substantiated by such "scientists" as Pranaitis, Shmakov and Sikorsky. From this interrogation, I received the impression that my indictment would not be quashed before the trial; that the trial would actually take place. I could not understand, however, the reason for the additional interrogations.

Chapter 15: My Attorneys are Persecuted

In this state of uncertainty, I spent the summer. The autumn brought no changes. Winter was approaching. During the months in question, I was not visited by anyone and therefore did not know what was taking place outside the prison walls. I had hoped before for a speedy date of trial, which could have revealed to the world my innocence. I was disappointed. Later, I expected the case to be dismissed, since I was told by Mr. Barsky that the charges against me were found baseless, and the case invalid. But the investigation began all over again.

Apparently, there was a new turn to the case, but just what was its meaning? Although the interrogations conducted by Mashkevich had been concluded several months ago, I was still kept in the dark. What was going on behind the stage?

I was informed later by one of my lawyers that Grigorovich-Barsky had been telling me the honest truth. All of my lawyers had been of the opinion that my indictment and the whole case would be dismissed and the trial would never take place.

This is what had happened. As I have already mentioned, the journalist Brazul-Brushkovsky, together with police-captain Krasovsky, had undertaken in earnest to find out the real murderers and to gather the facts for the evidence. They had made, with this purpose in view, the acquaintance of Vera Cheberyak and of her gang, visited them several times, interrogated her neighbors, collected considerable material, and presented it before Colonel

Ivanov.

Colonel Ivanov undertook a careful investigation in order to verify Brushkovsky's assertions. As a result of Brushkovsky's efforts, the colonel came to the conclusion that Yushchinsky's murder was the work of Cheberyak's criminal band. Ivanov conducted his investigations in strictest secrecy, and upon their termination sent the material to the prosecutor of the Superior Court.

At first, the prosecutor's office showed no interest in Colonel Ivanov's reports. Though these reports came from an official source, and what is more from the gendarmerie (the uniformed police arm of the *Okhrana*), the prosecutor ignored them. Nothing would have come of it had not my attorneys taken a determined stand. When my lawyers came to know that new facts had been discovered, they demanded that the investigation be reopened. This happened in the spring of 1912.

The higher judicial authorities and the Black Hundreds were much displeased by the new turn of events. They naturally feared a new investigation on the basis of Brushkovsky's discoveries; such action would result in the unmasking of the true criminals. This was what they feared above all. Yet they could not go openly against the letter of the law. When new evidence appeared, the law called for a new investigation.

Fenenko did not suit them for the new work. He was too "soft." He was therefore given a leave of absence, i.e. simply removed from any dealing with my case. Besides that, the prosecutor Chaplinsky was ordered to come to St. Petersburg for a conference with Minister of Justice Shcheglovitov concerning my case; the prosecutor was also to confer with the higher Black Hundreds leaders.

In the Ministry of Justice, there was at the time a group of officials who were inclined to have my case dismissed in order to "get out of the slimy bog." That tendency prevailed for a certain time, and it was then that Grigorovich-Barsky had announced to me the "happy tidings."

In the end, however, the Black Hundreds prevailed and won out. They insisted that if a new investigation was to take place, it had to be done "right," i.e. the new indictment was to contain the charge of "ritual murder" without any evasions.

The final decision was worthy of the corruption brought by Shcheglovitov into the administration of justice. It was decided to have a new investigation and an indictment based on its results, but the indictment was to come first. This time it was to be the "right kind," with "ritual murder," etc. The investigation was to be held just for the sake of appearance. And that was exactly what they did.

As I related, Mashkevich was put in charge of the investigation, replacing Fenenko. Mashkevich did not care for any "fine points." With him it was all very simple: he was looking for *Hasidim*, *tzadikim*, rabbis, white robes – in short, all the paraphernalia of "ritual murder" as written in the books of the fathers of the inquisition.

For the sake of appearances, the materials gathered up by Brushkovsky were also examined, but instead of sending them to the prosecutor, as was the rule, they were first dispatched to the Ministry in St. Petersburg, and then were sent back again with proper commentaries and annotations.

As I was told, the authorities were unable to find in the prosecutor's office of Kiev a man capable of formulating the indictment as it was desired, "with the teeth in it." Finally, a

---

suitable person was found. Even at that, the indictment was not prepared at once. It was turned "inside out" and doctored up several times. The work was done by an assistant prosecutor, Count Pashchenko-Razvodovsky. When the indictment was ready, it was forwarded to the Superior Court of Kiev for approval.

But the enemies of our people were not satisfied with their work. They now started to get after those who wished to discover the truth.

The Chief of the (non-political) secret police of Kiev,[e] Mishchuk, was prosecuted, together with the detectives Smolovik and Klein; they were charged with having been "partial" in their investigation, i.e. that they had leaned rather towards my side. Mishchuk was found guilty and received a year of imprisonment with deprivation of civil rights. The two detectives were punished in the same manner.

The police captain Krasovsky, who had a record of twenty years' service in the police, was charged with having embezzled the amount of seventy-five kopeks (about forty cents). This sounds like a joke when we think of the millions of rubles involved in the thievery of the higher officials. The case against Krasovsky, however, was dismissed.

The journalist Brushkovsky was prosecuted by Vera Cheberyak for criminal "libel." The same happened to the well-known journalist S. Yablonovsky. Of course, Vera Cheberyak didn't do it of her own accord. She was told to do so by those above.

Thereupon, the Black Hundreds turned their attention to my

---

[e] There was a political secret police (the *Okhrana*) and also a non-political secret police.

lawyer Margolin. First of all, because he published a book against the ritual murder calumny. The prosecutor based his charges on the assumption that Mr. Margolin was thus trying to influence the inhabitants of Kiev, from among whom a jury would eventually be selected for the trial. The second charge was that he had attempted to bribe the woman Cheberyak to have her assume the guilt of Yushchinsky's murder; that he offered to pay her forty thousand dollars in case she consented to "confess."

A similar prosecution was instituted against Mr. Barsky for having signed a public protest against the ritual calumny. He received a reprimand from the court. His subsequent appeal was lost in the higher court.

Hearing of all these events, I could well see that my case had taken an unfavorable turn. I saw a closely woven net about to entangle me. My lawyer tried to keep my courage up and assured me that in spite of all machinations, the truth would finally prevail. With these hopes, I set myself to wait for the long-postponed trial.

Chapter 16: The Attempt to Poison Me

The spring of 1913 came. I had not the fortune to appreciate, as did all other creatures, the awakening of nature. All were free and merry except me. It was the third year of my imprisonment in the dark cell, where I could not even move freely. For two years, I had scarcely seen my family. I had to wallow in the filth, to live in the sordid and damp air of the jail, hardly ever seeing God's sun which shines equally upon the righteous and upon the sinners; the rays of the sun could scarcely penetrate through my prison window.

Nevertheless, I felt more cheerful. It was not so cold in my room, and the mild winds coming through the gratings refreshed me. On one of these days, I received a visit from Mr. Grigorovich-Barsky. After the usual greetings, he told me he had a request to make of me.

"What could it be?" was my inquiry. "What could you possibly want of me?"

"Yes," he continued, "I want to ask you something. It will be hard, but you must do it."

"What is it?"

"You must cease to receive food from home."

"If you say so," was my answer, "I shall do so. You know, no doubt, why you are asking it. Could you tell me your reasons?"

"I certainly shall. I am asking you because the Black Hundreds have been writing in the newspapers lately that the Jews are attempting to poison you, out of alleged fear that you might slip

—

up with a word and confess your supposed guilt. This makes us, in our turn, afraid that the Black Hundreds may arrange your poisoning in order not to lose their case against you before the whole world. If you die now, they believe their accusations against the Jewish people will remain unrebutted. Those must be their intentions. We have therefore decided that you must cease to receive food packages from home, so as to stop the insinuations of those hooligans. If you receive no food from the outside, they will not be able to insinuate that the Jews are bent on poisoning you. Undoubtedly, it will be hard upon you, but it must be done."

I promised, of course, to do as he told me. Later, I thought over the matter. If the Black Hundreds insist that I am likely to be poisoned, it looks as though they are bent on doing it themselves. I became afraid it might be done through the prison guards. I therefore petitioned the warden that I be permitted to take my food from the common kettle myself, instead of it being brought into my cell as was the usual procedure. At first, when I was in prison with a number of men in the same room, we were given food in one large bowl for ten or twelve men. I was not then afraid of poison, for they would have had to poison the whole crowd in order to get rid of me. Now I was all alone in the cell, and was getting my food in a plate through an aperture in the door, and I did not feel quite assured of my safety.

My petition was at first refused. I was told, "If you want to eat, eat what you are given – if not, you can starve. No special privileges for you. We shall not poison you – it is your Jews that you have to beware of. They are not satisfied with using our blood and are inventing additional lies to make us appear ridiculous."

I had reasons to be stubborn. I declared a hunger strike.

Three days elapsed – whenever a prisoner doesn't eat for a few days, the prosecutor is summoned to investigate. The prosecutor appeared. I told him I should like to get my food myself from the kettle – not to have it brought into my room.

His reply was: "It cannot be permitted; you must not leave your cell. You are supposed to be under strict confinement. The other prisoners and guards must not even look at you."

"Well," I answered, "let them turn away when I draw my ration."

Somewhat to my surprise, after considerable bickering and argument I was allowed to get my food from the common kettle. I was again reduced to the half starvation diet. I was receiving no food from home, and the prison broth was unfit to eat.

Chapter 17: A Murderer's Suicide

About that time, I was told quite an interesting story, which I expected to be of great use to me. However, it proved to be a disappointment. Here is a short account of it. While the new evidence collected by the journalist Brushkovsky was being examined, the authorities arrested Cheberyak's friends, the thieves Rudzinsky, Singayevsky and Latyshev. They were arrested upon altogether different charges.

One day Latyshev, who was the principal murderer, was summoned by the investigating magistrate (it was still in the days of Fenenko). Fenenko commenced to ask his prisoner questions relating to my case. At the same time, he mentioned that according to some new evidence, Latyshev was implicated in Andryusha's murder, with the others of the band, and that they had done it upon Cheberyak's instigation. The investigating magistrate was giving such details, his information seemed to be so exact, that it all made a strong impression upon Latyshev.

After an interrogation which had lasted more than an hour, a confession was drawn up and Latyshev was told to sign it. He actually signed it. Apparently, he was at the time somewhat confused – and under the influence of the assurance with which Fenenko told him of the new evidence. Later, however, he must have regretted that he signed the confession in a hurry and thus implicated himself. He made a move for the desk in order to destroy, apparently, both the writing and the signature. But his

---

escort was on the alert and prevented him from snatching the document from the desk.

Three days later, Latyshev was again summoned before the investigating magistrate. Fenenko began to ask him further questions about the crime. This time, the questions were hitting so close to the point that Latyshev became completely confused in his explanations. The investigating magistrate began to write another confession. Latyshev noticed a carafe of water standing on the window-sill and asked for permission to take a drink. He approached the window leisurely and had his drink. The window was open, Latyshev jumped through it, fell from a height of four stories, and was instantly killed.

The reasons for his suicide were very simple. He was the arch murderer and leader of the gang. When he saw that the truth was finally discovered, he understood that he would have to spend the rest of his life in prison. He decided to put an end to his life.

Although his suicide produced a strong impression, it apparently did not influence the course of my case. The new investigating magistrate understood better than Fenenko how to do his work so as to please the Black Hundreds and those "higher up." The other two murderers, Rudzinsky and Singayevsky, were released shortly afterwards.

Chapter 18: The Second Indictment

One day I was again called to the prison office. In the office I found the investigating magistrate, Mashkevich, sitting quite at his ease at the desk and apparently in the best of spirits. After muttering something in answer to my greeting, he took off the desk a document of many pages and handed it over to me.

"This is your indictment," he said with an air of self-importance.

I was at a loss for what to think. The first indictment had been a short affair of five pages. This one was practically a book of about thirty pages. I expected no good out of this new visitation.

Quite downcast, I walked slowly back to my cell. Since I was very slow, feeling weak with apprehension and confusion, my guards cheered me up with a couple of blows on my back. In the cell I lay down upon my cot and could not raise my head, still less read the indictment.

I looked upon this roll of paper that represented what the higher officials wished to have written about me and my alleged crimes. And yet I was an innocent man who, as it is said, never hurt a fly in his life. I was being kept a prisoner while the actual murderers were promenading free on the streets, protected by what was called "Russian justice."

And so the die was cast; the lot fell upon me – they could not find anyone else. They were searching and investigating and finally decided in the "higher spheres" that I must be tried, and if possible convicted.

Well, then, let the trial take place, said I to myself, and let the whole world know what atrocious villainies are being committed in Holy Czarist Russia. I jumped from the bed and grabbed the indictment to see what these people were charging me with. I had to strain my eyes in order to see the small letters. My eyesight was affected by the darkness prevailing in the cell, and I could not read it except in short stretches. What were they seeking and what had they found?

This is what I read: when the autopsy upon the murdered boy's body was performed, a number of wounds were observed upon the various parts of the body. There were thirteen wounds on the throat, on the skull and around the ears – in all, forty-seven wounds were discovered upon the whole body. Upon the basis of the autopsy and analysis, Professor Obolensky of Kiev University, together with his assistant, came to the conclusion that the wounds on the neck and the skull had been inflicted while the heart had still been strong. The other wounds on the body had been inflicted when the heart became weaker. Thus, the first stabs were those upon the throat and the head – the last ones were those near the heart.

They were also of the opinion that the stab in the heart was inflicted by pushing a knife up to the hilt, which could be seen by measuring the depth of the wound. Their conclusion was that the assassins had been deliberately torturing the child.

Professor Kosorotov, whose opinion was also asked, confirmed that of his colleagues. He stated that the murder could have been perpetuated by one as well as by several murderers. He was also of the opinion that it was the intention of the culprits to inflict torture upon the child.

This was the expert opinion upon the murder. After that it became necessary to find the culprit – to find out why Andryusha had been slain. The indictment stated that at the beginning of the investigation, it was found that on March 12, 1911, at 6:00 in the morning, the boy Andryusha left his house for school. It was discovered later that he had not attended school on that day and had not returned home.

At first, his mother thought that he went to spend the night with a relative, Natalie Yushchinskaya. In the morning, his mother found that the boy had not been seen at the relative's house, and a search for him began. The search lasted for several days, until finally he was found dead.

In the beginning, there were rumors that Andryusha's mother had shown little interest in the fate of her son. Moreover, when he had been found dead, she was alleged not to have manifested any motherly feelings. She did not weep, nor did she seem to be particularly disturbed. Witnesses appeared, declaring that a day or two after the disappearance of the boy, his mother was seen dragging something enclosed in a heavy bag, in company with a man. Because of all that, Andryusha's mother was arrested, and the police searched her house. After several days of detention, the authorities reached the conclusion that the rumors were unfounded and baseless inventions of her enemies.

About the same time, rumors commenced to circulate that the Jews had murdered Andryusha. The indictment stated that the authorities did not at first attach much importance to those rumors, because they were still under the impression that Andryusha's mother was implicated in the murder.

The investigation also took up another trail in connection

with persons who could have been involved with the crime. The thieves Rudzinsky, Singayevsky and Latyshev were implicated. There were rumors to the effect that the boy Andryusha had known all the secrets of the band and had been threatened by them with violence in case he betrayed them. There was a possibility, because of that, of them having done away with him. Vera Cheberyak was also suspected, since Andryusha had often been seen in her house.

In reading this first part of the indictment, I felt rather pleased. Thus far, the investigation seemed to be on the right track. I began to hope the indictment would not be so terrible after all. In reading further, however, I saw a complete change in the story.

All this had taken place in the beginning. That is, the investigators had shared those views at first, but later … all gave way to a new version. The investigation, according to the wording of the indictment, was brought to the conclusion that the "gentlemen" Singayevsky and Rudzinsky (notorious murderers and thieves in the neighborhood) were simply paragons of virtue. The same high recommendation was extended to Cheberyak. She also had been the "purest of the pure." Yushchinsky's mother had been cleared sometime before, and really, how could such a calumny be leveled against so "perfect a mother."

In short, they were all decent, honest people, and simply could not have been charged with such an abominable crime. The real culprit, according to the indictment, was a Jew, Mendel Beilis, the manager of Zaitsev's brick factory. It was I who was selected for the role of Yushchinsky's murderer. Truly, I had been living on the factory grounds for a number of years, without ever having bothered anybody. But it really did not matter, for I had not murdered Andryusha for personal reasons, such as robbery or the like. I murdered him for religious purposes. There was a little hitch in this, however, for according to the indictment itself a *tzadik* (holy man) or a rabbi was needed for that. I, of course, was no *tzadik*, but was made such for the purposes of the indictment. A number of queer stories were invented to make me appear the murderer.

At the time, continued the indictment, when the journalist Brushkovsky found new facts and turned them over to Colonel Ivanov, suspicion turned again to Cheberyak. One of her neighbors, a Christian woman named Malitskaya, who lived in the lower story of the same house, was said to claim that she heard a child's screams coming from the story occupied by Cheberyak, and that on the day of Andryusha's disappearance.

But how could they say such evil things about Cheberyak? Who could believe it? Why, didn't she herself tell the story of her relations with Brushkovsky, who had taken her for a trip to Kharkov for a conference with an "important person," and had not that person offered Cheberyak forty thousand dollars if only she would take upon herself the guilt of the murder? The "person" was said to be no one else than my lawyer, Mr. Arnold Margolin. So Cheberyak averred. Of course, she indignantly rejected the tempting offer. She could not be bought with money. Hence, it was clearer than daylight that Cheberyak was innocent.

This, then, was the policy of the authorities. All the thieves and villains were to be whitewashed. The journalist Brushkovsky (who had a spotless name) and Captain Krasovsky were not to be believed. Cheberyak was given full credence.

In order to bring plausible charges against me, a Jew, it was necessary to make the crime a ritual one. Hence, it became imperative to base the charges upon the expert opinion of learned

---

Christians, who were to declare positively that the Jews used human blood for Passover.

I could not read further. My nerves were shattered, and I was exhausted. I fell on my cot. In the morning, I began to read the document again.

Just what were the expert opinions given by the scientists, and why were they sought? The indictment had it all clear. Yushchinsky had been murdered in a very unusual manner. Rumors began to circulate at once that the Jews had done it for religious purposes. The investigation authorities therefore were justified in asking for expert opinions in order to clarify the situation. For this information, they turned to Professor Sikorsky of Kiev University, to the professors at the Theological Academy in Kiev, to Glagolev, and to professors of similar subjects in the Academy of St. Petersburg, among them Troyitsky, as well as to the supposed "master of religious sciences," the Rev. Pranaitis.

The opinions of these experts were included in the indictment. Sikorsky and Pranaitis supported the prosecution, while Glagolev and Troyitsky gave opinions that favored me.

The question put to Professor Sikorsky probably was never equaled in court history. He was asked whether it was possible to express an opinion as to what nation the murderer belonged, and what motives had actuated the murderer to commit the crime. Though the question was most astounding, the great scientist (who by the way was a professor of Psychiatry, and himself somewhat unbalanced) was not abashed by it. He gave a "scientific" answer, to the effect that the crime had been committed deliberately and by a Jew for the purposes of racial vengeance, to "avenge the Children of Israel." The professor averred that the murder had been well

---

thought out. No insane person could have perpetrated it. The murderers had not gone straight for the heart. Their aim was not to accelerate the death, but to obtain their special ends, that is, to draw blood and to inflict torture. The professor laid down three points, distinct phases of the murder: the drawing of the blood, the infliction of torture, and the actual murder. That was why Andryusha had been stabbed so many times. The professor further opined that the deed was committed by one "used to that kind of work."

Such was Sikorsky's version. Crazy as that expert opinion was, even on the surface, it was accepted by the authorities as valid.

The two other professors, Glagolev and Troyitsky, who were the most prominent Russian authorities on the Bible and Talmud, were asked questions about Jewish laws and rites. Glagolev answered that there does not exist in Jewish literature any law or custom allowing Jews to use human blood, or Christian blood, especially, for religious purposes. He stated further that the prohibition against shedding human blood, or eating any blood whatsoever, was to be found in the Bible, and insofar as he knew was never retracted or abolished in any later writings. He did not find any specific prohibition to that effect in the Talmud or in the rabbinical laws.

Professor Troyitsky was also quoted as having said that the Jews were forbidden by their religious laws to use blood in food; also that they were strictly forbidden to murder any human being, whether Jew or non-Jew. The expressions "A Gentile studying the Torah is subject to death" and "Murder the good among the Gentiles" are to be found in the Talmudic laws, but he finds it difficult to explain them. He knows of no proper explanation. In

—

94

summing up, the professor stated that both the law and the Talmud prohibited Jews from using blood in general, and human blood in particular. As regards the Kabbalah, he was unable to express any opinion. He was unacquainted with the Kabbalistic literature, and did not know what, if anything, was said there about the usage of blood.

Hence, it became necessary for the indictment to turn to a Kabbalist, to the "great" authority on the subject, the Catholic priest, Pranaitis. This was quite interesting. The greatest Russian authorities, Glagolev and Troyitsky, distinguished professors at the highest theological academies, expressed themselves rather in my favor. That is, they explicitly stated that the Jews were forbidden to eat any blood, human blood especially. Hence, it seemed there could be no "ritual" in the case. But if there were no ritual, all the accusations leveled against me would fall to the ground. This, of course, the authorities did not like. They therefore began to tackle the Kabbalah. They searched high and low among professional clergymen, but they could not find anyone bold enough to say he knew the Kabbalah.

Finally, a certain priest Pranaitis, whose name had not been known to anybody, declared that he knew it all, the Talmudic as well as the Kabbalistic literature. The great Kabbalist gave his expert opinion: "All the Jewish rabbis and Jews in general are united in their hatred of the Christians. A Gentile is considered to be a 'beast harmful to men.'" Hence the explanation of the prohibition against murdering the alien. The prohibition, according to the priest, referred to the Jews alone, as only they were considered human. It did not refer to Christians, who were considered beasts.

Having done with the Talmud, the learned priest took up the

—

Kabbalah. "The ritual murder," he claimed, "must be committed in a specific manner as prescribed by the Kabbalah. Blood has a great part in the Jewish religion. It is used as a remedy in many diseases." When Jews need human blood, the practice is not to cut the victim's throat, but to stab the victim, to draw his blood out. The view that the Jews are actually forbidden to use blood is wrong, according to the priest. Even the Talmud likened blood to water, milk, etc.

Pranaitis then proceeded to enumerate a number of "scientists" (swindlers like himself), quoting their statements in regard to the question. He laid particular emphasis on the opinion of a certain renegade – formerly a rabbi, afterwards a priest – to the effect that the Jews could eat cooked blood. The renegade was alleged to have stated that Christian blood was good for eye diseases. Such were the discoveries made by Pranaitis in the renegade's name.

It is curious to observe that the renegade never said he knew these things himself. He declared that his father had told him so, taking the son's oath never to divulge the secret. While the renegade had been a Jew, he had kept the secret. Having changed his religion, he wanted to announce these things to the world.

The indictment was not satisfied with all this rigmarole. Its compilers turned back at this point, and told of certain evidence given by various persons. Cheberyak's boy, Zhenya, was alleged to have stated that he had seen strange Jews, *tzadikim*, in my house. I did not know whether Zhenya actually said so, for the boy had died in the meanwhile. However, his nine-year-old sister corroborated his story. They said that having once gone to Beilis, in order to buy milk, they had noticed through the window two strange-looking Jews, in funny hats and black robes. The children were said to have

—

96

become frightened and ran away.

Furthermore, on the day of Yushchinsky's disappearance, the girl said, she, with some other children, had been playing in the factory yard. Beilis started to chase them out, and they ran away and climbed over a fence to safety. She hid herself to see what Beilis would do. Thereupon she saw Beilis and the two Jews catch Andryusha Yushchinsky and drag him into the house.

Among other stories, there was also mentioned the story of my letter sent through Kozachenko to my family. The spy Kozachenko had quite a lively imagination. He related that having gained my confidence, he persuaded me to write a letter, and in doing so I told him many secrets. I was said to have asked him to do a job for me, once he was out of prison: to poison two "bad" witnesses. I supposedly promised him great remuneration from the "Jewish people." As a deposit, he was to be given fifty rubles and the required poison. If he did a good job, he was to be provided for the rest of his life.

The sum total of the second indictment was that I, in conspiracy with some unknown men who had not been discovered, had premeditated and committed the murder of a Christian child for religious purposes. For these purposes, we had taken Yushchinsky, gagged his mouth, and inflicted forty-seven wounds on his head, neck, and other parts, and had then drawn out his blood.

I received the second indictment in the month of March. Pacing my cell, I would often take out that document – what gall for them to call it a Court Indictment! – and read it again and again, till the blood would almost freeze in my veins. I was helpless. The whole of Black Russia, with Czar Nicholas at its head, willed it so.

When I was presented with the second indictment, I was

———

asked once more whom I was retaining as my lawyer. I answered that I wished to retain my former attorneys. A while later I was visited by Mr. Barsky. He told me that Mr. Margolin had withdrawn from the defense, because the prosecutor had summoned him as a witness. The law forbade one to be a witness and lawyer in the same case.

Mr. Barsky told me further that in addition to Gruzenberg and himself, I would be defended by Messrs. Maklakov and Karabchevsky. Some time later, I received another visit from Mr. Barsky. We spoke little of the case. He always told me to keep my courage and strength. He felt certain that the truth would rise, like oil upon water, and the Black Hundreds and anti-Semites would meet with ignominious defeat. He told me also to ask the investigating magistrate for a copy of the entire preliminary investigation. That was my right. My lawyers needed that copy. I sent a petition to the investigating magistrate for the copy.

The next morning, Mashkevich, the investigating magistrate, appeared in the prison. "Do you really wish to have a copy of the whole preliminary investigation?" he inquired.

"Yes, I must have it."

"If you insist, you shall have it, but I must tell you that it may make things worse for you. It may delay the trial date for another few months."

I asked why Fenenko [the previous investigating magistrate] had given me a copy without any quibbles.

He laughed at me. "You are foolish. Fenenko was a child. He believed all the stories you told him. Don't you compare me to Fenenko. He had drawn up an indictment that was good for nothing, while I made it to the point. Anyhow, if you wish to have

---

the trial delayed, you may have a copy of the preliminary investigation."

I was in a desperate dilemma. If I were not to have a copy, my lawyers would be unable to make a thorough study of the indictment in time. They would be unable to prepare their pleas or to get to the very heart of the prosecution's arguments. Were I, on the other hand, to get a copy, the date of trial would be postponed, and I had waited so long for that trial with so much impatience. It was possible that Mashkevich was just trying to give me a fright. But then again, he might be telling the truth. If he wanted to put any difficulties in my way, he was quite able to do so. His policy clearly was to inflict all possible suffering upon me.

Upon some pondering over the matter, I decided not to ask for a copy of the preliminary investigation. I believed that my lawyers would know how to get along without it. Or they would know how to obtain a copy by their own efforts. They had more chances of getting one than a helpless prisoner. Meanwhile, I would gain a least that much: that the trial would not be delayed.

A few days later, I was told that my wife and brother were coming to see me in the warden's office. Such meetings were the only consolation I had during my imprisonment. Entering the office, I saw my wife and brother sitting there. Mashkevich was also present. I began to ask them questions about the state of things in the family. My brother asked me: "Have you received a copy of the preliminary investigation?"

I told him that I had been informed that the process of trial would be delayed for another few months if I were to get that copy. Because of that I decided to dispense with the copy. My brother became angry and told me: "You mustn't listen to all these stories.

—

Get a copy and pay no attention to these stories."

The warden, who was present throughout the time of our conversation, jumped to his feet and turned to my brother with a shout: "Get out of here at once. What impudence!"

It was a long time before the warden regained his composure. He was pacing the floor and mumbling, "What insolence, what impudence." Thereupon, he ordered my wife to withdraw from his office too. I expected after that to hear that my brother had been arrested for his boldness, and I spent a few sleepless nights because of the worry.

A few days later, my wife came again for a visit. This time it was not in the warden's office, so we could talk only through a double grating. She told me, however, that my brother had not been arrested

It was with the greatest impatience that I waited for the much longed-for trial. Two and a half years had elapsed from that fateful day when the chief of the Kiev *Okhrana*, Kuliabko, had arrested me at my house. Kuliabko, meanwhile, had gone to his ruin, in part through his own fault. The well-known revolutionist, Bogrov, had managed to penetrate into the theatre at a time when Czar Nicholas had come to visit Kiev. It was there that Bogrov had assassinated Prime Minister Stolypin, in the presence of the Czar. Kuliabko's career thus came to a short and disastrous end. It did not, however, improve my situation a bit.

Now, at last, the great day was approaching. That day which not only I and my family, but the whole Jewish nation was breathlessly awaiting. Nay, the whole world; even many Gentiles were waiting for it, for all wished to know the truth, wished to know how the Russian people would decide my fate, as well as the fate of the Jewish nation.

I knew that I was to be defended by the greatest lawyers in Russia. I knew that the best elements of the Russian people were siding with me, with the truth, but what aid could the people render me? The situation depended not so much on the whole people as on the judges and the jury. In such a case, the ultimate issue and verdict hung, so to speak, on a hair. It could be swayed by a mood, by a caprice. What was it going to be? However, I firmly hoped that the bubble of lies would burst, and this gave me courage.

Chapter 19: The Trial at Last

Hard as it was to have spent over two years in prison, without definitely knowing what I was being accused of, it was harder still to wait for the great day when I would be put in the dock before the judges – that is, the day when the whole conspiracy would at last explode.

"But as long as we live, we live to see it," says the proverb.

One day I received a formal summons to appear for trial on the 25th of September, 1913. There were still over two months to be spent in anxious waiting. But the shore was at last in view; with every passing day, I was coming nearer to the longed-for end.

My joy was intense. I pictured to myself the procedure and incidents of the trial, the reading of the indictment, the questions I would be asked, and my answers to them. All my thoughts were concentrated on the approaching trial. I could not think of anything else.

About two weeks before the trial, I began to petition the authorities for permission to have my own clothes; they had been taken away from me when I was brought into the prison, when I had to exchange my own clothes for the usual prisoner's garb. I asked for my old clothes back because I was ashamed to appear at the trial in the prisoner's "royal raiment." I received no answer, however, to my earnest petition.

Two or three days before the trial, I was visited by my wife and brother. Of course, tears were rather plentiful and we were wishing each other to meet again in the near future in my own home, free and unmolested. Before leaving, my wife told me that I was to be permitted to have my own clothes, and that they would be issued to me on that very day.

The next morning, the thirteen locks of my cell began to click, preliminary to the opening. Usually, their opening filled me with apprehension and fear. This time, they seemed to have a different sound. They were clicking more encouragingly, as if bringing good news.

"Well," said the guard, "here are your clothes, dress yourself. Today your trial begins."

I was brought into another room, where I was given my suit of clothes, etc., that had been taken from me two and a half years ago. I was happy to be able to discard the ugly prisoner's clothes and to put on my own. I did not want to think at that moment that I might be putting them on for the last time. I was satisfied to be able, at least for one day, to appear like other human beings.

On that day, the authorities treated me with the greatest friendliness. All their former viciousness disappeared as if by magic. Some of them even helped me to put on my clothes. I could not imagine such politeness on their part after all the suffering they had subjected me to. When I was in readiness, I was handed over to the escorting squad. The command was given: "Forward march!"

As we came out of the prison yard, a pleasant sight awaited me. Previously, each time I had been conducted to the investigating magistrate, there was no one in the yard except for a few guards. This time, the yard was packed as if a great military review was on. A regular army; all the administration was there in full force. From the lowest guard to the warden himself, all were looking at me. I was the center of attention. Some of them smiled under the moustache; the majority were stiff and serious.

Besides these, there were several hundred Cossacks in the yard. Their lances were glistening, and the naked sabers were an indication that they had come to protect me from an "evil eye." I was seated in the black armored prison coach, which was surrounded by a whole army of officials and cavalry; and with all this pomp and grandeur, I was escorted on the road to the court.

From the window of my coach I could see that the streets were lined with people. The weather was far from propitious. It was very cloudy, and it looked as if the heavens did not view the whole spectacle favorably. But the crowds did not heed the weather. The Black Hundreds, who could be distinguished by their badges, were present in large numbers. I could see their ugly faces, popping up at every turn of the road. On the pavements, in the windows, and even on the roofs of houses, one could see multitudes of people.

During my progress I noticed Jewish faces, men and women, some wringing their hands, and wiping their tears with their handkerchiefs. I also did my share of crying.

Along the whole road, from the prison to the court, a distance of about two miles, a line of Cossacks on horseback stretched out, in order to insure order, and probably to watch me. Passing through the cordon, we finally reached the courthouse, which was surrounded by thousands of people. The gates of the courtyard swung open and our coach drove in. Alighting from it, I said to the driver with a smile: "I shall pay you on my way back." The chief of police and a police captain, who were standing nearby, could not refrain from laughing.

In the courthouse, I was led into a separate room, specially assigned to the prisoners under trial. I was impatiently waiting to be led into the courtroom. I had been waiting so long a time for this day. Now that it had come, I could hardly believe my sense that it had not all been a dream.

All those months and years passed before me as if in review: Kuliabko dragging me away from my family, the *Okhrana* headquarters, the investigating magistrate, the *tzadikim*, the *afikomen*, the prison, the days of hunger, the nights of sleeplessness, the guards, the swollen feet, the operation, the surgeon cutting endlessly and mercilessly, Fenenko, Mashkevich, the general and the lady, and all those endless tortures. My God, when was it all going to end?

Chapter 20: Karabchevsky

The door of the room opened and a distinguished, athletic-looking man with a flowing mane of hair came in and greeted me. I started, as if awakening from a nightmare, and looked at that handsome and friendly, smiling face.

"Good morning, Mr. Beilis. Don't be alarmed. I am your lawyer Karabchevsky," he said.

I had known that he was to be one of my lawyers at the trial, but I had seen only Messrs. Grigorovich-Barsky, Gruzenberg, Zarudny, and Margolin. They often came to visit me in the prison. The two others, Messrs. Maklakov and Karabchevsky, I had not seen before the trial.

The sudden appearance of Karabchevsky made a strong impression on me. It was as if a strong light had penetrated the room. His friendly greeting, his cheerful tone, not only liberated me from the nightmare of my thoughts, but made me feel as if I was to be liberated at once from my very imprisonment.

The famous advocate came closer and said: "Be of good cheer, Mr. Beilis. Keep your courage up. I should be happy to come nearer to you and to shake hands with you. Unfortunately, in your case, an exceptional rule has been laid down, and even we, your lawyers, cannot approach you nearer than within four steps' distance. It is not impossible that were I to break that rule, I should be severely reprimanded. How do you feel, how have you been?"

His cordial and friendly words had so strong an effect upon

me that I forgot I was a prisoner. I felt as if I were a free man, surrounded by friends. But a look at my escorts, who were ceaselessly watching my every movement, made me realize that I was still very much in their clutches.

I began feeling hungry, and wanted a smoke too. I therefore said to Karabchevsky: "I should like, first of all, to be permitted to smoke, and also to be given something to eat. I shall be completely starved if I am to wait till food is brought from the prison. I have money and could buy food from the courthouse restaurant."

While I was thus speaking, the colonel who was in charge of the escort came into the room. Karabchevsky turned to the colonel:

"Why is it that this man is not allowed to smoke?"

The colonel answered sharply: "Because prisoners must not smoke."

"That may be so," replied Karabchevsky, "but this man is not a prisoner. Besides that, he must be given something to eat. The trial which is about to begin will be a long and trying one. He will need every bit of his strength. It is a serious matter. I therefore earnestly beg of you to grant Beilis the two things he is asking for. If you do not grant him that – perhaps it is not in your power, but that does not matter – I shall be compelled to tell it to the public during the trial. Not many should be subjected to such privations, and especially not a man like him."

Karabchevsky's words made quite an impression on the colonel. He realized at once that he was not dealing with a downtrodden Jew, Mendel Beilis, but with the great Russian lawyer, Karabchevsky. And Karabchevsky's threat to tell all the public at the trial must also have made its impression. The colonel requested to be given a few minutes to communicate with higher authority about the matter, because the problem was no ordinary one, and he could not take the responsibility upon himself alone.

In the very act of leaving the room, the colonel turned around and said to the escort: "Well, he may smoke, at any rate."

"If so," said Karabchevsky to the escorting soldier, "go and bring him some cigarettes." He pulled out a three-ruble bill and gave it to the soldier. The soldier returned in a few minutes with some excellent cigarettes. Karabchevsky looked very pleased that he was at once able to obtain for me the privilege and the pleasure of smoking at my ease, and thus to rout my dark thoughts.

Meanwhile, the colonel returned and announced that the higher authorities, upon deliberation, had also granted me permission to procure my food from the courthouse restaurant.

"Well, Mr. Beilis," exclaimed my lawyer, "are you contented now?" He added: "If there is anything you may need or want, tell your lawyers about it. We shall certainly do all that is possible to help you. As for yourself, don't lose courage. After all, you are not altogether in the hands of your imprisoners. You are in the hands of God, and in ours; and my colleagues and I are happy to participate in your trial. Of course, I wish to God such trials never had to take place in Russia. We would be spared so much shame upon the good name of our country. But since we must go through with it, I want to tell you that it is the greatest honor for us to be able, as we hope, to show the whole world the falsity of the charges you face. You will see for yourself. The truth will emerge victorious. I am taking my leave for a short while. We shall be together again very shortly. Dosvedanya!"

Karabchevsky's utterances, so clearly heartfelt, inspired in me strength and confidence. I really felt full of energy, and my faith in a speedy liberation grew quite firm. The behavior and treatment of my guards changed rapidly. They became extremely helpful and pleasant. They could not understand, of course, how such an important person could speak in the manner he did to a common prisoner. They had never heard anything like it before. Moreover, had not the gentleman intimated that I was not a prisoner at all? Also, the cigarette incident, for which the soldier received a three-ruble tip from the lawyer; the tiff with the colonel in regard to the restaurant food – all had their effect in changing the escort's attitude towards me.

The soldier brought my meal from the restaurant, and every time he was to go to the restaurant, he would solicitously inquire just what dishes I would prefer; since we were paying money for it, he was quite willing to see to it that I obtained the best and most nourishing food. And all of it was done with a cheerfulness and politeness that I had never before encountered in any of the prison soldiers.

Soon, I began feeling considerably better. For one thing, I got the first good glass of tea I had had for months; and a decent meal made me feel much stronger. However, it was somewhat too early to rejoice. After all the past days of suffering, I had to face a good many more, and I needed a great deal of energy for the future. It must be said, nevertheless, that for a prisoner who had been secluded from the world of the living for long and weary months, even an hour of ease and pleasure is great good fortune in itself.

While I was thinking of my fortune, the door was opened and the colonel shouted abruptly: "Bring the prisoner into the courtroom; the trial is about to begin!"

I repeated that last phrase over and over again in my head.

Chapter 21: The Trial Begins

I was brought into the large courtroom and was told to sit in the defendant's dock. The soldiers stood on both sides of me with their swords drawn, but I paid no attention to them. Let them watch me if such were their orders. How contented I felt that now the veil of mystery was to be thrown away. Now the falsity of the charges against me would be revealed before the world.

I was very strongly impressed by the whole scene attending the opening of the trial. The large courtroom was packed with several thousand spectators; men of all nations and all classes were present. The ladies in splendid gowns, the well-fed generals in glittering uniforms and epaulettes, the high officials. But what impressed me particularly was the presence of the newspaper correspondents from all civilized countries.

The state prosecutor, the investigating magistrate, and some other officials were standing at the side engaged in animated conference. The dais was situated in the middle of the room, for the presiding judge and the two other judges.

All these people came to the spectacle as if to a play, to take part or to satisfy their curiosity. And all of them, participants or spectators, turned their eyes to me at the moment of my entrance into the courtroom.

The jury, the "twelve men, good and true," in whose hands my fate actually lay, made rather an uneasy impression upon me. As I surveyed them, I feared that I would lose the trial. I could not

110

believe that such a jury, composed of plain peasants, would be able to understand so complicated a case. If the jury had been as I expected, educated, scholarly men, I would not have had any fear of the ultimate issue. Such a jury would no doubt understand everything that was involved. But I feared that these peasants would not be able to understand even the arguments of my attorneys. Besides that, I knew how easy it is to impose upon so simple a class of people. They have not much of an equipment besides their native wits, and they have plenty of fear of the authorities. Therefore, I thought, it would be too easy for the officials to win over the jury with some glib talk and make them my enemies – the more so as the whole case revolved around a Jew. The prosecuting attorney and his assistants could be relied upon to heap every calumny on my head.

The jury saw on one side Russian generals, high officials resplendent with the Czar's authority delegated to them. True, on the other side, the jury could see a few Russian lawyers defending me. But would that make any impression upon them? Any defendant can hire advocates to defend him. Besides all this, the Russian peasant is well-known to be gullible, and the wilder the rumor, the more prone he is to believe it.

They were just the kind of people to believe that the Jews used human blood for Passover. For all I knew, they might all share that belief already. If so, it would look to them as if I were the murderer. But there was nothing to be done; the jury could not be changed. Trusting in God, we had to await the outcome.

I looked at my advocates and at the private prosecutors,

Shmakov and Zamyslovsky.[f] Scanning the faces of those in the courtroom, I noticed my wife sitting in a remote corner. She sat alone, with her head downcast, with tears in her eyes.

Upon my entrance, there had been considerable noise in the courtroom. Many people were holding conversation in loud tones. Some were walking back and forth. Various officials were coming in with their briefcases and reports. The confusion and din impressed one as though an orchestra was tuning up the instruments prior to starting the concert.

Suddenly, the sergeant-at-arms shouted: "Silence, the Court is entering." The public rose from the benches as one man. More officials came in, and immediately it became very quiet. One could hear the least sound, as if all had suspended breathing.

Presiding Judge Boldyrev interrupted the silence. He directed himself to me with a question: "To what religion do you belong?"

I did not recognize my own voice when I answered, in something approaching a shout: "I am a Jew!"

I noticed that the state prosecutor exchanged smiles with Shmakov, one of the private prosecutors, when I exclaimed that I was a Jew.

Immediately thereafter, the lawyers on both sides were involved in a controversy. The presiding judge asked my lawyers whether they objected to the fact that the private prosecutors were

---

[f] As explained in the Introduction, Russian criminal procedure in the Czarist period permitted the victim of a crime to participate in the criminal trial in order to receive an award of compensation from the accused. Following Maurice Samuel, we use the term "private prosecutor" to refer to the lawyers who represented Yushchinsky's mother in the trial. We refer to the official prosecutor as "state prosecutor" or simply "prosecutor."

seated so near to the jury. Karabchevsky immediately answered: "Yes, we are most emphatically against that. They are sitting too close to the jurymen, and every word of theirs is liable to prejudice the jurymen." Shmakov and Zamyslovsky attempted to deny that, but they were overruled.

The administering of the oath to the witnesses then began. This was no trifling matter. One hundred and thirty-five witnesses for the defense were summoned, along with thirty-five for the prosecution, making a total of one hundred and seventy witnesses. As the witnesses took their oaths, the silence heretofore prevailing in the courtroom was disturbed and a general hubbub began once more.

In coming up to take their oaths, the witnesses had to pass by me. All my witnesses, in doing so, greeted me in a friendly manner. Even a number of those summoned by the prosecution looked upon me and greeted me.

This procedure lasted throughout the day and was not over until late at night. I sat all the time as if nailed to my seat, and was near to fainting from boredom and exhaustion. When the swearing in of the witnesses was completed, I was carried back to the prison in the black coach.

During all the time of my imprisonment, I had slept practically on the bare floor, and nobody had ever thought of making it any more comfortable for me. Just the reverse: very often they tried to make it harder. Now I was pleasantly surprised, upon coming into my cell, to see it looking quite different than usual. There was a cot with a neat mattress. Also, the guards acted almost decently toward me; I could hardly recognize them.

I could not fathom the reasons for this change of heart. Did they begin to feel that the whole bubble of lies would burst and I would soon be liberated? But how could they have changed when the trial had barely begun?

Apparently, it was an order from their superiors that whatever the ultimate outcome, I should be treated in a milder manner for the time being. I thanked God for that. Let us accept an hour of relief, be it only an hour. Tired out with the excitement of the day, I threw myself upon the cot and fell asleep.

Chapter 22: The Testimony of Various Witnesses

The next morning, I was escorted to the courthouse with the same pomp and ceremony, by squads of cavalry and gendarmes acting as an escort of honor. The courtroom was as packed as on the day before, but the tension was greater this time, and the audience displayed more evidence of nervousness. For yesterday was only a formal ceremony of administering the oaths, but today was to begin the true drama, the real spectacle.

The examination of the witnesses began. The first to be called upon were the carters and drivers who had carted the bricks from the factory. These witnesses were to testify to a very important circumstance that played a large part in the trial. The lamplighter for the factory, Shakhovsky, had initially told the investigating magistrate, and it had been inserted in the indictment, that on Saturday, March 12, 1911, at 9:00 a.m., he had seen me standing in my house with two *tzadikim*, who were dressed in their long kaftans and skull caps, wrapped in their *tallesim* (prayer shawls) and absorbed in prayer. After prayers, I was alleged to have chased and caught Andryusha Yushchinsky in the yard, and to have carried him away to the kiln where the bricks were baked. He did not know what had taken place further, but from his statement it would seem quite clear that Andryusha had not come out of my hands alive. Shakhovsky had also stated that there was no one around the factory at the time, not even the workers. I was under the impression that the same story had been told to Fenenko by Cheberyak's little boy, Zhenya.[g]

When the prosecutor had asked me at the time what I had to say in regard to Shakhovsky's statement, I had exclaimed that there is a receipt book system at the factory. The receipts showed who the drivers and carters had been upon that day, to whom the bricks had been delivered, with the signature in each case of the carter who loaded and delivered the bricks to the customers. The books showed that on March the 12th, ten thousand bricks had been delivered, and that fifty drivers and carters had been engaged throughout the day in that work. It was preposterous, therefore, for anybody to say that there was nobody in the factory yard on that day, and that I had no other work but to chase after Yushchinsky.

One of the drivers gave the following testimony: "We were always at the factory. We even slept there. Beilis lived on the upper story; we lived in the lower one. Besides that, we know well that Beilis is an honest man."

Another driver said, "Beilis used to get up very early, about three in the morning. When we used to knock at his door he was always ready. He was very faithful to his employer and used to watch us pretty closely to see that we also got up early and went to work. He very often left his meals in the middle and would come over to see that we were not loafing. He never remained alone for an hour. All of us Christians were always around whether by day or by night." These simple and clear statements by plain peasants made a strong impression.

---

[g] This appears not to be the case; the story was concocted only after Zhenya died. See Samuel (1966), 188-91; Tager (1935), 84.

After the drivers, a woman – a complete stranger to me – was called up for testimony. Asked by the presiding judge whether she knew me, she gave the following answer: "Yes, sir, I know him – it is through Beilis that my family happiness has been ruined. I lost my husband because of Beilis. My husband had been a locksmith, and he was short of some piece of metal which he could not procure elsewhere. He noticed a suitable piece of metal at Zaitsev's factory, and, thinking that Zaitsev was very rich and would not notice the loss of that piece, he took or stole the thing he wanted. However, Beilis did not let the thing go and brought charges against my husband. My husband was imprisoned, became infected with typhus while in prison, and died there in a short while. Nevertheless, I call Beilis an honest man. He did his duty, he was true to his employer."

In this manner the court summoned one witness after the other, and these were shattering the indictment and the charges with their testimony. There could be no better proof for those who were really interested in getting the truth than the testimony which these plain people were giving. Of course, there remained the question how the jury would take that testimony.

After these witnesses, a Pole by the name of Visomirski, a man of over sixty years, came up before the judges. He was a neighbor of mine and lived in the third house from my own. His statements produced a powerful impression, and throughout his testimony the audience in the courtroom sat in perfect silence as if fascinated. When he finished, however, there arose quite a hubbub.

This Visomirski had been trading in cattle. Every time I needed a cow, I used to buy it from him. He was a frequent visitor in my house and knew everything in connection with my family, since he came practically every day. This Visomirski knew that at the time of the murder, I happened to have no cow at all. His testimony to that effect was a blow to the prosecution, since it showed the falsity of Vera Cheberyak and her children, who claimed that they had come to my house on the 12th of March to buy milk from me. That is why Fenenko at the first interrogation had asked me whether I had a cow, and whether I sold milk. Visomirski stated most emphatically that all the stories about the cow and the milk were absolutely false, since he knew positively that I had no cow throughout that whole year.[h]

When Visomirski finished his testimony, he still remained standing before the judges, as if absorbed in thought. It was clear he wanted to add something. The audience was, as the saying goes, "all eyes and ears," and a deaf silence reigned in the courtroom. What did the old Gentile wish to tell? And why was he thinking so long, why was he hesitating?

I myself felt quite uneasy. As to the cow, he had testified truthfully, but I was not sure what else he had to say.

Suddenly, he interrupted the silence. "I have something more to say," he proceeded very slowly. "I had not known I would be called as a witness – what have I to do with courts and trials and such things? I am an old man with one foot in the grave. During all my life, I have never been in court, whether as defendant or as witness, and I expected to end my peaceful life without having anything to do with courts, but lately I received the summons to come here – well, let it be so. What can I say? For the last two and a

---

[h] Testimony at the trial indeed established that Beilis had no cow at the time of the murder. Therefore, when Beilis spoke of having a cow, in his first interrogation by Fenenko (Chapter 3), he may have been referring to an earlier period.

———

118

half years, I have been ill on account of this case. It seems to me that it is likely to shorten my days. I have but one son who is very dear to me – because of him I would not do anything ungodly or dishonest. Besides that, I am under oath and I believe in God and fear Him. Because of that, I feel I cannot keep silent and must tell all that I know in connection with this trial.

"All that I have told you about the cow is proof sufficient how false the charges against Beilis are. But I am going to tell you more, which will put an end to all tales that Mendel Beilis is a murderer, that he could have murdered Andryusha Yushchinsky, or that he needed blood for the Passover matzah. I am telling you, all these charges are false from the beginning to the very end."

The silence in the courtroom was charged with intensity. The man stopped for a moment and apparently was gathering all his courage. He turned again to the judges and spoke in a straightforward and solemn manner. "I myself come from the city of Vitebsk. I had been the manager of an estate in the vicinity of that city. I had an assistant, a dear friend of mine and co-religionist, by the name of Ravich. Some time later, both of us had to migrate to the city of Kiev, where we settled and lived near one another, and that happened to be quite close to Cheberyak's house.

"The Ravich couple had no children. They lived in peace; they were very nice people and led an honorable life. He kept a grocery store and made a fine living.

"Thus several years elapsed. One day, Mr. and Mrs. Ravich came to me and told me they must bid me farewell, for they were going abroad, to America. I was amazed! How was it they were leaving the city, and suddenly at that? What was the matter? They were making out so well and were respected. What was the reason for leaving good friends and a profitable business and going to the other end of the world?

"Mrs. Ravich commenced to weep. I was deeply moved, for I knew something was wrong. With tears in her eyes, Mrs. Ravich told me, 'We must go to America.'

"'Why must you? Why is it you are leaving all of a sudden to face hardships in a new land? Have you friends or relatives there?'

"She wept the more. Mr. Ravich himself was sitting in silence and would not utter a word. I saw there was something oppressing their mind and soul which they would not tell. I begged her to tell me whether anything had happened. I said, 'I am a good old friend of yours. You must not conceal anything from me.'

"She said, 'My dear friend, I know I can tell you the truth, but I implore you not to repeat my words to anybody if you don't want to endanger our lives. Will you promise me?'

"'Yes, I will promise,' I said, 'but tell me the truth.'

"This is what she told me: 'We have been quite friendly all the time with Vera Cheberyak – you know we are neighbors. She would come frequently to get a loan of something, sometimes I myself would go to ask her for something – a pot or some other utensil. One morning I came into her house to ask for a chopping knife. I was so friendly with her that I knew where all these things were. I found Vera in bed, so I myself went to the kitchen to get the chopping knife. No sooner did I enter into the next room than I saw, to my utmost horror, a dead child lying in the bathtub. I was frightened out of my senses. I grabbed hold of the chopper and fled the place. Apparently, Vera noticed that I must have observed something, and she also became frightened.'"

The witness stopped once more – he spoke as if with

---

difficulty, and had to stop every few minutes. In the courtroom there was a wave of whispering and movement. Then the witness renewed his testimony. The rest of the story, as told to him by Mrs. Ravich, was as follows:

"A few days later, Vera Cheberyak came to see me and told me in a few sharp precise words: 'Look here, Ravich, I am mighty sorry, of course, that you saw the child, but it cannot be helped now – there is only one way out of it, you must leave Russia for good. If you stay here, you will have to leave this world altogether.'

"I said to her, 'Little sister mine, what is it you are saying? Why should I leave the country? Where shall I go, and what for?' She told me, 'I will give you the traveling expense to go to America. I know you would not squeal, but the spies will start nosing around. They will summon you to the investigating magistrate, and they will nag and question you, twist you back and forth, and in the end they will catch you and you will tell the truth. The best thing, therefore, is for you to disappear.'

"Well, what was I to do? I had to say I would consent and would leave Russia. Now I am coming to bid you farewell."

Visomirski concluded his testimony by saying: "In truth, gentlemen of the court, a few days later, they left for America, for New York."[i]

A veritable storm arose in the court when Visomirski ended his testimony. Vera Cheberyak, who was sitting there as a witness, bedecked in all finery in a gay hat, dressed as a "real lady," was near

---

[i] In a footnote to the original Yiddish and English editions of *The Story of My Sufferings*, Beilis states, at this point: "When I first came to New York and Mr. Ravich became aware of my arrival, he was one of the first to come to see me at the hotel."

121

fainting. She clearly became very agitated, was saying something and gesticulating frantically with her hands. Presiding Judge Boldyrev, who was apparently in quite friendly relations with Cheberyak, tried to quiet her, and instead of calling her "Mrs. Cheberyak," or "witness," as the official regulations required, he was calling her "Vera Vladimirovna," as if she had been a prominent person or a close friend of his. Those of the audience who were sitting close to her began to move away and shun her, as if she inspired them with fear.

This entire scene made, as I could well see, quite an impression upon the jury. When Vera Cheberyak saw all that, she took the gay hat off and threw a shawl over her head, so as to shield herself somewhat and to make herself less recognizable. She was white as a sheet and was visibly trembling.

The presiding judge, who was apparently quite shaken himself, directed himself to the witness. "If you knew all that you are saying now for so long a time, why did you keep silent to this day?"

Said the witness: "I did not think I would be called upon as a witness. I believed the truth would come out by itself. I will tell you more – I tried my religion. I kept silent in order to see whether we have a righteous God in the world – if there is a God, then the truth would surely come out."

It was clear the presiding judge did not intend to have the witness prolong his testimony. He was too good for the accused, and the judge wanted to get rid of him.

The next witness was a ten-year-old boy. His story was a new blow, not only at the indictment, but also at Vera Cheberyak.

The boy cast a glance at me and began to smile. The

presiding judge asked him, "Do you know Mendel Beilis?"

"Yes, I know him."

"Did he ever chase you from the factory?"

"I never had to be chased, and it was not up to Beilis to do that; he had other business to attend to. They had a janitor to chase us." (That question was asked several times, for the prosecution was trying to prove that I was in the habit of chasing Christian children from the factory yards, and that I had caught and made a victim of Andryusha).

"Yes," continued the boy, "we used to play around the factory, but Yushchinsky was never there, and Beilis never chased us from the factory."

He then added further: "Before you called me here, I was sitting near Vera Cheberyak and she said to me, 'Look here, boy, don't forget to say that Andryusha Yushchinsky had been playing at the factory yard with you boys – it's a long time ago, and perhaps you have forgotten it.' And I told her, 'Why should you teach me what I am to say? You are teaching me to tell lies – Andryusha never played around the factory.'"

By the expressions on their faces, the jurymen were moved by the boy's words. Vera Cheberyak was every moment faring from bad to worse.

I must remark here that it happened several times during the trial that not only was I being defended, but what was more, the witnesses declared themselves openly as being perfectly certain that it was Vera Cheberyak who had committed the murder. The grim humor of the situation was in the fact that instead of being on trial herself, she was summoned as a witness against me.

A series of important witnesses were interrogated during the first few days of the trial. Several witnesses were summoned to tell about the fire which had happened at the factory. I didn't know about the fire myself, but I came to know of it during the trial.

This is how it happened: Some time after my arrest, there was a fire at my house, apparently as a result of incendiarism. While the culprit was never discovered, there is little doubt that Cheberyak's gang had their hand in it. The anti-Semitic newspapers, however, began printing stories to the effect that it might have been my relatives who set the house afire, in order to obliterate the vestiges of my crime. The witnesses were therefore asked (they were mostly workers at the factory) when and where the fire had broken out. This was important, for the anti-Semites were insisting that the furniture from my house had first been removed, and only thereupon had my house been set afire.

The employees stated that the fire had broken out at midnight, and had they not been awakened betimes, all would have perished in flames. It was owing to a fortunate coincidence that they did awake at all. One of the workers happened to be drunk on that evening (it was Sunday). He was so drunk that about midnight he felt sicker than a dog – he commenced to scream and generally raise a racket. This awoke the others. All of a sudden, they saw smoke and then fire. The smoke and fire were coming from my part of the house. My family was fast asleep, and (thus ran the statement of the workers) "had we not awakened the Beilises, they would all have been burned to ashes."

Two young sisters by the name of Dyakonova were called up next. One of the girls gave highly interesting testimony. She said: "My sister and I frequently spent nights in Cheberyak's house because of her children, with whom we used to play. One night she asked us to come and spend the night. She told us her husband was going to do orderly duty that night at the telegraph office, and that she felt very lonely at the prospect of remaining alone in the house. We came to her, and about midnight, when she was already asleep, I noticed that on the floor there was something rather large wrapped up in a bag. I was curious and wanted to see what it was. When I uncovered the bag, I saw a dead child lying there. I was frightened almost to death and ran to wake up Vera. 'Look here,' said I, 'there is a dead child lying there – isn't it Zhenya (Cheberyak's boy)?' Instead of giving me any answer, Vera Cheberyak began to snore, and pretended that she didn't hear me. I was afraid to stay in the house – I woke up my sister and we ran home in the middle of the night."

State prosecutor Vipper and the private prosecutors, upon hearing the girl's testimony, were making wry faces and tried to confuse the testimony. The presiding judge put in another question: "Why didn't you tell all this before?"

The girls answered, "We were afraid. Vera is a dangerous person. She could easily have done away with us. We had to keep silent, but now we can tell the truth as it actually took place."

I could see that both the audience and the jury were deeply moved by the girls' story. The jury exchanged glances throughout the testimony.

A new witness, a barber, was called up. He said he had been arrested and brought to the police station, where he found three other prisoners: Vera's chief gangsters Rudzinsky, Singayevsky and Latyshev. That night, the barber overheard a conversation among the trio. He heard Rudzinsky telling Latyshev he was a stupid beast and without brains – "You should have thrown him into the factory yard – near the Jew's house." He did not hear anything else. This story he had told before to Fenenko.

I must say here that the trial was rich in revelations about things that I myself had no idea whatsoever, as I had been kept isolated for over two years. I listened with the greatest curiosity to the testimony presented in court, and I learned of all that had taken place around me while I was behind bars. Only thus did I realize what powerful evidence the authorities actually had against Cheberyak. And yet she was sitting in the court as a "witness," while I was on the defendant's bench!

Another witness was a Mrs. Malitskaya. She was in charge of a government dram shop (government liquor dispensary) with premises in the same house where the Cheberyaks lived. The Cheberyak family lived on the upper story; the dram shop was on the ground floor. This Mrs. Malitskaya told the court that on the night of March 12, she heard something heavy being dragged on Cheberyak's floor. She listened attentively and could hear the screamings of a child – she did not know what was actually taking place, but that much she heard.

Chapter 23:

An Honest Priest and a Disgusting Renegade

The presiding judge was apparently becoming tired of listening all the time to evidence given in my favor; all that evidence clearly tended to show that the murder had been committed in Cheberyak's house. Whether it was Visomirski, or the sisters Dyakonova, or the ten-year-old boy, or Mrs. Malitskaya, they all implicated Vera Cheberyak. In order to change the impression, the court began to summon the witnesses for the prosecution – to weaken the impression which my witnesses created at the time upon both the public and the jury.

A deacon was called (something like an assistant priest), which was meant to have its effect upon the peasant jurymen. The witness began to speak quietly and a length. I felt that his words were making their impression upon the peasants. The presiding judge put the usual question to him: "Do you know anything about the murder?"

He began to answer, "I know a great deal."

"What precisely do you know?"

"I had known Andryusha Yushchinsky as a dear little boy. I could almost say a saintly boy. He wanted to become a priest when grown up. I was preparing him for the seminary. When I asked him once why he wished to become a priest, he told me he liked the vestments very much. All of a sudden, I heard one day that he had been murdered. It made a tremendous impression on me. Since I had known him, his mother asked me to assist at the funeral ceremonies. When the boy was about to be lowered into the grave, I saw pogromists' circulars spread among the public. As soon as I read these circulars in which it was being said that Andryusha had been murdered by Jews, I saw that Andryusha's death had nothing to do with saintliness. I understood that the whole thing had been done in order to arouse pogroms against the Jews."

In the courtroom there was considerable movement and whispering by that time. The presiding judge threatened to clear the hall if order was not maintained.

The next witness on the stand was a monk. "What do you know about the murder?" he was asked.

Here is what he said: "I am over sixty years old. I think more of the world to come than of this world. Therefore, I must tell you the truth. My dear brethren, if only the earth was to give up its dead, and you could see how many Christian children had been murdered by the Jews."

It was obvious that the monk was not out so much for giving testimony, as to make a pogromist's speech for the benefit of the prosecution. A lively commotion started in the courtroom. The presiding judge interrupted the witness by a question: "Have you seen it yourself, or have you just heard it told?"

"No, I was just told so."

"Well, then, sit down," said the presiding judge.

The monk sat down quite angrily. As I was later told, the presiding judge was severely reprimanded for this action of his by those higher up. He was given to understand that he would lose his post if he behaved in this way toward the prosecution witnesses.

The monk had come to save Russia. At least, so he thought.

———

He was out to save the honor of Russian justice, and then to receive such an insult from the presiding judge! The latter actually had the cheek to ask the monk whether he had seen any child murdered by a Jew. What if he had not seen, was it not the truth just the same?

My lawyers, however, were not yet through with this individual and subjected him to cross-examination. It was Gruzenberg's turn to take this witness for cross-examination. Since, however, the witness was a Russian priest, tact demanded that a Christian lawyer should take up the task. Gruzenberg therefore wrote a note to Karabchevsky, and Karabchevsky proceeded with the work. The first question asked by Karabchevsky ran thus:

"Little Father, I ask forgiveness for this question, but I must ask it. Tell me, please, are you not yourself a Jew by origin? Is it not the truth?"

The priest stood somewhat disconcerted. Apparently he had not expected the question, and he did not quite like the idea of revealing before the Christians his former Judaism. But he had to give an answer.

"Yes, I had been a Jew for fifteen years."

"Did you ever hear in your father's house that the Jews used Christian blood for Passover?"

"No," he said, "I never heard it in my father's house, but I came to know of it since I became a Christian."

Karabchevsky turned to the jury. "Look here, gentlemen," he said, "the Father says himself that he never heard of any such charges when he was a Jew. In the house of his Jewish father, he never saw or heard of such a thing. He came to hear it for the first time after he turned a Christian. What does it mean, if anything? Why, that there are such Christians who invent all sorts of wild stories and cruel calumnies, and you can readily understand that his new co-religionists told him this story for the simple reason to make him hate the Jews and never return unto his old fold."

The cross-examination of the priest was thus ended, and he was no more interrogated. The day's session was also at an end with this witness. It was quite late in the evening, and all were very tired. The people went to their respective homes, and I was sent back to the prison.

The next morning at the beginning of the session, the college student Golubev, one of the leaders of the Black Hundreds organization in Kiev, was called to the witness stand. He was dark-complexioned and looked like a regular desperado. His appearance created something of a sensation. For he had been instrumental in demanding that a charge of ritual murder be brought, and he was expected to show great prowess and wonders. The state prosecutor, the private prosecutors, and Presiding Judge Boldyrev all received him with great friendliness and respect.

Golubev came up to the stand. Everyone was looking at him. Apparently nervous, he became paler and paler. The presiding judge inquired formally: what did the witness know about the case and the murder? The witness was silent. This alone caused a disappointment. He was asked whether he did not feel well. He was told to cheer up and collect himself. He was given a chair to sit down, and no sooner had he sat down than he fell into a swoon. The Black Hundreds professors, the "experts" Kosorotov and Sikorsky who were present, turned to the famous Professor Pavlov, the life physician to the Czar, who was also there as a witness. They appealed to Professor Pavlov to help Golubev to regain consciousness.

Said Pavlov: "Well, why do you remain sitting; is he not your witness? Why don't you do something for him?"

Finally, Golubev was carried out by the attendants, half dead and unfit for testimony. He did not say a word on that day. Why he became so frightened, nobody could tell. Was it pangs of conscience? Nobody knew. The best guess was that he was afraid of the galaxy of lawyers he was certain to face. He would have been cross-examined by the greatest legal talents in Russia, and he may not have remembered all he had told to the investigating magistrate. Of course, had he told the truth, there was nothing to be afraid of.

I must say right here that Golubev's father was a very fine and noble person. He was a professor at the University of Kiev and had an honorable reputation. When the father Golubev was once asked how it was he permitted his son to be implicated in such suspicious doings, he answered: "What do you want of my son? For a while he was in the insane asylum at Vinnitsa. Later, when he recovered somewhat and returned home, he became a member of the Black Hundreds organization, and of course they led him astray. He was made Secretary of the 'Double-headed Eagle,' and he is their leader. But he himself is misled, the poor boy, and is unbalanced. Let him alone, and do not mention his name to me."

Chapter 24: Lies and Calumnies

After Golubev was carried from the courtroom in a swoon, a new witness, a priest by the name of Shainevich, was called to the stand. His story ran thus:

"A lady had been living near my home who began to build a big house for herself. One day a Jewish broker came over to the lady and asked her whether she needed any money to complete the house; he was able to procure the sum if she needed it. He was told by the lady that no money was needed. The Jew, however, was not so easily put off. 'Impossible,' said he, 'that you should not need any money. No matter how much one has, it always proves insufficient when building a house. I know it from experience.' The lady still refused him and he had to leave. About three days later, he reappeared again and told the lady a story about her being presently summoned as a witness for Beilis's trial, and again proposed to her that he would lend her any amount that she might want. This time, the lady told him to come the next day. She would think the matter over and find out exactly whether or not she needed any money. She came to me, as her priest, and told me the whole story. She also asked me for advice: whether she should take any money or leave it alone. I told her: 'Don't take any money from the Jews. Chase him out the next time he comes. Have no business with him whatsoever.'"

I saw that the priest's story was making no impression at all on the audience. That much one could see easily; all of it was pure invention from beginning to end. He gave no names, nor any proofs whatever. A pure fabrication about a Christian lady who was building a house and about a Jew. The whole story was so clumsily concocted that it palpably did not fit. The audience smiled while the priest was talking.

After that, the court clerk began the reading of the testimony of a witness who was unable to appear in person in the court and whose deposition had been taken down in writing. His story was also as poorly fabricated as the previous one. That was the reason, apparently, why the witness did not appear in court.

This is how his story ran: He was in the same cell with me. I had already been there when he arrived. Why was he in prison? Because of being a sort of attorney and having had cases before the court. In connection with one of his cases, there had disappeared from the court some important protocols and documents. Since he was conducting those cases, the suspicion fell on him and on the court clerk, and they had both been imprisoned. When he was brought into the cell where I was kept, I supposedly embraced him and kissed him, imploring his aid to save me. I had in the past several lawsuits and he, the witness, had helped me out of many a "tight place." I was said in this case as well to have asked him for his assistance in getting free. I was said to have told him that I had actually murdered Yushchinsky, the circumstances of the murder, and the reason for it. I was said further to have implored him for advice in order to get out of the mess in which I found myself.

Furthermore, he declared that I confided in him all the "secrets" of the "ritual." I gave him all the inside story. I told him that ritual murder demanded, among other things, the participation of a physician who knows just what thirteen spots on the human

133

body ought to be stabbed in order to draw the most blood. I was alleged to have told him the name of the physician with whom he was to get in contact and from whom he was to receive a sum of several hundred rubles in order to "get through with the case."

Who was this mysterious witness? It came out presently that he had been in jail for a certain crime. He had been in danger of being condemned to a severe punishment. Being a desperate sort of fellow, he wrote a letter to the minister of justice himself, stating that he had important evidence to give against Beilis; if he were to be freed, he would tell all and create a strong impression against Beilis. The minister of justice, the notorious Shcheglovitov, bit only too readily at the bait. Shcheglovitov apparently believed he had hit upon a veritable find. The individual was promptly liberated. The minister gave orders, and the judicial authorities had to carry them out. However, when this witness began to rehearse his testimony, the judicial authorities were not pleased one bit. Truly, there was a chance that the peasant jurymen might be influenced with such wild stories properly rehashed, but there was also every prospect that my lawyers would reduce the man's story to pulp and ashes at the cross-examination. Therefore, he was kept away from appearance in person at the court.

Of course, Gruzenberg immediately inquired why such an important witness had not been brought to court. The presiding judge answered that the witness could not be found by the authorities. They had lost his address.

After this, the testimony of the spy Kozachenko was also read from a deposition. Kozachenko also offered wild stories that so palpably did not hold water that he had not dared to come to court in person. His deposition was that he had spent several months in the same cell with me, and that during all that time we frequently conversed about Andryusha's murder. Since I knew that Kozachenko was to be released presently, I asked him first to transmit a letter to my wife, and secondly to have a couple of witnesses poisoned. As, for instance, the lamplighter and a certain shoemaker. I was alleged to have told Kozachenko he would be given the poison strychnine by the doctor of Zaitsev's hospital. I was further said to have promised him a handsome reward, which he was to have obtained from "certain Jews."

The story being read, Gruzenberg asked at once why so important a witness was not brought here. We would like to hear all that from him in person, Gruzenberg said, especially since the indictment was based in considerable part on this man's statement. The presiding judge gave the same answer: the police were unable to find the witness.

Chapter 25: The "Tzadikim"

Real gaiety broke out in the courtroom when the sergeant-at-arms brought to the witness stand the two "*tzadikim*," Ettinger and Landau, who were alleged to have been seen at my house dressed in kaftans and skull caps, wrapped in *tallesim*, etc. The actual story about these two "rabbis" is as follows: the lamplighter, Shakhovsky, had at one point given a statement to the effect that on the Sabbath morning before the murder, he had seen two *tzadikim* in my house. The authorities therefore checked the register of the factory and the office, and found on the books the names of two persons, Ettinger and Landau.

Ettinger was a young man of about thirty years of age, clean shaven, completely "Europeanized" and hardly much of a Jew. He was very wealthy, and was Zaitsev's brother-in-law. Mrs. Zaitsev was his sister.

Ettinger was Austrian. He had come to Kiev to visit his sister's family, but as a foreign Jew, he had no right to live in Russia outside the "Pale." Even his millionaire brother-in-law Zaitsev could not help in this case. Zaitsev himself lived in the most aristocratic section of Kiev, in the Lipki district, and it was precisely in that locality that his dashing young relative had no right to reside. Legally, at least, he could not have been shown on the house register.

To surmount this obstacle, a police captain of Zaitsev's district found the way out – as most Russian policemen knew how to do when there was a prospect of remuneration. His idea was to have Ettinger register in the Plossky district, where Jews had a right to reside. So Ettinger registered there, but spent his nights and generally lived in Zaitsev's house. Thus, the law was obeyed in a form which was perfectly *a la Russe*. Ettinger was duly registered at the factory, but as a matter of fact did not even know where it was located. He never put his foot inside of the factory.

The same was the case with Mr. Landau. He was a young man of twenty-five and was studying on the Continent. He was a grandson of the old Zaitsev, and was for similar cause also registered at the factory as a resident. The register showed that both these men had "checked out" about five months before the murder of Yushchinsky. Nevertheless, the two young men were summoned as witnesses for the trial, since the "experts" had decided that the murder had been performed with the participation of *tzadikim* in accordance with a supposed Jewish ritual.

When the two neatly-dressed young men were put on the stand, Mr. Gruzenberg, well known for his wit, introduced the two to the judges and to the public. "These gentlemen," he said, "are the two *tzadikim*, who are said to have been praying wrapped in the *tallis* and dressed in the kaftans with their skull caps on." As most residents of the city of Kiev knew the Jewish customs only too well, the public were quick to catch the joke, and a roaring peal of laughter rocked the courtroom.

Ettinger could not speak Russian, and his testimony was given through an interpreter. He was asked questions of which he certainly had never dreamed before. He was asked whether he was a *tzadik*, whether he ate the ultra-Orthodox *shmura* matzah,[j] whether he partook of the *afikomen*, and similar theological riddles. He shrugged his shoulders perplexedly, but answered the questions patiently. The whole procedure apparently smacked to him somewhat of an insane asylum, but he was willing to go through with it. His statements were immediately translated into Russian.

The prosecutor, Vipper, who had built up the whole indictment on the *tzadikim* allegation, became quite nervous when he heard the testimony. It did not fit to Mr. Vipper's taste, and why should this young gentleman deny being a *tzadik* and eating *shmura* matzah? Vipper got up and turned upon the witness with asperity. "Now, tell the truth; I also am German and understand everything."

Vipper clearly wanted to create the impression with the jury that Ettinger was giving false testimony. Since the prosecutor came out with an open accusation to that effect, the jury was likely to be impressed accordingly, and in fact, the peasants commenced to exchange glances between themselves.

The thought struck me: How could those plain farmers realize that a dashing young man, spending his nights in chorus girls' parties, could not at the same time be a *tzadik*, wrapped up in a *tallis*, and eating *shmura* matzah? I could hardly restrain my tears from anxiety and fear. When Vipper saw that, he started to laugh, and the more he looked at me, the more pleased his laughter sounded.

I mentioned previously that Vera Cheberyak had told the investigating magistrate that she had been invited to come to the

---

[j] Matzah made from grain that is guarded after harvesting to ensure there is no leavening.

city of Kharkov to see a prominent person (whom she later insisted upon identifying as my lawyer, Margolin), and that she was there offered forty thousand rubles to take upon herself the guilt of Yushchinsky's murder. She stated also that besides Margolin, there was present at that Kharkov conference an associate editor of the paper *Kievskaya Mysl*,[k] Sergei Yablonovsky. It was Mr. Yablonovsky's turn presently to take the witness stand. He bluntly stated that he had never been to Kharkov.

Madame Vera Cheberyak was called upon to confute his testimony. The presiding judge naturally asked her: "Would you recognize the man who offered you that sum in Kharkov?"

"Yes, I could recognize him."

Yablonovsky was brought up again on to the stand. The judge proceeded with his questions to Cheberyak. "Do you know this man?"

"Let him sit down upon a chair, and I'll recognize him," said Cheberyak.

The Judge began questioning Yablonovsky: "Is what Vera Vladimirovna has told us true, that you and another man offered her money if she were to assume the guilt in this murder?"

Yablonovsky smiled. "One of us is telling the untruth. It is for you, of course, to find out which of us is the liar."

"Well, Vera?" queried the Judge.

"You want me to sit down?" asked Yablonovsky. He seated himself comfortably in the chair and folded his hands.

"Yes," said Vera, "that is he, that is the way he was sitting at the time – with his hands folded."

---

[k] *Kiev Thought*, a liberal paper.

A roar of laughter broke out in the courtroom. The presiding judge inquired: "How is it you recognized him only by his manner of sitting and not by his face; one recognizes a man by his face, is that not true?"

She answered with an air of tranquility: "On that occasion, he was sitting just as he is now; that is why I recognized him." The public was quite merry at this testimony, and though I felt embittered enough, I myself could not refrain from laughing.

An important witness, Shakhovsky the lamplighter, was called to the stand. The advocates and the public were ready for another sensation. This witness was one of the props of the prosecution, for the indictment rested on him in large part.

"What can you tell us about this case?" inquired the presiding judge.

To the astonishment of all, Shakhovsky said: "I know nothing."

Nothing! The records were brought up and the previous statement of the witness was read aloud, wherein he had claimed that on that Saturday morning, at 9:00 a.m., he had seen the *tzadikim* in Beilis's house – skull caps, *tallesim*, prayers and all. How was it possible that he knew nothing?

He gave a straightforward answer: "Now I tell you the truth. I told it differently before, but then I was drunk. The detective Polishchuk plied me with vodka. I was angry at Beilis, for he had threatened to have me arrested for stealing wood from the factory yard. Well, I did say all that stuff against him. I was not under oath at that time. Now I have sworn, and must tell the truth. I am a Christian and fear God. Why should I ruin an innocent man who knows nothing about the charges brought against him?"

This plain statement was like a bomb thrown in the courtroom. All the Black Hundreds who were there were completely dumbfounded. Practically the whole indictment was based on Shakhovsky's statement. So much had been expected of him, and all of a sudden such a shameful disappointment. Shmakov and Zamyslovsky jumped to their feet and began to cross-examine the witness.

"How is it," almost implored Shmakov, "did you not tell before about the woman Volkivna who met your wife and mocked you both because you, who lived so near the scene of the murder, knew nothing about it, while the whole world knew that it was Beilis who had murdered Andryusha?"

The witness kept on repeating: "I know nothing. I was drunk."

Thereupon Shakhovsky's wife was brought to the stand.

"What do you know?"

The same answer: "I know nothing."

"What did you talk about with Volkivna?"

Shakhovsky's wife answered sullenly: "It was Volkivna who did the talking. But what does it amount to? I myself do not know a thing. If you are not satisfied, ask Volkivna."

Madame Volkivna was brought in. She proved to be an old peasant woman, barefoot and clothed in rags.

"What do you know about this case?"

Volkivna seemed to be quite peeved, and not a bit abashed. "Leave me alone, all of you. I don't know a thing."

"What is your profession?"

"Collecting alms, when I get them."

"What do you do with the money?"

"That has been my occupation for years and years. At times I buy some vodka to drown my sorrows."

The public naturally laughed.

"Shakhovsky told us that you had been boasting that you knew all about the case, while they themselves knew nothing."

"Will you leave me alone?" The old woman was becoming quite angry. "What do you want of an old woman like me? I was drunk on that day and slept that night in the market. Leave me alone, and don't annoy me."

Her testimony produced quite a hilarious effect on the courtroom audience, and even on the judge.

Chapter 26: The Bubble of Lies is Bursting

The testimony hitherto presented in court clearly indicated that truth was on its way to victory. Not only was I being proved innocent by the witnesses for the defense; even the prosecution witnesses were exonerating me. Especially Shakhovsky proved a terrible disappointment for the prosecution. He changed the whole aspect of the case.

Apparently, all was going for the better with me. Nevertheless, every time I looked at the jury, at their plain, peasant faces, a chill ran down my spine. I did not know what impression all the testimony was making upon them. Perhaps they were not grasping all the import of it, not understanding the meaning of the whole proceeding.

There was a short intermission, then the witness Krasovsky was summoned to the stand. This Krasovsky had formerly belonged to the (non-political) secret police force and had risen to the rank of a detective captain. He retained that position for twenty years and had really distinguished himself by his cleverness and efficiency. There was no capital crime, no murder, but that he was capable of solving it.

When Yushchinsky's murder first came to light, public opinion demanded that Krasovsky be put in charge of the police investigation. Such was the confidence he enjoyed. But the authorities were averse to such a course. The Black Hundreds actually feared that Krasovsky would find the real murderers, and this was the last thing the anti-Semites wished to see. Only half a year later, when my lawyers commenced to insist that the investigation be undertaken by a reliable police official – that is, by Krasovsky – was he put in charge. Immediately, he found the right scent, and was about to discover the entire band, when the governor himself interfered, finding some pretext or other with which to trump up a charge of malfeasance. Krasovsky was deprived of his captain's rank and was put in jail. There, he had to go through all sorts of humiliations. Krasovsky was acquitted by the court, but lost his post and was never reinstated in the police service. His sin, of course, was to have discovered the truth.

Krasovsky's testimony was not long. But what he said was quite sufficient.

"I used to come to Cheberyak's house quite often after the murder was discovered. I used to go to see the boy, Zhenya, at home and ask him questions. Once while I was sitting and talking with him, he turned pale and stopped in the middle of a word. I turned quickly and saw his mother standing behind me, in the act of making a sign with her finger that he keep silence.

"During the time she was in jail, two of Cheberyak's children, Zhenya and the older girl, fell ill. They were removed to a hospital. Immediately upon her release from jail, Cheberyak ran to the hospital to take the children home. She was told by the physicians not to take the children, for the boy was so weak he might die on the way home. But she would not listen to reason. She insisted on taking him home, come what might. She did it because she feared he might reveal something. She feared the questions he might be asked.

"Thereafter I came to see them. Zhenya was in bed. He did not feel well. Cheberyak said to the boy: 'Tell them to leave you alone. Tell them you know nothing.' Zhenya retorted: 'Mother, will you ever leave me alone with your fibs and instructions?' A short while later the boy was dead."

Krasovsky and the journalist Brazul-Brushkovsky gave many new facts in the course of their testimony – facts indicating clearly that the murder had been committed by Cheberyak and her associates Singayevsky, Rudzinsky and Latyshev. No less clear and convincing was the testimony against this quartet given by the advocate Margolin, who appeared in court not as my lawyer, but as a witness.

For the first time during the trial, I became fully aware of the remarkable work performed by Messrs. Brazul-Brushkovsky and Krasovsky; of their heroic efforts to uncover the highly-protected murderer. While in prison, I had only a vague idea of their energy and the results achieved by them in my behalf. I had already received some information about Mr. Margolin. I had never imagined, however, that "real" Russians, non-Jews such as Messrs. Yablonovsky, Brushkovsky and Krasovsky, would actually sacrifice their safety and positions, all in the interest of truth. Never will I, or my family, forget, to the last day of our lives, these wonderful and enlightened men.

Investigating Magistrate Fenenko was also summoned, and he told the story of the investigation he had made when he was in charge of the case, before he was replaced. Fenenko had not seen any grounds on which to base an accusation of ritual murder against me, or any charge of murder at all. He knew that Shakhovsky the lamplighter was talking "through his hat," but he was unable to do anything. Since there were witnesses to testify against me, he had to draw up an indictment.

Young Zaitsev was then called up. The presiding judge put a series of questions to Zaitsev: did he ever pay homage to the *tzadikim*; had his father ever done so; and similar questions. The last question was: Why had it occurred that Beilis was the one put in charge of baking all the matzah that Zaitsev himself had ordered for home use, when there were dozens of other Jews in Zaitsev's employ besides Beilis?

The story about the matzah runs somewhat as follows: The elder Zaitsev (who had died some time before the trial) was one of the wealthiest Jews in Russia, owner of fifteen sugar factories. He had a large sugar factory, with a beet field, in Rigorovka, twenty-five miles from Kiev. On that field, there were set aside several acres to be sown with wheat, and from that wheat several hundred-weights were usually set aside for *shmura* matzah. That grain was locked in a separate granary, the key to which was kept by Zaitsev alone.

About a month before Passover, a rabbi would come, and under his supervision, about five hundredweight would be milled for matzah. The matzah would then be baked, packed in cases, and one case sent to various members of the family or friends. This was the old man's habit, which was known to the family for long years. I myself had already been engaged in supervising the work for about fifteen years. When I was arrested, the correspondence between Zaitsev and myself, in which I was ordered to go to Rigorovka for the matzah flour, was discovered in the house. That is why the authorities started the whole story about the *shmura* matzah.

When asked why the elder Zaitsev had always sent me for the matzah, his son told the court the following: "Beilis's father had been a very religious Jew and always ate *shmura* matzah. My father knew old Beilis very well. We had some commercial dealings with the old man. I myself asked my father why it was that he had selected Beilis particularly to handle the matzah. My father told me that he had known old Beilis to be strictly religious and to have trained his son accordingly, and he therefore felt that no one was better fitted to do that sort of work."

The most important witness who followed was Vera Cheberyak. Throughout the trial, the witnesses had always pointed to her and insisted that she was the actual murderer of Yushchinsky. Naturally, the public was giving her a wide berth. Early in the trial, she had appealed to the presiding judge for protection, alleging threats against her safety. Every time she would go home, she asked for a policeman to escort her, for she feared to be assassinated.

It is interesting to observe here that whenever the witnesses who were supposed to testify for the prosecution were asked why they had changed their previous testimony, and were speaking in my favor, they invariably answered: "We are Christians, Orthodox churchmen. We don't know a thing about the Jewish religious customs, whether they use blood or not. Maybe it is true, maybe it is a lie. What do we Orthodox Christians know about such things? As soon as we began to investigate this case, we discovered that it was Vera Cheberyak's deed. Then why should we accuse an innocent man? We are under fearful oath to tell the truth, and we know that the murder was committed in Cheberyak's house."

A great deal was expected from Cheberyak's testimony. She was relied upon to supply the best material thus far for the prosecution. As a matter of fact, she did not go beyond telling a couple of old stories, and when asked whether she had seen any of the things she spoke of, she replied that it was her children who had reported them. Since the children had been transported to the better world by this time (apparently with their mother's help), it was impossible to verify the truth of her statement.

Yushchinsky's mother was then summoned, and she gave an altogether different version from the one expected of her. Asked whether she knew Beilis, she said "No." Shmakov interposed the question: "Had you seen any Jews around the cave where your child's body was found?" She said "No."

My attorney Gruzenberg asked her the next question: whether she recognized the shirt shown her by the investigating magistrate, and which was considered an important exhibit according to the indictment. Her answer was "No, the shirt is not Andryusha's." This produced quite an impression. I noticed that some of the jurymen exchanged glances and shrugged their shoulders.

The presiding judge was next with a question: "Had your boy gone to visit Jews during the month of March?" Once more she answered: "No."

Testimony was taken for a period which seemed interminable. The long list of witnesses was finally exhausted, however, and the court decided to go in a body to the factory where the murder was alleged to have taken place, and also to see my own house and that of Vera Cheberyak.

Chapter 27:

The Reenactment of the Crime and a Bomb Thrower

I began to feel somewhat more cheerful. For one thing, the witnesses were now finished testifying. Of course, there were still many difficult things to be endured. But I felt as though the greater part of the load was removed from my shoulders. And I welcomed the chance to see my house after two and a half years of imprisonment.

It was about three in the afternoon. Despite a heavy rain and a quite slippery ground, the streets were packed with people. The jurymen were surrounded by cavalry and police, lest they come into contact with outsiders. In order to avoid any demonstration, I was driven to the factory through unfrequented side streets.

At last we arrived at the factory yard and approached the house that had been my Kiev home for so many years. I remained in the coach. Some of the neighbors came out to see me. Through the little windows of the prison coach I could see them pointing their fingers at me and shouting "Beilis! Beilis!" Some wrang their hands and wept with excitement.

The presiding judge permitted me to go with my escort into the house and take a look at my old residence. My wife and children were not there; they had been warned to leave the house. I saw there only a new clerk, a Christian.

Outside again, the mud was so deep we could hardly walk.

Nevertheless, all of us – the judges, the jury, the experts, the journalists, and the student Golubev – made a complete survey of the factory. Everything was examined: the place where the children were wont to play; the spot where "the Jew with the black whiskers" had been reported to have been seen; the cave where the body had been found (here it was so dark that lanterns were needed); and the entire factory.

Standing near the kiln, Shmakov, the private prosecutor, turned to the jury. "Look," said he, "there is from here a straight road to the cave where Andryusha's body was found." Mr. Karabchevsky immediately retorted: "But permit me to draw your attention to the fact that the road from Cheberyak's house to the cave is shorter and straighter."

We now went to Cheberyak's house. The police had brought along a little Christian boy to reenact the murder scene. They took him to Cheberyak's rooms on the top floor, held him fast, and told him to scream. The lawyers Zamyslovsky and Grigorovich-Barsky remained downstairs and listened – and they found that the boy's screaming could be heard quite distinctly.

The staging of this scene took about two hours. Then I was sent back to the prison, and the others went home.

Ever since the beginning of the trial, the prison officials had been treating me with unwonted consideration and even a bit of respect. My every request, instead of being insolently unheeded, was granted with celerity. This time again, when I came back from the trial, the officials tried to outdo each other in courtesy to me. Whether my jailers were thus metamorphosed into real gentlemen because of orders from their superiors, or because of the impression created on them by the numerous witnesses, I can't tell.

The next morning in the prison coach, on the way to the trial, I was alarmed by the explosion of a bomb. There was great confusion for some minutes, and I feared the attack might have been directed against me. The coach stopped, but the officers ordered the driver to proceed. The reason for this assault was never discovered by the authorities. I learned later that one of the soldiers of the cavalry escort had been so badly wounded by the explosion that his leg had to be amputated.

This was the day put aside for the testimony of the experts and the scientists. The previous witnesses had been summoned only to tell of what had actually happened – to make clear who had committed the murder. The task of the experts was to throw light on the question of ritual blood murder. It was for them to prove either that the Jews were accustomed to use Christian blood in the making of the Passover matzah, or that all these stories were infamous lies. Which, of course, they were.

The star expert for the prosecution was the Catholic priest Pranaitis. He was not a Russian Orthodox priest – indeed, there was not to be found a single Russian Orthodox priest to do the "dirty work" for the authorities. So this Pranaitis was a veritable find. He was supposedly well learned in the Talmud as well as the Kabbalah. In short, he had been announced as a great Hebraist. But when this "expert" began to talk, it became obvious to all that the man was an amazing ignoramus, just a charlatan with a glib tongue. However, since the authorities stood in need of this creature, they had to pretend respect for him. For it was only this adventurer with his foxy Jesuitical expression who was willing to help out the anti-Semites.

Pranaitis began his story by saying that the Jews offered

human sacrifices and that the Jewish religion commanded its followers to murder Gentiles. He quoted from the Talmud, "Murder the best of the Gentiles." Then he swung off from the Talmud to the Kabbalah. In spite of all that, however, when the prosecutor asked him the direct question – if he knew for certain that the Jews used Christian blood – he said he did not. His expert opinion was making no impression on anybody. In fact, the public laughed more than once when he clearly became confused at some of the questions asked by my attorney.

A sensation was produced by an incident connected with the number thirteen, a number supposed to have great meaning in the Jewish ritual. The prosecution insisted that the thirteen wounds which Professor Sikorsky discovered on a part of Andryusha's body had been obviously inflicted in accordance with "ritual." But it was afterwards discovered that there were actually fourteen wounds, further discrediting the ritual story.

All the vagaries and prevarications brought forth by the priest Pranaitis were completely refuted by Rabbi Mazeh, the well-known and universally respected chief rabbi of Moscow. Rabbi Mazeh delivered a long speech, quoting passages from the Torah, the Talmud, and other books, in order to reveal the depths of ignorance of Pranaitis. Rabbi Mazeh showed that the priest had no knowledge whatsoever of the Talmud and could hardly read a passage of Hebrew.

The jury listened with attention to all these explanations which they undoubtedly were unable to understand fully. Such things as Talmud, Kabbalah – what had all that to do with these plain peasants? I was watching the jurymen with the greatest attention. It was they who were to be my judges. They were to give their verdict upon the basis of the testimony and all these explanations and arguments. But how was I to know if they themselves did not believe in the story of the Jews using Christian blood? If there were secret Jewish books, why shouldn't there be secret things written in them, customs hidden from view? It was then that I saw in all its clarity the depth of the misfortune which had befallen the Jewish people, the horror of the calumnies heaped upon our nation by villains like Pranaitis.

Chapter 28: The Verbal Battle

At last began the final fight for my liberation, for my very life, as well as for the honor of the Jewish nation against the terrible accusation leveled against it. The battle was between the prosecution on one side, and my attorneys on the other.

The prosecutor addressed the jury in approximately the following manner: "I have spent about thirty years in the Czar's service. It is my task now to prove, on the basis of facts, that this man, Mendel Beilis, who is now sitting on the defendant's bench, murdered the boy Yushchinsky, and I shall demonstrate it so clearly that there will be no doubt left whatever. The world must know the truth. The world is awaiting the truth, and to my lot it falls to demonstrate that very truth. And you gentlemen of the jury, you also are facing a great task. It is your duty to consider and to weigh all these truths and testimonies. You must decide what shall be the fate of a man who has committed so horrible a crime.

"I am not telling you that all the Jews are guilty and that pogroms should be instituted against them, but it is true that there is a religious sect among the Jews, the so-called Hasidim-Tzadikim, who commit their crimes in secret so that the non-Jewish world never becomes aware of them. It is they who are murdering Christian children, and Mendel Beilis belongs to that criminal sect.

"The whole world has been deeply moved by this crime; the world is in an uproar. Why is it so? Because Mendel Beilis (here, he pointed his finger at me) is sitting on the defendant's bench. You just catch one Jew and all the Jews will be set in motion and will exercise all their influence and their untold millions to get him out. Do you remember the Dreyfus case in France? The whole world was set agog, and why? Because he was a Jew.

"But let us take up the other aspect of the question. Two and a half years have passed, and Andryusha is lying in his grave; he has been forgotten by all. Who is playing the leading part? It is Mendel Beilis (again he pointed his finger at me). Had such a case happened with us Christians, would anybody have said a word, would the world have displayed any interest? Do not forget, gentlemen, that Andryusha is one of our own. We must not forget him. We cannot forget him! We Orthodox Christians who are wearing the cross, we must carry out the most terrifying verdict, to avenge the Christian blood shed by this man."

Here, the prosecutor made a fine semblance of weeping. Then he continued his speech with new asperity: "Just imagine the scandal of the thing. In broad daylight, in this holy city, where there are so many cathedrals and monasteries with all the holy shrines of Russia, here of all places the murderers got hold of a young child, a saintly child, a boy who has been preparing for the priesthood; and it was a Jew, actuated by his religious fanaticism, who seized that child, gagged his mouth, tied him hand and foot, and inflicted thirty-four wounds upon one part of his body, and thirteen wounds upon another part, in order to draw five pints of human blood. I am asking you, how can we remain so unfeelingly charitable, so soft and unmanly, as not to avenge ourselves on this man? Do you remember when our presiding judge asked Beilis at the beginning of the trial to what religion he claimed allegiance? Beilis answered

---

155

with a defiant shout, 'I am a Jew!' You understand what it meant. It meant, 'I am a Jew, and I laugh at you Christians. We Jews can do to you what we please.'"

Throughout his speech, the prosecutor kept on drinking water. At this point in the speech, he seemed to have become exhausted, and he asked for a recess.

I was completely distressed by the prosecutor's speech. I felt as if the knife were at my throat. I thought that a speech of this kind was sure to produce the most pernicious effect upon the jury. But Mr. Maklakov, the famous lawyer, came over to me and cheerfully slapped me upon the shoulder. "Mr. Beilis," he said, "keep your heart up. It isn't as terrible as it looks. He speaks well, but we shall speak much better."

In a few minutes, the prosecutor was again continuing his harangue. It seemed to me that there was no end to his speech. He was making desperate efforts to prove that it was I who had murdered the boy, only I and no one else. How could Vera Cheberyak have had anything to do with it? Who could be low enough to invent such a falsehood about her?

Among other things, the prosecutor shouted, "There are good minutes even with the worst of men. On this very table there was lying the bloody corpse of the murdered boy. Once, when Beilis was brought in here, he looked at it and began to weep. Why did he weep? Surely, because he became remorseful for having murdered an innocent child. At that moment Beilis was rueing his crime."

It was with the speech of the prosecutor that the court session of that day came to a close. I, and apparently all the audience, left the courtroom with a heavy heart and full of apprehensions.

The next day saw the beginning of a series of statements and speeches delivered by the experts and by my lawyers. The following lawyers made their speeches: Messrs. Gruzenberg, Karabchevsky, Maklakov, Grigorovich-Barsky, Zarudny; also the experts Rabbi Mazeh, the professor Troyitsky, Kokovtsev, and others. Each of them made splendid retorts to the arguments of the prosecutor and to the whole indictment against me.

Mr. Maklakov, a famous lawyer and a Christian himself, paid the following respects to the prosecutor's "proofs" and especially to the latter's anger at the Jews for setting all the world agog: "I listened with special attention to that part of the prosecutor's speech where that gentleman was telling us with a smile that the Jews always created a stir whenever one of their number was caught in anything. Will you tell me, gentlemen, how would we behave if, for instance, we Orthodox Christians were to find ourselves amongst the Chinese, and the Chinese were to accuse one of us of a crime similar to that ascribed to Beilis? Wouldn't we try to 'set the world agog?' Why should the prosecutor be surprised at that? How could it be otherwise? How else can they protect themselves? By sitting quiet and keeping silence? Nor must you forget that we Christians have no fear of pogroms. The Jews, however, are in constant fear of pogroms and pogromists, and should they do nothing in order to prove their innocence?

"Another thing: we heard the prosecutor reproaching Beilis for having wept. We know why he wept. He was weeping because there had been a time when he was a man like all of us, free and unconcerned, and today he is facing so overwhelming a disaster. And are you surprised to see him weeping? Why did the prosecutor not mention the fact that after the Black Hundreds leader Golubev was brought to the witness stand with so much respect and honor, the man fell into a swoon and did not say a word? Was it because he knew he would have to tell a lie?"

It is difficult, of course, to give here the contents of all the speeches. I shall mention, however, some of Gruzenberg's words which made a particularly moving impression at the trial, both upon the jury and the public. Among other things, he said: "Not long ago, I studied together with Christians. I lived together with them, ate together, enjoyed and suffered together with my Christian friends. And now, all of a sudden, I and my co-religionists are faced with this shameful, disgraceful accusation. We are charged with such an abominable crime. I am telling you now, and you know my words will be heard by all my co-religionists, that if I thought for a moment that our Torah allowed us to use Christian blood, I should not remain a Jew for one hour.

"I am certain that Mendel Beilis will not be convicted, and must not be convicted. But should he be convicted, then let it be so. Why should he be more fortunate than ever so many of our brethren who have in the past lost their lives as a consequence of these indescribable calumnies and falsehoods? Beilis, if ever you are convicted, proclaim: 'Hear, O Israel, the Lord is our God, and He is one God.' Be of stout heart and good cheer."

The audience was sitting as if petrified. There could be no doubt of the strong impression made by this speech upon the jury. They were listening to it with rapt attention; for that matter, the speeches of all my lawyers made a most favorable impression. It seemed that the efforts of the prosecution and the Black Hundreds were doomed to disgraceful defeat. But who could be certain of the thoughts and decision of the jury?

Chapter 29: I Barely Escape Being Shot

The great day had come at last. It was the thirty-fourth day of the trial, the 28th of October, 1913. It was the day for the jury to give their decision. As it happened, an incident occurred that day which might have cost me my life, and would have dispensed with all the formalities of a verdict.

At eight in the morning, I was called as usual to the prison office to proceed to the courthouse. On each previous day of the trial, the soldiers in my escort had searched me and started on the drive to the court immediately. But on this particular morning, after I was already in the custody of the escort, the deputy warden sent word to bring me back. He wanted to search me once more.

The searches were a veritable inquisition. The mental and physical humiliation can hardly be described.

In accordance with the law, my escort initially refused to comply with the deputy warden's order that I be searched again. Once a prisoner was in the hands of the escort, no one else had any authority over him. Since the escort had signed a receipt for the prisoner, the escort alone was responsible for him, and no one else could touch him.

The deputy warden insisted, however, that a special telegram had come from the Imperial Court, from the Czar himself, ordering that I be searched very strictly. My convoy was naturally impressed, and they surrendered me to the deputy warden. Though the deputy warden could easily have availed himself of my escort for the purposes of the search, he called his own men, the prison guards, to do the work.

I was told to undress, and I complied with the order. I had never removed my undershirt during these searches. This time, however, the deputy warden ordered me to remove the undershirt as well. I became irritated, and in my excitement I tore the undershirt from my body, tore it to pieces, and threw it into his face.

He snatched his pistol and aimed at me. He was so inflamed with anger that he looked more like a wild man than a human being. It was fortunate for me that the convoy, attracted by the noise, came on the run. Had not the convoy been responsible for my safety at that moment, they would not have dared to protect me. But since they had already signed for me, they felt responsible. One of the escort soldiers grabbed the revolver from the deputy warden's hand.

The alarm was sounded. The officials and guards came on the run. The warden came in very excited and turned to me. "What are you doing? Is it not the last day of your trial, and you are starting new trouble?"

"What do you want of me," I exclaimed. "Why does this man subject me to new insults? Was I not once searched? Why does he search me again in that most insulting manner?"

The deputy warden left. A few minutes later, he returned and put down my escorts as witnesses of the incident. He intended, apparently, to press charges against me. "Don't you imagine, Beilis, that you are free. I will square my account with you yet. You will not escape from us, and we will see you with chains on your hands."

I replied, "You will never live to see it."

"Never fear," he assured me, "even if you are acquitted, you will be given a month of arrest."

That was, so to speak, my breakfast. A breakfast after which I might not have survived for another meal. The deputy warden would have been entirely within the law had he shot me. My action constituted an "assault," and he had the full right to shoot. However, as it happened, I got off with a scare and nothing more.

Chapter 30: Freed

The courtroom presented a holiday appearance. It was almost over; nothing remained but the formulation of the end, the final touch.

The presiding judge asked me with solemnity: "Beilis, what have you to say in your defense?"

I rose weakly to my feet. "Gentlemen, I can but repeat that I am innocent. I am too weary for anything else. The prison and the trial have made me tired of words. I can only request that you scrutinize all the evidence you have been hearing the thirty-four days of this trial. Examine it carefully, and deliver your verdict, so that I may return to my wife and children, who have been waiting for me these two and a half years."

The presiding judge began to sum up the case, in a way that amazed me: "Gentlemen, it is my duty to say nothing good or bad. I must be impartial. But this trial has been an exceptional one. It has touched upon a matter which concerns the existence of the whole Russian people.

"There are those who drink our blood. You must not take into consideration any of the things that have happened here: Neither the witnesses who wanted to whitewash Beilis, nor the experts who stated that the Jews do not use Christian blood, nor the stories of Vera Cheberyak's guilt. You must disregard all this testimony. You must think of one thing alone: a child, a Christian child, has been murdered. Suspicion and the accusation have fallen upon Beilis. He is now before you on the defendant's bench. It is him you must try!"

This, and much more, was said by the judge in what he called an impartial tone. His summing up amazed not only me, but a great many in the courtroom. Everyone was astounded to hear the presiding judge speak as though he were the prosecutor. But he continued his summary until sunset.

It was about five in the afternoon when the questions to be put before the jury were decided upon. First, "At what place had the child been murdered?" And second, "Who murdered the child?"

At last the moment had come. The peasants who composed the jury, in whose hands my fate rested, rose from their box and retired to deliberate upon the questions. I was led to my room.

The last moments of terrible anxiety! I had been waiting for them for years, and now they were here. My fate was to be decided in a few moments. Was I doomed to eternal darkness, were my wife and children to die from shame and grief? Or would I come out a new man, free, and with all of life before me?

I was again brought into the courtroom. The jury was to give its decision, signed and sealed. It was to be read aloud. A deathly silence fell over the room. People almost stopped breathing.

The state prosecutor, the private prosecutors, and all the Black Gang looked about themselves triumphantly. They seemed assured of victory. Only two of my lawyers, Zarudny and Grigorovich-Barsky, remained in the courtroom. Gruzenberg, Maklakov and Karabchevsky had left. They were afraid of an adverse verdict, and they did not feel strong enough to withstand the shock. After the exertions of the trial, they felt unable to endure it.

The jury had not yet entered the courtroom. All eyes were directed toward the door, toward the door through which the great revelation was to come. At last the door swung open and the jurymen slowly filed in.

During the thirty-four days of the trial, whose outcome concerned not only me, but the fate of all the Jewish people, I had never removed my eyes from the jurymen. I had wanted to gaze into their very souls. What were they thinking about, these plain Russian peasants?

They had been listening for more than a month to various stories: about the murder itself, about Jewish life, about our religious customs and laws. Had they believed all they were told? Did they realize that the accusations brought against me and the Jews were lies? Only a minute ago, and they had decided the fate of me and, to a certain extent, of millions of Jews. My life depended upon a single word of theirs. And at times, their decision is based on the persistence of one or two jurymen! God, could I stand it to the end?

Why was it dragging on so long? Why not deliver the verdict? I looked into the eyes of the jurymen to read their decision. I had seen them so often during the trial, but I had never seen them like this. In the past they always had a smile on their faces, looked friendly. But now their faces were somber and downcast. They must be inhuman.

Suddenly the conviction rushed in on me that they had given a verdict of guilty. I tried to pull myself together and pray to God to sustain me in the face of that horrible verdict. Let them shoot me, let them hang me, let them do as they please with me. I tried to find consolation in the thought that the whole world, the world of honest

164

men, would say that I had been a victim of flagrant injustice. All the world would know that the verdict was a colossal blunder. This gave me courage to hold out to the end.

By this time, the silence in the courtroom had become funereal. I cannot describe the rigidness with which the audience held itself, afraid to stir that it might not lose a word. The air became so intense that one felt it would suddenly break and tear apart.

The foreman of the jury rose to his feet and began reading the decision. "Where had the crime been committed?" The jury decided upon the Zaitsev brickworks. It was in the factory of which I was superintendent that the boy had been murdered.

Certainly, then, they had decided that I had committed the murder. I held myself rigid and clenched my teeth. If the boy had been done to death in my factory, and I was the only Jew in the neighborhood, the jury would surely find me guilty.

The foreman continued reading: "If it has been proved that the murder was actually committed at Zaitsev's factory, who committed it? Was it the defendant, Mendel Beilis? Did Beilis take the boy Yushchinsky and inflict forty-seven wounds upon the boy's body, drawing the blood out of the child's veins, and use it according to the Jewish religious laws? In short, is Mendel Beilis guilty or not?"

The jury had decided: "No, Mendel Beilis is not guilty."

I cannot describe the noise and shouting in the courtroom that followed immediately upon the announcement of the jury's decision. First of all, there was a gasp of relief, and then many began to weep. I myself, with great joy, wept like a child. My advocate Zarudny ran to me, shouting: "Beilis, my dear man, you are free!"

The colonel in charge of the escort, who was standing near me, poured out a glass of water and wanted to give it to me. Zarudny snatched the water from his hand and did not let me drink it.

The colonel was deeply offended. "Why don't you let me give him a drink?" he demanded, "Is he not under my protection?"

"No," shouted Zarudny, and I had never seen him so excited. "He is not in your hands any more. At last you have no authority over him." He kissed me.

Then Grigorovich-Barsky came over. "Well, let us all go," said Zarudny. "Let us tell this wonderful news to our friends and congratulate them."

At that moment, the presiding judge rose again and read the formula, to the effect that by the order of His Imperial Majesty, I was freed and could take my place among the people in the courtroom. As a rule, this was sufficient, and after the announcement of the verdict in this manner, the soldiers ordinarily sheathed their swords and the defendant left the dock. I, however, remained seated. I did not know what I was to do, and the soldiers who surrounded me were still standing with their naked swords and made no move to put them into their scabbards.

I glanced at Shmakov, one of the private prosecutors. He stood as if dumfounded and was muttering to himself. When one of his friends approached him, I heard Shmakov say: "It cannot be helped; all is lost; a terrible blow for Russia."

There could be no doubt, however, that the public was rejoicing over the verdict. People were shaking hands, kissing each other, shouting their congratulations to me, wiping their eyes – and all these were people, most of them influential Russians, whom I had never known before the trial. I saw that many of them wanted to come over to me to extend their congratulations in person, but the gendarmes and police did not permit them. So the public greeted me from a distance, women waving their handkerchiefs. The presiding judge finally ordered the courtroom to be cleared.

The Russian gendarmes were experts at that sort of thing, and the room was cleared in a few minutes. In the meantime, I was finally recognized by all as the innocent Mendel Beilis.

I was still sitting on the defendant's bench, with the soldiers, swords in hand, guarding me. While the people were leaving the hall, a very distinguished and gigantic looking Russian came over to me and spoke: "I am a merchant from Moscow. I left three large factories, left them almost without supervision, and have spent more than a month's time here. I have been awaiting the moment of your liberation. I could not leave before; I knew I could not rest at home. And now, the Lord be blessed, I can go home rejoicing. I am very happy to be able to shake hands with you. I wish you all the happiness in the world, Beilis."

This Russian giant was weeping like a child, and was energetically wiping his eyes and blowing his nose. "God bless you, Beilis," were his last words while being propelled to the door.

Chapter 31: The Prison Becomes My Castle

I remained sitting on the bench. My faithful guards, the soldiers, were still there. I was becoming impatient: why was I not being told to go home? Two and a half years of prison seemed to be about enough. But apparently, they did not feel like parting with me yet.

In the meantime, I thought of my home, of my wife and children. I thought of the mercy that the Almighty had granted to me and to the people of Israel, saving us from such a disaster. I thought of the joy which must prevail at my house. An official came over and told me that the presiding judge wished to see me in his chambers. I felt certain that I was to be told at last to go home.

In the presiding judge's chambers, I found the jury, the peasants who had judged me. When I came in, one of the jurymen tugged at my coat. As I discovered later, he was one of those who had stood up for me. And by this quiet tugging he wanted me to understand that he was my friend and had done what he could for me. Apparently, he was afraid to say it aloud, but he wished to say: "Well, we pulled you out, didn't we?"

The presiding judge asked the jurymen to leave his rooms, and we remained alone. "Mr. Beilis, he said, "you are a free man. I have no right to hold you even for a moment. You can go home."

I was about to bid him good-night when he raised his finger, as if to detain me, and began speaking slowly: "Wait one minute. I have something to tell you. I think that after all it would be better for you to spend this night in prison."

I could hardly believe my ears. Had they become insane, all these fellows? Had I gone through endless sufferings and humiliations, and finally reached the great day of freedom – to then go back to prison? And for what earthly reason? Why should they begrudge me the joy of my final reunion with my family?

Of course, I thought, I could expect no good from this judge, especially after hearing his summing-up speech, which had been really biased and inflammatory. He at once noticed my anxiety. He understood the apprehension which I felt and tried to reassure me.

"Calm yourself, Mr. Beilis. I assure you that I mean it all for your own good. Our verdict was one that the people did not expect. Mob feeling has been aroused, and you know how difficult it is to be responsible for eventualities in such a situation. You must also remember that it was in this city of Kiev that Prime Minister Stolypin was assassinated in His Majesty's presence. You know what that means. It did not occur so long ago. No one can be responsible when the people are aroused. Besides, since you have been so miraculously aided, and have withstood the tribulations of two and one half years, surely you will be able to endure it for an additional night.

"Do spend this night in prison. Meanwhile, the people will cool down somewhat. In the morning you will be able to go home."

I felt that he was not telling me this out of sheer sympathy for me. But what else could I do? I feared that in case of my refusal to comply with his request, he was very capable of playing some trick upon me. At least, I had no guarantee against it. I was quite afraid of the prison officials with whom I had clashed just that morning. Nevertheless, I agreed to spend that night in prison.

"In that case," said he, "we must write a formal application. The question is: what motive shall we put forward?" He thought for a minute and then said: "Good, we shall write in your own name, that you request permission to spend this night in prison in order to return the government's clothes and to square up your accounts with the administration." He wrote up the application and I signed it.

Meanwhile, the chief of police came into the chamber. "Well, Mr. Beilis, do you wish to go home? I congratulate you on your acquittal."

The judge made a sour face. Apparently, he did not like the friendly tone of the chief of police, and he said to the latter: "Beilis will spend this night in prison. Please see to it that he gets an escort."

I left the courthouse and was driven back to the prison by an escorting policeman, but this time as a free man, not as a prisoner. I was in the same black coach, but things were quite different. Usually it was dark inside. This time there was a lamp burning in one corner. Before, I had always been alone. Now the chief of police was in the coach with me, and he was most friendly and polite.

The chief of police honored me with a cigarette, and we chatted while on the way to prison. He plied me with questions all the time. He wanted to know how I felt during the trial; he wanted to know the whole history of my stay in prison. "Well, the Lord be thanked," he said. "The whole business is over. I myself have almost become ill with anxiety. I was responsible for you and for the order in the city during the last two months. I had to be on guard lest any harm befall you. It was no trifle, I assure you, to control the

170

excitement of the mob. I feel real joy in knowing that you have been released."

Once more we were nearing the dark and forbidding prison building, but I felt light at heart. I was free. On one of the streets, the coach suddenly stopped. Upon inquiring the cause, the chief of police was informed that it was due to the military patrols which had been posted along the road in order to clear the streets of people.

Chapter 32: Home at Last

The coach stopped at the prison gate. A door opened and a squad of prison officials and guards came out. In the past, they used to be surly. They would jeer at me and treat me in a rough manner. "Move on," "Don't crawl," "Walk like a man, you blood-drinker." This time, however, there was a change of attitude. Not only did the officials refrain from pushing me, but they behaved with extreme gentleness, and even used a title unheard of by a prisoner: "Mr. Beilis, Sir." The politeness increased in proportion as I advanced into the prison.

A guard rushed to get a chair "for Mr. Beilis to sit down," as "Mr. Beilis must feel tired." The warden then came to me. This man was really a heartless individual, and he rarely used to call me anything but "bloodsucker" and "murderer." He had often offered me "consolation," telling me the gallows awaited me.

This time I could hardly recognize him. He was human! He said: "Mr. Beilis, I congratulate you most cordially and extend to you my best wishes. Do allow my wife and children to shake hands with you." He shook hands with me, and thereupon his wife and son came in and greeted me with true cordiality. The whole office staff gathered around and vied with each other in heaping congratulations upon me. All seemed to be pleased. The prison official who had threatened me in the morning stood there, but seemed to be more frightened than anything else. He had no authority over me, and he knew it.

The warden exclaimed: "By the way, do you know, Beilis, that we have some of your money, about nine rubles and fifty kopeks. You will get it at once. Some of your personal belongings, however, are in the storehouse, and you will get them later."

I was given the money and a few personal effects. When the warden read my application, signed at the court, asking for permission to spend the night in prison, he protested: "No, no, that won't do. Take the man home. He has spent enough time in prison. Let him go home and see his family." Upon hearing this, I forgot all the alarms with which the presiding judge had tried to impress me, about the danger threatening me because the anti-Semites were aroused.

"I want to go home," I said. Apparently, there was no order from "above" that I spend the night in prison. The application stated that I myself was asking for it. The warden therefore had the full right to refuse my application. He gave orders for a cab, and a policeman was summoned to act as my escort on the road.

It was the rule in Kiev that any Jew released from prison, and not possessing the right to live in Kiev, had to go to the police station to be sent to his home under police supervision. I actually enjoyed the great privilege of "the right to reside," because of my boy who was a student in the Kiev Gymnasium. This was a special regulation which applied to Kiev alone, of all the cities of Russia. In other cities "outside the Pale," the children acquired the right of residence because of their parents. In Kiev, however, it was the parents who acquired this sacred right because of their children who attended the schools; the children were not supposed to be left without parental care. But although I had the "right to reside," I was still given a police escort.

Since Zaitsev's factory was situated in two police districts, I had to go through two police stations: the Plossky and the Lukianovsky. I was driven along with great pomp. A squad of cavalry rode ahead of the cab, and two gendarmes sat on the driver's seat. Finally we reached the Lukianovsky police station.

The captain of the station was a notorious Black Hundreds anti-Semite. He could not endure the sight of a Jew. It was he who was one of the first to have entered my house on the unforgettable night of my arrest. But all of that had been in the past. Apparently, the hearts of all the authorities had changed: they all became different men, with different manners. No sooner had I entered the police station than the captain came out with arms outstretched. "I am very happy to see you." He shook hands with me very cordially. "I want to ask a favor of you, Beilis, and I hope you won't refuse me."

"What can I do for you?"

"My daughter wishes to see you. She wishes to congratulate you upon your liberation. Will you permit her that pleasure? She is a *gymnasium* student, who was terribly excited during the whole period of your trial. Every time she read the papers and saw that something had gone wrong with your affairs, she wept like a child. She neglected her studies because of you. She used to go around moaning: 'Oh, my God, how the poor man must be suffering.' Now you must permit her to come and greet you."

During the course of this speech, the policemen at the station looked at their captain as though he were a madman. It was an unusual picture for them to see their savage captain imploring a Jew for a favor; it was usually the reverse. And the official apparently considered it an honor for his daughter to talk to me.

Of course, I was only too glad to grant him his request, and said that I myself would be pleased to meet his daughter. The captain rushed to the phone. "Is that you, Marcia?" he called. "Your friend has come, the man Beilis. Come over to see him, and be quick about it."

While waiting for his daughter, he wanted to entertain me. "Would you like to drink something – tea or beer? I shall prepare the necessary papers in the meantime." Tea was brought in; the policeman who offered me the cup gave me the military salute.

The captain's daughter entered a few minutes later, accompanied by a girl friend. The two seemed quite bashful and hesitated to come over. "Well," encouraged the captain, "don't be shy. Greet your friend Beilis."

The girl finally came over and asked very timidly: "Are you Mr. Beilis? You must forgive me for being so bold. Here is a friend of mine; we both used to weep for you and pray for your liberation."

The two girls seemed to be sincerely overjoyed at my freedom. I could see how genuine and honest was their sympathy.

"We suffered so much because of you," said the girl. "We did not sleep whole nights, and always talked of your sufferings, but of course it was nothing compared to what you have gone through. But now, justice and truth have won out. I wish you peace and happiness together with your family."

I refer to all this because, as it happened, it was the first greeting that I received, upon liberation, from pure, innocent children who had really suffered because of the falsehoods and calumnies that had oppressed me and the Jewish people. There came to my mind at that moment the words of my Gentile friend, Zakharchenko, who had said: "The stones of the bridge may

175

crumble, but the truth will out."

When all the formalities were over, the captain accompanied me to the street and saw me seated in the cab. We now had to go to the Plossky police station. A large crowd had assembled there, composed of thousands of Jews who had learned that I was coming. The streets were packed, and the police had a difficult task keeping order.

No sooner had we reached the station that a police lieutenant ran out and embraced me. He took me by the hand and led me inside. The papers had apparently been prepared in advance, for the whole proceeding did not take more than three minutes. Then the lieutenant smiled at me and offered to take me home. "I must have the signal honor of bringing you safe to your wife and children, and to see to it that your house is properly guarded. Let us go."

I did not recognize my house, as the old one had burned down during my imprisonment. But I recognized the neighborhood which I had known for so many years. It seemed as if it were only yesterday that I had been taken away from it, and my heart pulsed with joy and impatience.

In the house itself the children fell over me, shouting "Father, father," and they clung to me as if afraid that I might once more be taken away from them. They and my wife cried and danced wildly at the same time.

Not all of my family was present, however; my wife had sent three of my children to another part of the city, fearing for their safety. She was right to be afraid. On the day on which the verdict was to be given, the excitement in Kiev, and especially in my district, was really fierce. The Jews were naturally apprehensive in case of my being convicted, for a terrible massacre would undoubtedly have broken out in Kiev. The Black Hundreds were all set for it. They expected to see me convicted; and had the jury come out with a decision that I was guilty and that the Jews use Christian blood, there is no doubt that the pogromists would have avenged themselves on the Jews. At our factory, this fear was at its height, for this was naturally the first place for the Black Hundreds to begin their activity. That is why my wife had sent the three children away.

After I arrived home, some of the neighbors began to gather. The lieutenant who remained in the house would not admit anyone, except upon my request. There were few people around, except for the usual residents of the factory, but there were many soldiers in evidence. An army of them was posted on the adjoining streets. Guards were thrown around the house and at the gate, and no one was admitted without my permission. The lieutenant sat in one of the rooms with two policemen, and every half-hour or so the telephone would ring from the governor's palace, inquiring as to my well-being.

After a while, telegrams commenced to reach me from all parts of Russia, greetings from a group of intelligentsia from Tsarskoye Selo, from the Jewish deputies of the *Duma*, from the famous Russian writer Korolenko, from the student bodies of the Universities of Moscow and St. Petersburg, from various private persons, Jew and Gentile alike. I gave the lieutenant three rubles as a tip for the police messengers who were bringing the telegrams.

I tried to go to bed about two that morning. I was completely exhausted by the events of the day, by the biased speech of the presiding judge, by the anxiety and tension of waiting for the verdict. I lay down, but could not sleep. The excitement was apparently too strong for me, and then – who could sleep on such a night, the first night of freedom? Who could spend the most precious moments of a life in sleeping? I arose; tea was made and we recommenced our conversation.

No sooner did the dawn of the next day break than virtually thousands of people swarmed around and into the house. The street car on our street ordinarily stopped two blocks from our house. This time, however, somebody had a signboard rigged up in front of my house, reading "Beilis Station," and the street car brought guests by the thousands.

Chapter 33: A Rejoicing World

I had believed that once freed, I would enjoy my former quiet life. It was not meant to be, however. My house was daily besieged by people coming to greet me and to express their joy at my liberation. Not only individuals, but groups of fifty and sixty people would come to the house at one time. The cabmen at the railroad stations, seeing groups of Jews descending from the trains, would straightaway ask: "Are you going to Beilis?" The cabmen would drive them straight to me.

Dozens of automobiles always stood in front of my house. One party would leave and another would come. People brought flowers and chocolates; everyone wished to bring me something. The house was turned into a flower garden and a candy shop.

The whole experience gave me great moral satisfaction. I saw the world taking an immense interest in my tribulations, and coming to me in order to express their joy at my liberation. I was very thankful, of course, though I must admit that the continuous handshaking was anything but pleasant for my hands, which became swollen after a time.

One day, two gentlemen came to visit me, one from St. Petersburg, the other a doctor from Lodz. Neither of them spoke at first, and finally one began to sob. The doctor spoke up: "Don't cry, it affects Mr. Beilis. He is still very nervous." In a few minutes, the doctor himself was in the same condition, and he went to the window, turned his back to us, and was very busy with his handkerchief.

In a short while, I actually became ill witnessing such scenes, all of which affected my nerves. I was finally sent to Zaitsev's hospital. Many of the visitors who came to my house and did not find me became hysterical with disappointment and with anxiety for me. Some insisted that they must see me or they would commit suicide. "Why, we have suffered so much with him and through him, and now we don't want to go away without seeing him. He ought to be taken out of the hospital."

I therefore had to go back home. The numerous visitors again began their daily pilgrimages, in and out, out and in. The official who was in charge of the guard around my house used to jest, saying that in another month of such duty, he would be able to retire; he received so much money in the form of small gifts from my visitors.

One day a Russian priest came to see me. He entered the house, and without saying a word, he fell on his knees, made the sign of the cross, and wept like a small child. "Mr. Beilis," he said after a while, "you know that my action puts me in some danger. I should not have come to greet you at all. I could have sent my greeting by letter, but I decided to come. My conscience would not let me do otherwise. I came to ask forgiveness in the name of my people." He kissed my hand before I had time to withdraw it, and immediately left the house.

This incident created a profound effect on me. I felt it to be a unique occurrence that a high Christian clergyman had come to a Jew to kiss his hand, and to bend his knees before him. What strange creatures the Russian people are! On the one hand, there are the Zamyslovskys, the Shmakovs, and the whole nefarious band of Black Hundreds; and on the other hand, one finds Russian clergymen coming to beg forgiveness of Jews for the persecution inflicted on them.

On another occasion, a military colonel, accompanied by a college student, came to my house. The colonel was a giant of fierce and forbidding appearance. He greeted me and introduced his student son. Then he began pacing the room in silence. His spurs clicked, and the house shook with every step he took. I was overawed. At last he stopped and turned to me. "Permit me to congratulate you most sincerely upon your liberation. I myself am posted in the Far East with my regiment. My family is also there. But I took special leave for a month in order to come here. I had to see you, and to greet you in person." Again I was shown how difficult it is to read into the soul of a Russian. Here was a military colonel with the air of an executioner, and yet so gentle and humane.

We talked for a while, but he was silent for the most part. I noticed that he was oppressed by something. He arose in a while and bade me farewell, and left with his son. A moment later the bell rang; the colonel was there once more. "Do forgive me, Mr. Beilis," he said, "I must be annoying you, but you must allow me to spend another five minutes in your house. I am leaving for distant lands; we shall probably never see each other again." Before he left he asked for one of my cigarettes as a souvenir. I gave him some cigarettes and was rather sorry to part with him.

The famous Russian writer and friend of the Jews, Vladimir Korolenko, came to my home also. "Do you know," he said, "I have been envious of you. I would have been happy to wear your prisoner's uniform, to sit in jail for you. You must have suffered very much, but you suffered for the truth." He spent considerable time with me, inquiring about everything with the curiosity of a child, and consoling me with the sincerity of a loving brother.

There were no less than seven or eight thousand visitors a day at my home. During the period immediately following the trial, I received eleven thousand letters in all European languages, from all parts of the world, and seven thousand telegrams. Some of the telegrams were long messages. Twenty thousand visiting cards completed the collection.

I received the following letter from a lady in St. Petersburg: "I am a Christian from a well-known military family, but the militaristic spirit has not affected me. Jews have always been dear to me; it is an atrocious calumny to say that they want our blood. The truth is that we want their blood. It gives me great joy to know that you are free. My child shares my feelings. During your trial he used to look at your picture and say: 'The poor man. How much Beilis suffers, and all unjustly. All on account of that murderess Vera Cheberyak.'"

It was during this time that the rumor began circulating that I was receiving money from many sources. The truth is that some people sent me a few rubles. But the papers had it that I was becoming a millionaire. The result was that I was deluged by hundreds of letters asking for financial aid. Talmud Torahs, rabbis, hospitals, charity institutions, and innumerable committees asked for money. Students appealed for money to see them through college. One Jew had to marry off his daughter, and therefore he demanded a dowry. Some people had to pay their promissory notes, and I was summoned to come to their rescue. And these were not requests for meager sums; they went in for big money. No one asked for less than a few thousand rubles.

Meanwhile, the truth of the situation was that I needed help myself. I had not a cent left of my savings and did not know what the near future had in store for me. Among the numerous letters of sympathy that I received were also a number of messages from the Black Hundreds, threatening me with death. I could not, therefore, feel completely assured even of my safety.

Chapter 34: Provision for the Future

The threats addressed to me by the Black Hundreds multiplied. Each day brought its quota of ominous letters. In addition, the governor of Kiev insisted that I leave the city, for he could not be responsible for my safety.

My situation was a difficult one. If I could not remain in Kiev and return to my former position at the factory, I would be deprived of any source of income, and I would be unable to support my family. Financial worries began. Instead of renewing my quiet life as I had expected, I had to begin thinking of moving somewhere else, of starting life anew.

About this time a committee of three was formed, consisting of Dr. Bikhovsky, of Zaitsev's hospital; Rabbi Aronson; and the well known financier, Joseph Marshak. This committee was to provide the ways and means of bettering my financial situation, and thus enable me to leave Kiev and earn a living elsewhere.

One day a representative of the *New York American* newspaper came to me, with an interpreter. This man made me a proposition to come to America for a tour of twenty weeks, for which I was to get $40,000. I told the man from the very beginning that I did not want to go there, but he told me to take my time and to think the matter over.

A few days later, he appeared again. He told me he was leaving, but left his proposition open. "Of course, it is fortunate that you have been liberated, but you must not forget that you have to make a living. You cannot live long on hopes and sympathy. You won't be able to continue here. If you are going to America, you ought to accept my offer. I will attend to everything; whatever other proposition you may get, I am ready to double the amount offered. For the time being, give me a few autobiographical facts, and I shall pay you well," continued the newspaperman.

I related some of my experiences; the conversation lasted a few minutes, whereupon he produced $1,000 and paid me. "This," he said, "is for permission to print my conversation with you in our newspaper." Before leaving, he gave me a personal souvenir: a golden watch.

A few days later I received a telegram from H. Marcus of New York, proposing a contract for three years in his banking house, with a salary of $10,000 a year.

I must admit that it was a great temptation listening to all these offers, especially in view of the difficult situation in which I found myself. I was losing my health, had lost my position, and could not remain any longer in Kiev. Nevertheless, I turned away all offers, and the Kiev committee of three agreed with my decision.

A certain Jewish woman of Paris offered to present me with a house worth about three-quarter of a million francs, if I would come to Paris with my family. I thanked her very cordially, but refused. In addition to the difficulties of going to a country, the language of which I could not learn, I did not care to accept this munificent gift, somehow.

Among the many other generous offers given me was one extended by a factory owner from Odessa, a Mr. Gershovitz, who told me that his son in New York, worth a million, had asked him to give me $25,000 and send me to America, where his son would take care of me. I referred Mr. Gershovitz to Dr. Bikhovsky, who was the chairman of my committee. Dr. Bikhovsky refused to listen to this offer, which made Mr. Gershovitz angry.

"Will I gain anything from this? I want to do something for Mr. Beilis as one Jew for another; why then won't you listen to my proposition?" said Mr. Gershovitz. "It matters not to me whether Beilis goes to America; the thing is, he ought to be provided for. If you want to send him to the Land of Israel, very well; but he must also be able to live there in decent circumstances and suffer no privations. If you cannot send him to the Land of Israel, let him go to America, where he will be able to live in comfort. If, as a result of your advice, Beilis should find himself in need, you will never forgive yourself. His fate is in the balance; what is your decision?"

But Dr. Bikhovsky refused.

Similar propositions came from Berlin, Vienna and London. In London, a comfortable house was prepared for me at Rothschild's expense.[1] The house was to become my property, fully furnished, immediately I arrived in London. A young Jewish student was specially sent from London to take me to England. I was told, however, that the climate in London, being damp, would adversely affect my health, since I was already suffering from some of the effects of prison life. When the public learned that I had refused the London offer, it occasioned some comment in the Kiev press.

---

[1] Beilis's life intersected with the lives of several members of the Rothschild family. Reference here is apparently to Lord Leopold Rothschild. During the Beilis trial, Leopold Rothschild successfully appealed to the Vatican to authenticate the statements prior Popes had made denouncing earlier blood libels against the Jews.

Chapter 35: Toward the Land of Israel

During the deliberations as to where I should go, I missed the counsel of Mr. Gruzenberg, my former lawyer. I knew he would be the best person to advise me. With his experience, he would know what I ought to do and what to avoid. I felt certain that this man, who was ready to sacrifice everything to save me from prison, would also do a great deal to aid me for the future. However, Gruzenberg was abroad at the time, taking a rest from the exertions of the trial, which had told heavily upon him. While he was abroad, I received a letter from him, in which he asked what I was doing and expressed surprise that I was still in Kiev. He wrote: "I have suffered much less than you and yet I feel completely exhausted and broken down. You, Mr. Beilis, have suffered much longer, and I am sure you feel the consequences. Why don't you go away somewhere for a rest? I understand your situation very well; the same occurred to Hilsner.[m] After the thing is over, the people forget about you. I cannot think of your living insecurely in Kiev. How is it no one seems to be doing anything for you?"

I heard people talking about my future, but nothing practical seemed to result. I had nothing more tangible than words. Finally the committee got together to make a definite decision. The

---

[m] Hilsner was a victim of blood libel in 1900. It is possible that Beilis misremembers Gruzenberg's letter here, and that Gruzenberg actually wrote that "the same occurred to Blondes." Blondes also was a victim of blood libel in 1900; like Beilis, he was successfully represented by Gruzenberg.

proposal was that I be sent to the Land of Israel. Mr. Marshak and Dr. Bikhovsky were initially opposed to this plan; they wanted me to settle some place else. But Rabbi Aronson prevailed in the end, and it was decided to have me go to the Land of Israel.

Then the committee wanted to know what occupation I would choose for myself. "We shall give you the means to take up whatever you like. Do not consider it as a gift. It is merely our duty to you."

I could hardly decide upon anything specific. It was all so definite and concrete. I had to say: "Gentlemen, I cannot decide upon anything just now. I believe that it would be best if you were to make up my mind for me. I would not be averse to having a little house which would bring sufficient income for a modest living, and a piece of land connected with it which I should be able to work. I like farming very much, and I always wanted to live on the land."

"In that case," said Mr. Marshak, "there is no better place than the Land of Israel. We shall give you the necessary means."

The plan was to have me go to Trieste first and get a month's rest there, and then to embark for the Land of Israel. I began preparing myself for a parting with mother Russia. I must confess that it was not easy. There were many Black Hundreds in Russia who were eager to shed Jewish blood, but on the other hand there were so many wonderful people. How many Christian prisoners had wept with me in jail; how many Christian children had not slept nights and prayed to God for my release? And then the Russian intelligentsia, what an interest they had displayed in my case, how much energy they had spent for my sake, and how great was the joy of these people, when their efforts resulted in my liberation!

My impressions were obtained not only from the hundreds

of Christians who had come to my house to greet me and to rejoice with me, but from the numerous letters I received and the indirect reports. In addition to harboring a fondness for these people, it was difficult to part with my native land, where I had been born, grown up, had suffered and enjoyed life.

It was planned that my departure was to be kept a secret. No one, not even my relatives, were to know. We had to take these various precautions because my life was in danger.

One day I went to the governor's palace in order to get my passport. There was a line of about seventy people waiting for their passports. I was recognized immediately, and one man, one of the first in line, let me have his place. In the governor's office I was received with considerable pomp. A chair was brought in, and my passport was ready in a few moments. I was carefully escorted to the cab and was bid a hearty good-bye.

My departure was planned for December, 1913, and although we hoped it had been kept a secret, events showed that it had not. A few days after I secured my passport, the newspapers had big headlines that I was to go abroad. We were not very anxious to have the anti-Semites know that I proposed leaving Russia. Fortunately, the day and hour of my departure were not known. We selected a day when the crowd would be busy with their vodka.

Chapter 36: From Kiev to Trieste

Goodbye, Kiev, farewell my native land, farewell all my friends with whom I have spent my life! I am leaving for the land of our fathers, for the Holy Land, where once flowed milk and honey, and which has always been dear to my heart. I am going to rest body and soul in the Land of Israel. These were the thoughts that passed through my mind.

On the evening of my departure from Kiev, I was supposed to be invited to a party given by a friend, to camouflage my leaving. Dr. Bikhovsky went ahead to the station to buy the tickets, so that I could go onto the train at once and not be seen at the station, in case any of the Black Hundreds were prowling around.

I did not even bid farewell to my brother and sister; they were not even told that I was leaving. A coach drove up to my house in the dark. I put on spectacles and was dressed in a huge cloak, so that I would not be recognized. My wife and children had gone ahead on an earlier train; they were waiting for me at Kazatin. There we took another train which was going direct to the Austrian border. We were accompanied by the manager of Zaitsev's factory, Mr. Dubovik.

The whole night we sat in the train coupe as in a dungeon. We did not let anybody see us, for fear of being recognized. At break of day, I went into the passageway for a minute. I noticed two Christians pacing back and forth. The moment they saw me, they approached and asked: "Aren't you Mr. Beilis?"

I was suspicious. It seemed to me that these two might belong to the Black Hundreds gang, possibly they had been sent to do away with me. Of course, my suspicion might be unjustified, but I had to be careful. Therefore I answered: "I should like to be Beilis, but he is already in America. Do you know him?"

"Yes," said one of the men, "I was in his house."

When some of the Jewish leaders in Berlin learned that I was going abroad, they sent two men to the Austrian border to assist me in crossing the border. Upon their arrival at the border station, they told the officials whom they were expecting.

We finally reached Podvolochisk, on the Austrian border. There, a couple of Austrian officials came into the train and asked for our passport. The moment they saw I was Beilis, they didn't even look at my baggage; they told us we were free to proceed.

On the other side of the border, we had to wait a short while for the train to Lemberg. During that interval, the people of the little town on the border came to know that I was there. Jews came running from all directions, and as is the general custom at a Jewish celebration, a general weeping ensued.

Apparently, the Jews of Lemberg had also been informed of my arrival. As our train came slowly into the station, and as I looked through the car windows, I could hardly believe my eyes. The whole platform, the station house, and the adjoining streets were lined with people. The shouting was deafening. Had the train left immediately, it would not have been so bad. The trouble was that we had to stay there for a time. The crowd insisted that I come out and show myself. I was not inclined to do so, however. The station master thereupon came into my car and begged me to come out for a minute; he feared that the crowd might somehow damage the station. Besides, a number of people had threatened to post themselves on the rails and not permit the train to go further. Therefore, I had to go out. I bade farewell to the assembled multitude, and a few minutes later our train left for Vienna.

We reached Vienna in the early hours of the morning. There we were met by the representatives of the Jewish community: Adolph Stern, Kaminka, and others. We had tea in the train and were driven to our hotel, where we expected to have a little rest. But we were hardly there a few minutes when we heard knocking at the door. It was Mr. Stern, announcing that some of the foremost Jews of Vienna had come to pay their respects.

Mr. Stern engaged an additional suite of rooms as a reception chamber to accommodate the many people who came to visit me during my stay in Vienna. That first day there was an aggregation of professional men: lawyers, professors, and doctors. Some of the doctors declared that they would like to examine me to see if I was well. I gave them this permission, and they declared that I was well, only very much run down and exhausted because of the many things I had been through. A special dinner was arranged for that day, and about sixty persons were present. Some of the most eminent men in town attended the dinner, among whom was the editor of the Vienna paper, *Neue Freie Presse*.

We were kept pretty busy by visits and official receptions. I was driven about the town in an automobile and shown the sights of the wonderful city of Vienna. We drove to the Jewish musical school, where the choir chanted a blessing, and the cantor sang the appropriate chapters from the Psalms.

After two days we were ready to take our departure to the

192

South, for Trieste. In the latter city, we were met by Rabbi Chajes, who later became the chief rabbi of Vienna. My sojourn in Trieste was to be kept a secret, and since all hotels required guests to show their passports, a special place was found by Rabbi Chajes so that I would not have to show the identifying passport. We took our meals with a certain *shochet* (Jewish ritual slaughterer), who did not know who I was. It was arranged between me and my family that my name should not be mentioned aloud.

One Friday night when we came to our host for the meal, there were about thirty Jews around the table. At one point, conversation shifted towards the Beilis case, and one Jew said it was known that Beilis was in Trieste at the time, but unfortunately he had to travel incognito so that the Black Hundreds would not persecute him.

At these words, one of my children could not restrain herself from bursting into laughter. Some men looked at the child and one of them asked why she laughed. The Jews became suspicious; they began to exchange glances and whispers. At last they discovered I was Beilis. And that was all that was needed to start things going.

A tumult arose in the streets; people ran to Rabbi Chajes's house, in order to reproach him for having kept secret my whereabouts. A reception was tendered me in a big hotel, and thousands of people came to see me. I was besieged with requests for autographs, and in the end I stayed in Trieste for a whole month.

Chapter 37: In the Land of Israel

Finally the day came for us to bid goodbye to Trieste and to Europe. We boarded the ship and started on our voyage to the Land of Israel, the land in which I expected to pass the remainder of my years. The moment the passengers on my ship became aware who I was, there was no lack of demonstrations of sympathy from both Jews and non-Jews. The captain and the ship's doctor asked for permission to come to my cabin for a visit and a conversation. The doctor showed me my picture, which he had clipped from a magazine. A group of Christian passengers presented me with a gift.

The nearer we got to the Land of Israel, the more cheerful I felt. We had to pass one port on our way to the Land of Israel, and that was Alexandria. Thousands were on the dock to see me.[n] While the ship was entering the port, a number of people came out in small boats in order to meet the ship and bid me welcome. I was met by a band of representatives of various Jewish societies. No sooner had we reached land than I received an invitation to attend the circumcision celebration of one of the local Sephardic families. I felt very tired, but excuses were of no avail. At the party I was honored with all sorts of testimonials.

We finally reached the port of Haifa on the 16th of February, 1914, in the land which was to be our new home. A delegation came

---

[n] There was at the time a large Jewish community in Alexandria in Egypt.

194

aboard to greet me, including Rabbi Kook,[o] Rabbi Ben-Zion Uziel,[p] and Messrs. Levitan, Schenken, Mosesson, and Dizengoff. Rabbi Kook delivered a speech in which he stressed the fact that I had selected the Land of Israel as the country of my residence in preference to the many lands from which I had received tempting offers. Afterwards, Rabbi Kook pronounced a formal blessing on me.

In addition to the deputation which came on board to meet me, a boat was sent out to carry us ashore. The Arabian boatmen came out in full force, shouting "Long live Beilis!" On the shore, I was awaited by the students of the Jewish *gymnasium* (college preparatory school), who bore flags and flowers. The children sang and a band played.

One of the Arabian chiefs, who owned the finest coach and pair of horses in the whole district, honored me by having me driven to Tel Aviv. This honor had been conferred in the past only upon the most exalted guests, for example Rothschild when he had visited the Land of Israel.[q] But the Arabian chieftain went even further. Not satisfied with having left his coach at my disposal, he himself, accompanied by a retinue, rode in front of the coach, acting as my guard of honor.

On the way to Tel Aviv, the road was lined with Jews. A great number of them had come from the agricultural colonies

---

[o] Then the Ashkenazi chief rabbi of Jaffa-Tel Aviv, later the Ashkenazi chief rabbi of Palestine under the British Mandate.

[p] Then the Sephardic chief rabbi of Jaffa-Tel Aviv, later the Sephardic chief rabbi of Palestine under the British Mandate and the first Sephardic chief rabbi of Israel.

[q] Reference here is apparently to Baron Edmond James de Rothschild, a major benefactor of the Jewish community in Palestine.

especially for this occasion. In Tel Aviv I was put up at Herzliya Hotel, and there too I was greeted by representatives of various organizations and colonies, by Hapoel Hatzair, Poale Zion, the city board of aldermen, the ICA (Jewish Colonization Association), the Shomrim, etc. Numerous speeches were delivered, naturally, at all times.

The Land of Israel had an invigorating effect upon me; it gave me new life and hope. Nature itself, the life of the people, inspired me with vigor and the desire to live. When we had left Kiev, it was cold and the fields were covered with snow. Here everything was green, and the sun was warm. It was the most beautiful season of the year in the Land of Israel. Everything was blooming; the hills and the fields were covered with vegetation.

I could not get too much of the atmosphere. For quite some time I would wander around, inspecting every corner of the country, breathing the refreshing air, deep-lunged. At first I could not sleep at night; I felt as though I did not want to lose one moment of the fragrant, inspiring nights in the Land of Israel. In the meantime, of course, I continued to be feted, received and greeted in various districts. The first Saturday in the land, Rabbi Kook invited me to attend his synagogue, where he held a two-hour discourse about me.

A week after my arrival in the country, a deputation of Jerusalem Jews came to me, inquiring where I planned to settle: in Tel Aviv or Jerusalem? It would be a humiliation of Jerusalem for me to settle anywhere else, they declared.

"But Jaffa and Tel Aviv belong to the Land of Israel too," I answered.

"Yes, but it was we who prayed for you at the Western Wall," they protested.

I began preparing to go to Jerusalem in a week or two. I would constantly receive messages from them, asking when I would come. They wanted to prepare a reception for me. I answered that I preferred to arrive secretly, that I was ill and weak, and that receptions tired me out. And moreover, I was afraid that the reception would keep me from seeing Jerusalem as I wanted to.

As a matter of fact, the receptions during my first weeks in the country tired me very much. They were almost as numerous as the ones following the Kiev trial. It was almost Passover, and innumerable tourists were arriving in the Land of Israel for that holiday. Almost every ship brought seven or eight hundred people, all of whom wanted to meet and greet me, to shake my hand, and to express their sympathy.

Before I left for Jerusalem, I inspected the colony of Petach Tikva. I visited the place in company with Isaac L. Goldberg, Sholem Asch, Polakov, and Mr. Brill, and we spent some time there. My first contact with an Israeli agricultural colony gave me the utmost satisfaction and joy.

The next day we went to Arsuf, where I spent three days. At the local celebration I was the guest of the pupils of the Jaffa Gymnasium.

At last I decided to visit Jerusalem. Some of my party wanted to go along with me. Upon our arrival, we put up at Amdursky's Hotel. My name was kept a secret, however.

A few hours after our arrival, one man recognized me. The proprietor of the hotel was very much insulted. He could not understand why my name should have been kept a secret from him. Especially since he had prepared a special suite of rooms for me. Within no time, the news spread throughout the town, and the endless receptions began. In the three days which I spent in Jerusalem, I had to visit all the synagogues, inspect all the hospitals and charity institutions, and inscribe my name in all the albums.

The greatest point of interest, for me, was the Western Wall and the site of the ancient Temple. Approaching the Western Wall, I was reminded of the words of the Jerusalem Jews: "We prayed for you at the Western Wall."

Of course, Jews throughout the world had prayed for the happy outcome of my fate, during the whole time of my imprisonment until the day of my liberation. My misfortune was the misfortune of the whole Jewish people. But there was something closer to me in the fact that Jews had prayed for me at the Western Wall – here, where Jews had wept and prayed for almost two thousand years, bemoaning their great national loss, the supreme tragedy of the Jewish people, their bitter exile. My trial was but an episode in the history of our life in the Diaspora; it was but a part in the record of our national sorrows. Surely the praying for me at the Western Wall was most appropriate.

It was with mixed feelings that I came close to the old wall, to the silent witness of ancient Jewish glory and present sorrow. I relived the whole Jewish exile and also re-experienced my own sorrows. As I was standing at the wall, absorbed in thought, I saw H. Berlin, one of the members of my party, crying. It was surprising from a man who had no Jewish characteristics whatsoever; he had been supposed to be far-removed from Judàism altogether. His daughter, a doctor, who could not even speak any Yiddish, was crying hysterically.

Berlin later explained to me that he had cried both from sadness and joy. "I reminded myself of our exile, but I also thought of the new hope for a Jewish homeland," he said.

On the site of the ancient Temple, as everyone knows, there now stands a Mohammedan mosque. Pious Jews go nowhere near it; and the Moslems permit no "unbelievers" to enter it. In my case, however, an exception was made.

"We will permit you to enter the mosque," I was told by one of the leading Arabs. "You belong to the three great Jewish heroes and martyrs." One of the others he mentioned was Dreyfus.

I was given a guide to take me through the place, and was shown all the curiosities. I saw the place where Solomon was supposed to have kept his horses, and the rostrum from which he addressed the people.

From Jerusalem I returned to Tel Aviv, and I gradually began the process of becoming a resident. For a month we lived in the hotel, then we took up residence with the *Hakham Bashi*.[r] The fetes and celebrations continued until after Passover. In the first place, the stream of tourists who wanted to see me was uninterrupted, and secondly, the natives themselves let pass no opportunity at which they could hold some kind of celebration for me. At Purim time, for example, hundreds of Jews came to my house for the big repast, and danced there and made merry until the small hours of the night.

On the second day of Passover, which is already a half-holiday in the Land of Israel, everyone goes to the public squares. I was present at one of these gatherings; at that time Nahum Sokolow was visiting the town. Mr. Eisenberg, the chairman of the affair,

---

[r] Evidently referring to Rabbi Ben-Zion Uziel, who held this title as Sephardic chief rabbi of Jaffa-Tel Aviv.

welcomed Mr. Sokolow and myself as the two guests of honor, and Sokolow spoke in honor of the occasion.

As time went on, I became more attached to the Land of Israel. The climate was doing me good. It healed my physical and spiritual wounds. In a short time, I felt as though I were a native of the country, as though I had been born there and had lived there all my life. I was pleased by the country and everything in it, from the people to the inanimate things. In Tel Aviv, for the first time, I began to appreciate what the true Jewish life is. I saw for the first time a race of proud, uncringing Jews, who lived life openly and unafraid.

When people would plead with me to go to America, I answered:

"Before, in Russia, when the word 'Palestine' conjured up a waste and barren land, even then I chose to come here in preference to other countries.[s] How much more, then, would I insist on staying here, after I have come to love the land!"

Even if it had been only for the fact that I could give my children a Jewish education, I preferred to stay in the Land of Israel. I came there with five children, three sons and two daughters. In Russia I had always lived among Christians, one Jew among four thousand non-Jews. It was extremely difficult to raise my children as Jews. My children knew no Yiddish, and it was still more difficult to teach them Hebrew, not to speak of the impossibility of giving them a thorough Jewish education. In the Land of Israel, my

---

[s] The original Yiddish edition is a play on words. Beilis writes that in Russia, the word "Palestine" recalled to him the word *"Pushtina"* (a Russian word meaning wasteland). This is one of the few places where Beilis uses the term "Palestine" in place of "the Land of Israel."

children had the opportunity of living in an unadulterated Jewish environment, received the best type of Jewish education, and in three months were able to speak Hebrew. How glad and overjoyed I was at this last accomplishment.

In deciding the question of education for my children, there was the difficulty of choosing between the old and the new Land of Israel. Rabbi Kook advised me to choose a school of the former type. The instructors at the Jaffa Gymnasium came to me, however, and pleaded that if I would not send my children to the Gymnasium, it would be a blow to the school. I told them all that I was so happy that my children had the opportunities of receiving a Jewish education that it mattered little where they got it.

I finally decided to send my oldest son to the Gymnasium and the others to the Academy.[t] There were many who volunteered to coach my children after school hours. Among these was Mr. Engel, of the Academy, and Mr. Berlin (not the same Berlin as mentioned earlier), and Mr. Berlin's two daughters.

At last, I thought, I was comfortably settled, with the fates of my children adequately secured; now I could retire to a peaceful existence. But just at this time the War broke out and shattered all my well-laid plans and hopes.

---

[t] In the Yiddish edition, Beilis actually writes that he decided to send his eldest son to the Academy and the others to the Gymnasium. However, that appears to be an error, as there are references below to Beilis's eldest son attending the Jaffa Gymnasium before entering the Turkish army.

Chapter 38: My Fortune Changes

The War broke out, and like a prairie fire it caught everything in its path. It swept from country to country, finally including Turkey, and of course the Land of Israel. The Garden of Eden was turning into the Valley of Gehinnom.

Even just before the war, the poetry of my life had become diluted by quite a bit of troublesome prose. The question of money came to the surface, the question of "how shall we eat," how shall I provide for my children. The committee which had been selected to take care of me in Kiev had decided that I should go to the Land of Israel, and I had been satisfied. They had said: "Beilis, do not worry. We will do everything. We will provide for you adequately." But these promises were not being fulfilled so quickly.

I had traveled from Kiev to the Land of Israel at my own expense. As I forgot to mention before, the representative of the *New York American* had paid me an additional $2,000 for other material I gave him. In all, I had $3,000, or 6,000 rubles in Russian money. I deducted 500 rubles for my expenses and left the rest with Zaitsev.

Even in Trieste I had begun to feel the lack of money. Now that I was in the Land of Israel, day followed day and week followed week, and I was being feted, wined and dined, but the questions became more insistent: What will the future be? What will be the outcome? How will I provide for my family?

At that time, Baron Rothschild of Paris visited the Land of Israel, and the plan was that I should meet him, but somehow or other that never came to pass.

At Passover time, Dr. Bikhovsky of Kiev came to visit me. He told me that the 5,500 rubles had been deposited to my account in a Paris bank, and that I would always be able to get the money at the Anglo-Palestine bank at Jaffa. He said: "Rest assured, you will get everything we promised you. You will get the house, and you will have the means to live in peace. Don't worry about anything."

Before his departure, he selected three men who were to "look out" for me.

A few months passed, and I saw that nothing was happening. I asked them to let me go to some place where I could make a living, but they answered my fears by advising me not to be concerned. Everything would be done in the proper manner.

I had been patient enough for two and a half years in prison, had been able to endure the taunts of my jailers and the daily physical and spiritual suffering. I supposed that I could wait a few months to see that these promises were kept, the promises that had been made all around.

It never rains but that it pours! A whole summer passed in waiting and hoping, and suddenly the War broke out. Instead of breathing freely, I again became a sort of prisoner.

As soon as Turkey entered the War, foreign subjects were the first to be aware of it. Everybody was told to leave the country. There was only one escape for me: to become a Turkish subject. And thus, in my old age, I became a Turk.

Because of the War, Mr. Levantine, the director of the Anglo-Palestine bank, had to leave, and a German Jew was appointed in his place. When I came to the latter asking for money, he refused, saying that he did not know me. I immediately went to the local committee of three, but they did not recognize me either. Nobody knew me, all of a sudden, they had never seen me.

What was one to do, how to provide for oneself?

The Turks decided to take my eldest son, Pinchas, for the army (the one who attended the Jaffa Gymnasium). I myself was driven to Petach Tikva. While all those who were driven out had supposedly been provided for in the matter of housing, I was one of those who, upon arriving in Petach Tikva, had not been provided for. In order to pay for some sort of lodging, I had to sell some of my possessions.

My son went into the army in company with a group of other students. When Jemal Pasha came to Jaffa, he had decided that the students of the last three classes – the sixth, seventh and eighth – should be sent to the officer's training camp in Constantinople, but that they would not be sent into battle. My son was in the fifth class at that time, and was barely seventeen. He decided, however, to enter the army.

I opposed it, and pleaded with my son against it. "You are still young," I said. "You should not do it. I cannot permit it."

"I want to do something for the Jewish people," was his answer. "If we should serve Turkey faithfully, the government will treat us more leniently after the War. Our possibilities for acquiring the Land of Israel will be much greater."

"But my service suffices for both of us," I returned. "I have suffered enough for the both of us."

"I am a man already, and I must fulfill my own obligations. I can no longer be satisfied with your achievements. At my Bar

---

Mitzvah, did you not say the sentence: 'Blessed is the son who hast rid me of him?'"

He needed only one more reason to strengthen his determination to fight: Turkey was fighting against Russia.

At last he won. He saw to it that he was counted among the students of the sixth class, and thus became a Turkish soldier. He was sent away with a hundred other Jewish lads to Constantinople. Jemal Pasha, however, did not keep his word. After a short time, they were all sent into the field of battle. And while our children were fighting for Turkey, we were driven here and there. Jemal Pasha lost all his former humanity. He changed his entire demeanor. He declared that in view of the fact that England might be the victor, he would see to it that none of us, at least, would ever see an Englishman. Wherever he would go, he would take us with him.

The command to leave Jaffa staggered me. I became so nervous and hysterical that when I walked upon the porch of the house, on the morning when we were supposed to leave town, I fell down in a faint and bruised myself. I am deaf in one ear to this day, on account of it.

The field of battle came nearer and nearer. When the battle of Gaza took place, we could hear the thunder of the cannons. I naturally thought of my son, who was in the battle, and was in danger of his life – who might be giving up his life for Turkey while the leaders of that country were driving us mercilessly.

One day, as I was walking in the street, a young man came up to me and whispered in my ear: "Your son is at my house."

In great anxiety for the safety of my son, I grasped the hand of the young man with such a grip that he began shouting. I had the strength finally to ask: "Dead or alive?"

"Alive," was his answer.

Then I must see him at once. But the young man would not take me to him under any circumstances. He told me that my son had deserted the army in company with another Jewish officer, and that they were hiding at his house. They would undoubtedly be hunted. He was afraid to take me to my son in the daytime, in order not to lead the Turks to any traces of his whereabouts.

But I could not wait until night. I could not endure the agony of it. At last he gave in.

Thank God, my son was alive and well. But why had he deserted the army, and how? How could he have dared to do such a thing? I was told the following story:

My son had heard about the indignities to which we were being subjected by the Turks, and he could not remain with them any longer. So one day he confided in another officer, older than he – the father of three children – that he had decided to desert. He proposed that the other officer should do the same.

The other officer attempted to dissuade him. "It is impossible," he said. "It means certain death."

"Then I will do it myself, if you are afraid," said my son.

The other man finally gave in.

They decided upon this plan: that they would both go to a nearby village to buy food, and would leave from there. After they had been traveling for some time, they were met by a squad of German intelligence officers, who offered to take the two Jewish-Turkish officers with them. That fitted in with their plan. But what happened was that the Germans lost their way, and instead of leading the two deserters away from the camp, they were carrying them back. As luck would have it, they discovered this in time to turn back.

At one point they went into the house of a Jew, where they took off their clothes and burned them, and put on other clothes. Afterwards, they were put into a wagon, covered with oranges, and brought to Petach Tikva.

On the one hand, I was happy that I was to see my son. On the other hand, I recognized that he was in mortal danger. My troubles then increased: my son became ill with typhus.

Here I was, driven from Jaffa, wandering from pillar to post in Petach Tikva, without any money, and here was my son, a deserter, down with typhus. At this time, the order was given to go back, because the English were coming. The Turks disposed of things in heavy-handed fashion. Those who were rather slow were bound and led like sheep. To add to things, Turkish officers were going around inquiring where Beilis was.

My son finally recovered from the typhus, but he was still weak from its after-effects. A certain Jewish officer, in order to save us, attached a certificate to our door, certifying that the house was quarantined – that there was a typhus patient within. As the Turks were very much afraid of infecting the army with typhus, they did not even approach my house. Of course, they did not know that it was I who was within.

Then the English entered the town; we were thus saved from death. I took advantage of the interval to walk to Jaffa in order to get some money for my starving family. Having gotten the money, I turned back to Petach Tikva. On the way back, I encountered the stringencies of military law. There was a battle in the vicinity. After a great deal of difficulty, I finally succeeded in getting into Petach

---

Tikva, rescuing my family from there, and bringing them in safety to Jaffa.

A miracle occurred for me at this time. A few hours after I left Petach Tikva with my family, the Turks recaptured the town and razed my house to the ground. Whether by accident or providence, I do not know, but the fact is that had I remained there another hour, there would have been nothing left of any of us. Not only were the Turks incensed against the Jews in general, accusing us of too great an intimacy with the English, but they were particularly angry with me.

With the arrival of the English, things became much easier. New hope was aroused for the establishment of a Jewish homeland in the Land of Israel. My son, who had formerly been anxious to join the Turkish army, and then deserted it, became the first recruit in the Jewish Legion, which aided the English in defeating the Turks. Rothschild embraced him as the first member of the Legion.[u]

Colonel Patterson,[v] the commander of the Legion, was very much attached to my son. Patterson regarded the Legion as sacred. He felt that it had done more than its share. He himself never took leave of absence, nor did he permit others to do so. Furthermore, the parents of the Legionnaires received a certain amount of aid. Patterson saw to it that there was no difficulty in our getting the pension. My son was finally sent to Alexandria to train for officer.

---

[u] The original Yiddish says that Rothschild "kissed" Beilis's son, suggesting that reference here is to one of the French Rothschilds, either Baron Edmond James de Rothschild, or his son, James Armand de Rothschild, who was later naturalized as a British citizen and became a member of the British Parliament. The son – James Armand de Rothschild – was involved in setting up the Legion.

[v] John Henry Patterson, an ardent Christian Zionist.

After the war, Patterson still maintained that the Legion should be kept up, in order to protect Jewish interests in the land. As for his leaving the Legion, there was no question about that. He did not leave the Legion until the last moment.

But I have gone past where I had intended, and I must turn back at this point. When the English became masters of the land, the situation was much easier. After all the privations and hardships, I again began thinking of a future. I hoped anew that at last the people who had promised me so many things would do something for me.

Chapter 39: Many Promises and Few Fulfillments

In the meantime, I learned that in the year 1914, two persons, one of them James Simon of Berlin, had made up a fund of 41,000 francs for me. The money had been set aside to buy me a house. Besides these two people, no one gave anything. At that time, one could have bought a nice house with the sum. But where the money disappeared, I don't know to this day.

During the time of the War, my own money was reduced to almost nothing. It was paid out to me in small amounts, and because of the difference in the rates of exchange, I lost a great deal. In the end, there was still no house.

When the English entered the Land of Israel, a certain Mr. J. Goldberg advised me not to be concerned about the future; everything would end happily. He was going to Paris to see Baron Rothschild, and everything would be settled. In the meantime, he gave me a loan of 50 pounds.

When he returned from Paris, J. Goldberg told me that he had talked with the Baron, and the latter had given orders that things be done for me. A representative of the Baron was supposed to visit me in the near future, and then the whole matter would be settled.

We have thus reached the year 1920 – that is, seven years have elapsed since I was freed from prison, since I was given my first promise in Kiev. Seven years have gone, and nothing has yet been accomplished. Eminent visitors have come to the Land of Israel in the meantime, including Justice Brandeis. They all visited me and advised me to wait, urging me not to be concerned with the future, dissuading me from thinking of going anywhere else, telling me to remain in the Land of Israel, where my future would be amply provided for. Time did not remain stationary, however. Month followed month, and I kept on waiting.

Finally the representative of Baron Rothschild came to me. Mr. J. Goldberg said: "Now, Beilis, tell them what you want, and you will surely get it." I could only say that I wanted that which had been promised me. It had been spoken of so long to me that I began thinking of it as my right. I told the representative of Baron Rothschild that I would like very much to be given a small house with land attached.

A few days later, I ran into Mr. J. Goldberg and asked him how things were getting along, whether there was any change in my status. He said that he was going to Paris to settle things, and if he could not arrange it with Baron Rothschild, it would be with somebody else.

I am sure that Mr. J. Goldberg was thoroughly honest; there is no doubt that he tried to do a great deal for me. The question remains, however: why did he not see the thing to its logical end, why was I fed with stories for so long a period?

It was a short time before the San Remo conference[w] that Mr. J. Goldberg went to Paris. I remained without any money. My situation became desperate.

Summer – and J. Goldberg returned from his trip. I wrote to

---

[w] The April, 1920 conference of victorious World War I powers in San Remo, Italy.

———

him and asked him for a few pounds so that I could leave the country. I was deeply humiliated to ask for money in this fashion, but the endless promises had brought me to this pass. I had no alternative.

J. Goldberg answered that I should not think of leaving the Land of Israel. I must remain there, and he would see to it that I got money. In July, he again left for Paris, and I was left with the promised fortunes. He returned, but left again in December.

I began to realize that affairs must be straightened out. I began thinking seriously of leaving, but where was one to go? What was one to do? As matters became worse from day to day, I decided to go to New York; at least, to get some money there, the money that had been set aside for me by the American Jewish Committee some years ago. Also, I might find some means of making a living there.

It was certainly not easy to make up my mind to leave the Land of Israel. I did not want to leave the country; I had come to love it; I had become so attached to the Jewish life of Tel Aviv. I had wanted to bind my future, and that of my children, to the land that held the future of the Jewish people. I liked working the land and I wanted to devote myself to agriculture. I surely had no desire to remove my children from the land where they had grown to be such upright, stalwart Jews.

In addition to the fact that I had no desire to leave the country, my oldest son was strongly opposed to it. When I told him that I was thinking of going to America, he became deathly pale. It was only after I had convinced him of the exigency of the situation that he even partially consented to let me go, but he begged that I should not stay in America for a longer period than three months.

I myself thought that I would stay there only a short time. I did not even think of taking my wife and children. After getting some money there, I would return and live quietly with my family in the Land of Israel.

Isaac L. Goldberg kept pleading with me: "The Land of Israel is an out-of-the way place; the world has forgotten you. Go to America and tour the country; the American Jews will remember you and do their utmost. I am sure that they will provide for you amply and send you back here where you can live comfortably."

It was decided that I should leave. Where was I to get the money, however? I went to Jerusalem, where I met a young man by the name of Aronson, who was kind enough to give me 40 pounds and letters of introduction to the young Baron James Rothschild, and to Judge Mack in New York.[x] I was given minor sums by other people, and I began preparing for my journey. The American consul was very friendly to me, and when he heard that I was Beilis, he was very quick in getting me a visa. He wished me a happy journey.

I arrived safely in London, where I was besieged by everybody. But instead of inquiring about my future, they were interested in the past. They overwhelmed me with questions as to how the whole thing had happened; they rehashed all my old troubles and sufferings. What could one do?

Do not imagine that the people of London did not flood me with promises. They all promised, and urged me to be assured about the future; everything would come out all right. But could I live on promises? I explained the circumstances to all of them. I told them that I required nothing of any of them. I told them how

---

[x] The reference is evidently to Julian W. Mack, an American judge active in Jewish affairs.

originally I had been advised to go to the Land of Israel, where I was to be bought a house, from which I would be able to make a living. I had acquiesced and gone to the Land of Israel. And now I had been there for eight years, and none of the promises had been fulfilled.

I merely requested that I not be misled by further promises. The fact was that had I wanted to make money, I could have made huge amounts, and all in an honest way. I could have provided for myself for a lifetime. I did not do it, however. Furthermore, I was not allowed to do it, and that furnished the basis of my complaint. The Kiev committee took full responsibility upon themselves to provide for my future. But I wasn't going to suffer any hardships any longer.

My London friends admitted that my plaint was just, and nevertheless they did nothing for me. As I had a letter for James Rothschild, I expected to await his return from America. However, my ship left the same day his arrived, and I had to send him the letter by mail.

Just before I left, I ran across Mr. Marshak of Kiev. He was surprised that I was going to America. He tried to assure me that everything would be alright, and that he had not forgotten his promises to me. Whatever he had said in Kiev would be done. He declared that it was through him that Rothschild himself had promised 10,000 francs.

But we parted – he to Paris and I to New York.

What a remarkable meeting. Eight years ago, this man had come to my house and assented to my going to the Land of Israel, had finally even urged me to go. Eight years later, his promises not yet made good, we meet on the way, as I return from the land where he had persuaded me to go.

Chapter 40: In America

(translated from the Yiddish by Jeremy Simcha Garber and Miriam Stein)

Editors' Note: Following is the last chapter of Beilis's Yiddish-language memoir, presented here in English translation for the first time.

I was at last on my way to America, where I had been invited eight years before, right after my trial, and had been promised mountains of gold. At that time, I had not wanted to make the trip, nor would it have been proper for me to do so. It would have been blasphemy to permit my tragedy, which was of course the tragedy of the entire Jewish people, to be used as a vehicle for profit for entrepreneurs and business men. I had turned down even those offers that did not appear to be connected with any business deals.

On the ship Aquitania I did not want anyone to know who I was. I was already so worn out from my mournful fame. But I could not keep my identity secret for long. I received a telegram from London while on the ship, and the secret was out. A man approached me and asked me in Russian, "Are you Mr. Beilis?"

It turned out that he was the secretary of the English ambassador to the United States, and that the ambassador, who was also on the ship, was eager to speak with me. By the way, the secretary let me know that the ambassador was among the first to protest against the false blood libel allegations made against me.

Naturally, I could not refuse the honor of having a conversation with the ambassador, nor did I want to. After that meeting, many other passengers came to visit me in my cabin. They did not let me rest. Everyone was discussing my former plight.

When we reached New York, I was met by some representatives from HIAS (the Hebrew Immigrant Aid Society) and was approached by some reporters. One of the HIAS men insisted that I stay at the HIAS residence. I declined, so they took me to the Broadway Central Hotel. I was released from the ship without having to be examined by a doctor.

Without delay, I sent a letter to Judge Mack, informing him of my arrival. I waited more than three days, however, before I heard from him.

The first greeting from him that I received was through a young Canadian staying in the same hotel. "Greetings to you from Judge Mack," he said to me. "He could not see you until now, but he does want to see you."

At last the judge phoned. He explained why he could not see me when I first arrived, and we set up a time to meet.

He told me, "It's not good for the Jews to have permitted Beilis to leave the Land of Israel. However, I was told that Beilis himself wanted it." I explained to him that these reports were not true.

"This is a difficult time for the Jewish people as a whole," he continued, "and it is hard to do anything for any one individual Jew. But Beilis is an exception. Toward Beilis we have special

216

obligations."

At the same time, I read in a newspaper an announcement that the American Jewish Committee had allocated a $5,000 stipend for Beilis, which they had sent to Palestine and which had then been returned.

I received an invitation from Mr. Herman Bernstein to come to the office of the American Jewish Committee. Mr. Louis Marshall, the president, could not see me personally because he was not well. Mr. Bernstein told me about the $5,000 and said: "It would be a big blow if you were to stay in America. But I am sure it will not be necessary. We are prepared to do even more for you so that you will be able to return to the Land of Israel. What can we do to make your return possible?"

I responded, "The only option for my family would be to establish a dedicated trust fund in the Land of Israel, the interest from which would sustain us. Before the war, $10,000 would have been enough. Now, we would need a full $30,000."

"We'll see," he replied

In two days they had reached a decision: "Bring the family here to America and we will see to it that everything is done properly for you."

"Do what you are able, and what you think is best," I replied.

Thereafter, a committee was formed to look into doing something for me. Meanwhile, from home they were still writing me: "For God's sake, come back home to the Land of Israel."

At a meeting of my committee, Mr. Zemel, one of the members, asked me, "So, what's new?" I told him of the letters from home and asked him, "What would you do in my place?"

He replied, "For the sake of your children, you shouldn't stay here. We will establish a $30,000 fund for you. We can raise the money with no trouble."

But it turned out that it was not so easy to raise the funds. The *Morning Journal* (a New York Yiddish daily) did start the public fundraising.

Then, out of nowhere, I received a telegram saying that my eldest son, Pinchas, had died. It was like a death blow to me. And even deadlier was the second blow, when I learned that he did not die a natural death. He took his own life. He shot himself. And, God in heaven, what circumstances had led to this!

He had, more than any of my other children, been aware of and lived through my whole misfortune. Because he was older than the other children and could comprehend more, he felt more alone. What is more, the authorities involved him in the proceedings. They wanted to show that he was a friend of Yushchinsky and that was how Yushchinsky became a victim of "ritual murder". They dragged Pinchas to the *Okhrana* headquarters and interrogated him.

After that, he enlisted in the Turkish Army. He hoped that through his life and his blood he would serve the Jewish people, by furthering the establishment of a Jewish homeland in the Land of Israel, within the Ottoman empire. Later, he put himself in danger by fleeing from the Turkish Army and, with the same love for the Jewish people, and in order to give substance to its hopes, decided to sign up with the British-sponsored Jewish Legion. He was the one in our family who did not even want to hear about our leaving the Land of Israel. It was he who made me give my word that I would not stay in America for more than three months.

The disappointment he faced in the Land of Israel and the pain that he felt from the news that reached him from America

218

drove him to suicide. As I learned later, the manner in which they were collecting funds for me in America made him physically ill. He often saw the *Morning Journal* there in the Land of Israel and he felt mortified as they announced the receipt of paltry amounts. He began seeking employment there, but could find no work. Finally, he traveled north to Galilee to do the hardest and dirtiest labor. And there, while working, he took his own life.[y]

In the letter that he wrote me before his death, he asked my forgiveness and expressed his bitter disappointment. His death knocked me off my feet and caused my mind to whirl with grief. I could no longer continue to be separated from my family. However, to return to the Land of Israel after barely arriving in America would make no sense. I hastily sent for the family to join me in America. However God would provide for us – at least we would be together.

Here in America, in the meantime, everything was up in the air. Day after day passed, week after week. At one point, the publisher of the *Chicago Courier*, Mr. Ginsburg, came to me and started pleading with me to leave immediately for Chicago.

"You should have come to us sooner," he said. "But now you simply must do it. Chicago must have the honor of seeing you. We'll organize a committee and we'll invite you."

I decided to take him up on his offer and traveled there. Chicago gave me one of the most beautiful and heart-warming receptions I had received in America. About 700 people met me at the train station. Among those who greeted me was the famous American, Miss Jane Addams.

---

[y] It is possible that Beilis here overstates the role that his own fortunes played in Pinchas's suicide. A Beilis family legend has it that Pinchas was despondent over a broken love affair with a girl he had met in Palestine.

219

"I am happy," she said, "to shake your hand and to see you in person. In America, I helped organize the protest against your persecution and against the false accusation that you faced."

Miss Addams requested of me that immediately upon leaving the terminal, I should pay a visit to her home and be her guest for a cup of tea. She told me that she had also invited some of her good friends, who were intensely interested in my fate. I granted her request and went. In the parlor, where a sizable group of people had assembled, they greeted me warmly, after which my hostess gave a speech.

The large official reception for me, on the other hand, was not very satisfactory. Only a very small audience attended. The organizers explained that this was because they had called for the meeting to take place in a theater. Some Jews had complained that a theater was not an appropriate place to host Beilis, that the reception should have been held in a synagogue or study house.

From Chicago, I traveled to Cincinnati. At the train terminal, I met the famous matzah baker, Mr. Manischewitz.

"I've been coming to the train station to look for you for the past two days," he said. He invited me to stay at his house, or at least eat a meal with him. After that he proposed, "I want to make a banquet in your honor, to which I will invite a small number of the most prominent Jews."

There were about forty people at the dinner, among them judges and bankers. They asked me to say a few words to explain what I thought would be necessary to do for my family and what I would like from them.

I told them, "I would like to return to the Land of Israel." And I repeated what I had said in New York. "With a trust fund in the Land of Israel I would be taken care of for the rest of my life. Years ago, before the war, a sum of $10,000 would have been enough. Now, three times that much would be required."

They responded, "It is duty of all Jews to do that, and it is never too late."

They voted to collect in the United States a fund of $30,000-$40,000, which would remain a perpetual fund, that is, the principal would not be touched and we would live off the interest.

"Cincinnati is ready to give you its share, $2,500." And they began to berate New York, complaining, "What has New York done for you?"

I also visited Cleveland. There, the most significant thing was that the Reform Rabbi, Rabbi Wolsey, showed an interest in me. "I will raise $2,000 for the fund here," he assured me.

And with that, I returned to New York. Time was again flying by: day after day, week after week. A year went by. But when it came to the fund it was all "*sha shtil*", still and silent. I heard from no-one, I saw no-one. What, if anything, are they doing? Are they even beginning to do anything? I realized that I would no longer be able to return to The Land of Israel, and my plans for staying in America were unsettled. But we had to live.

So my children went out to look for work. But the same happened with them as with my eldest son, may he rest in peace, in the Land of Israel. It was impossible for them to find a position in business, for the very reason that they were Beilis's children. People were reluctant to hire them lest others think it was done solely out of duty.

In the beginning, I went with them to look for work. Nothing! Nobody had any work for them. Finally, it occurred to me what the problem was and I told the children, "Go look for work on your own, and do not tell anyone our name." And that is what, in fact, helped.

But myself, what was I to do? How could I earn my small piece of bread? It goes without saying that if the name "Beilis" was a hindrance to my children, it was even more of a misfortune for me. I was ready to accept whatever position came my way, however humble. But it always came down to the same consideration: How can one offer Beilis an insignificant, unworthy position?

That was the long and short of it, until someone proposed a business venture to me. A printer approached me and suggested that I become his partner. He would take me in as an equal partner, and I would receive a certain sum each week to live on. He would be the skilled worker and manage the printing establishment while I would bring in the orders. I agreed. Finally, an end to my troubles. At last I would have something to do. I would not be a superfluous man, dependent on others.

I was not the only one pleased with this development. Those who had actually taken an interest in my plight were pleased as well. Some proclaimed, "We take our hats off to Beilis, who with a wave of his hand dismisses all offers of charity and goes right to work." Judge Mack expressed great satisfaction with my decision, and he recommended me to people who needed printing work done. I brought in work for the printing house, and my heart was light. Again I was a doer, again I was working. I had become, once more, a solid man, standing on my own two feet, not beholden to anyone.

But what was the Almighty doing? "Beilis," He said, "You have not suffered enough in this world."

Just two or three weeks into the venture, my partner

---

declared bankruptcy. No more business, no more livelihood, no more happiness.

But I quickly entered into the same type of business with another printer. Orders came in from all directions. A number of private individuals, as well as organizations, decided it was their obligation to give me their printing orders. From miles around New York, they sent us orders. So I thought things were good again. But my happiness did not last long. First of all, the printer took advantage of the fact that my name was bringing in orders and raised his prices. Second, within a few weeks it became apparent that my partner was short of money and had nothing left to pay the weekly salaries. Third, there were simply troubles without any particular reason. After struggling and laboring for six months, I finally left the business.

Once again the old question arose: What was I to do? And again, I was ready to do anything that others proposed, but the main hindrance was my unfortunate fame and my tragic history. For example, I was about to receive a position in a Jewish owned bank to stand by the door, answer questions and keep order. But the old story repeated itself again: that is to say, how would it look for Beilis to be a guard? For me, it is true, it would have been a dark and bitter pill to take such a position, but 1 would have swallowed it. But others could not tolerate my accepting such a low level job. So those who were able to offer me these lesser positions were afraid to begin doing so. They complained: "The Jewish community will stone us if they find out the manner in which we employ Beilis."

Ten years ago, when I was first freed from the false accusation and from prison, a New York Jewish owned bank had offered me a $10,000 a year salary. Now even the low paying job of a guard in a Jewish bank was hard to find.

A plan arose to arrange a position for me at HIAS. Some good people emerged to intercede on my behalf with the president of HIAS, seeking to persuade him to give me a job, even if it were a door guard, like the job at the bank. But Mr. John L. Bernstein did not even want to hear of it. "As many bricks as there are in New York," he said, "that's how many the Jewish community would throw at our heads if they found out we hired Beilis for such a job."

And that is, up to now, the last chapter in the story of my sufferings.

What the Almighty has planned for me in the future, we can only see, provided He grants us life.

BEILIS IN NEW YORK

The last two chapters of Beilis's memoir are anticlimactic and indeed somewhat depressing, with their description of his decision to leave Palestine, the suicide of his son, and his difficulty finding work in America. The last chapter was omitted from the original 1926 English edition of *The Story of My Sufferings*.[89] The last three chapters (38, 39, and 40) were omitted from the version of Beilis's memoir published in 1992 under the title *Scapegoat on Trial*.[90] We believe, however, that the full memoir should be available in English.

When Beilis was released from prison in 1913, he could have become wealthy through what would now be called celebrity appearances, and by otherwise capitalizing on his fame. In the Jewish communities of America and Europe, there was at the time an insatiable interest in Beilis. The extent of this interest can be discerned from Joel Berkowitz's article "The 'Mendel Beilis' Epidemic on the Yiddish Stage":

> Anyone wanting to see the major stars of New York's Yiddish stage on Thanksgiving weekend in 1913 had three choices: *Mendel Beilis* at Jacob Adler's Dewey Theater, *Mendel Beilis* at Boris Thomashefsky's National Theater, or *Mendel Beilis* at David Kessler's Second Avenue Theater. Earlier in the month, other versions of the headline-grabbing story ran at three of the smaller Yiddish theaters in New York, and the phenomenon was duplicated on a smaller scale in a number of other North American and European cities.[91]

Beilis turned down an easy life in America and chose a hard life in Palestine. In the early twentieth century, wealthy Jews generally did not move to Palestine; they sent money to poor Jews in Palestine. Beilis was aware of possible hardship when he allowed himself to be persuaded to move to Palestine, as indicated by the response he initially gave to those who urged him to leave Palestine and move to America:

> Before, in Russia, when the word Palestine conjured up a waste and barren land, even then I had chosen to come here in preference to other countries. How much more, then, I would insist on staying here, after I have come to love the land![92]

In retrospect, perhaps Beilis should have moved to America in 1913 and taken opportunities to enrich himself. Beilis, however, clearly thought that his ordeal imposed a special obligation on him, to continue to act in a way befitting a symbol of the Jewish people.

When Beilis finally did move to New York, in 1921, his celebrity was in decline. He was still something of a celebrity, however, at least in the early years. In a 1999 interview, Beilis's daughter Rachel, then 90, described some of the scenes:

> I don't have to tell you about the Jews, how they carried on. Jewish landlords let Mendel Beilis live rent-free. The Hunts Point apartment was full of visitors.... When I saw the crowds I'd run out; I didn't want to hear about [the blood libel] every minute. After a while my father would say, 'My dear Jewish people, you put such a big monument on top of me, I'll never get out of my grave!'[93]

In New York, Beilis worked only irregularly. After the failure of his printing ventures, he became an insurance salesman, but he was not successful. Beilis did earn some money from the sale of his memoir. The 1925 Yiddish version,[94] at least, evidently sold fairly well, as a second Yiddish edition was published in 1931.[95] At the end of the 1925 Yiddish edition, as well as the 1926 English edition, there is a long "Honor List of Organizations Subscribed for the Book," listing many labor unions,

Workmen's Circle branches, and other organizations that had agreed to buy various numbers of books at $3 each.[96]

The 1931 Yiddish edition includes a letter from Rabbi Abraham Isaac Kook, Ashkenazi Chief Rabbi of Palestine under the British Mandate (reproduced, in translation, as Appendix C).[97] Beilis had met Rabbi Kook when he lived in Palestine. In flowery language, Rabbi Kook exhorts American Jews to support Beilis by buying Beilis's book, which "has become like the Book of Lamentations for our generation."[98]

On December 24, 1933, about six months before Beilis died, the English-language *Jewish Daily Bulletin* published an interview with him. In this interview, Beilis recalled some of the offers he had received in 1913 to capitalize on his fame, such as by appearing on stage. All those offers, he said, "involved my exploiting myself as a Jew and as a Jewish victim of a cruel and unjust persecution. So I refused. And I would still refuse today." When asked whether he enjoyed his life in New York, Beilis replied, "No, I have never become used to American life. It moves too fast for me. I still long for Palestine."[99]

A definite impression one receives from this interview is that Beilis was highly intelligent. Beilis had help in producing his memoir, and some might wonder how much of it is his own work. The 1933 interview indicates that Beilis's memoir is his authentic voice, as the interview is very reminiscent of the memoir.

Beilis died in relative poverty on July 7, 1934.[100] At his death, his fame returned. As noted in the Introduction, Beilis's funeral was attended by about 4,000 people, and the Eldridge Street Synagogue – a large synagogue – could not contain the crowd.[101] In her 1999 interview, Rachel Beilis recalls that a Jewish millionaire paid for Mendel Beilis's funeral, in part so that he could "someday share a... cemetery with the great Mendel Beilis."[102]

PULITZER PLAGIARISM:

WHAT BERNARD MALAMUD'S *THE FIXER* OWES TO THE MEMOIR OF MENDEL BEILIS[103]

The remainder of this book is about the relationship between Beilis's memoir, *The Story of My Sufferings*,[104] and Bernard Malamud's 1966 novel *The Fixer*,[105] a fictionalized retelling of Beilis's arrest and imprisonment. *The Fixer* was a commercial success for Malamud and a critical success as well, winning the 1967 National Book Award for fiction and the 1967 Pulitzer Prize for fiction. The novel has been translated into numerous languages. It has become part of the standard English curriculum in many high schools across the United States. A film based on the novel, also called *The Fixer*, was released in 1968.

We demonstrate in this essay that in writing *The Fixer*, Malamud plagiarized extensively from Beilis's memoir. Malamud copied, without attribution, many verbatim or almost-verbatim passages and many key events. We detail thirty-five such instances of copying.

Regrettably, the issue of Malamud's plagiarism escaped notice in the literary world for forty years, until the publication in 2007 of Philip Davis's biography of Malamud, titled *Bernard Malamud: A Writer's Life*.[106] Citing a previous, unpublished version of this essay, Davis acknowledges that there are "close verbal parallels" between *The Fixer* and Beilis's memoir.[107] Davis also offers a justification of Malamud's behavior, which we address and reject below.

While the main topic of this essay is Malamud's plagiarism, our criticism of Malamud is not limited to the issue of plagiarism. In writing

The Fixer, Malamud also debased the memories of Beilis and his wife through the characters of Yakov Bok (the protagonist of *The Fixer* who is based on Beilis) and Bok's wife Raisl. The actual Mendel Beilis was a dignified, respectful, well-liked, fairly religious family man with a faithful wife, Esther, and five children. Malamud's Bok is an angry, foul-mouthed, cuckolded, friendless, childless blasphemer.

Malamud's work has thus caused two kinds of confusion, which we illustrate through the reaction of literary critics to *The Fixer*. Some critics have given Malamud credit for inventing parts of *The Fixer* that were not in fact invented by Malamud, but rather copied from Beilis's memoir. At least one other critic has falsely imputed to Beilis the negative characteristics of Malamud's character Yakov Bok. As the historian Albert Lindemann has written, "By the late twentieth century, memory of the Beilis case came to be inextricably fused (and confused) with... *The Fixer*."[108]

Subsequent to the publication of *The Fixer*, Malamud added insult to injury by both denigrating Beilis and by failing to acknowledge his debt to Beilis's memoir. We correct the record. We also express the view, which we are sure not all will share, that Beilis's memoir, in its truth and directness, is a better book than the often-labored fictionalized version produced by Malamud.

There is one matter as to which we commend Malamud. In response to a complaint from David Beilis (son of Mendel Beilis and father of Jay Beilis), Malamud wrote that he was attempting to arrange for the republication of Mendel Beilis's memoir, with royalties going to Beilis's surviving family. Though this plan did not come to fruition, we give Malamud the benefit of the doubt by assuming that he sincerely attempted to make amends in this fashion.

When quoting from Beilis's memoir in this essay, we quote from the 1926 English edition, because that is what Malamud read. Citations to Beilis's memoir, given in the endnotes, are first to the 1926 edition, and then to the relevant chapter in this edition.

A. *Malamud the Borrower*

Malamud's protagonist, Yakov Bok, works at a brickworks in Kiev. He is accused of ritual murder and imprisoned. The novel follows the general outline of the Beilis case, except that it ends before the trial.

There are of course many differences between Malamud's novel and Beilis's memoir. We discuss some of the differences below. Here, we detail many instances in which Malamud copied material from Beilis's memoir. Some of the instances involve so much verbatim copying from Beilis that we believe each of them, standing alone, would justify a conclusion of plagiarism. In other instances, Malamud copied a small amount of material verbatim or copied events described by Beilis. We believe it is useful to present a relatively full account of Malamud's debt to Beilis, including items that might be considered minor if they were not part of a pattern of extensive copying. In each instance, we first give Beilis's version and then Malamud's version. As to some of the borrowings, we add an additional comment.

* * *

(1)   **Beilis**. Beilis discovers that a child has been murdered:

> The window which I faced while at my desk overlooked the street. As I looked through the window on that cold, dark morning, I saw people hurrying somewhere, all in one direction.... I went out to find the cause of the commotion, and was told by one of the crowd that a body

of a murdered child had been found in the vicinity.[109]

Malamud. Yakov Bok discovers that a child has been murdered:

> From the small crossed window of his room above the stable in the brickyard, Yakov Bok saw people in their long overcoats running somewhere early that morning, everybody in the same direction.... Outside the yard a black-shawled, bony-faced peasant woman, thickly dressed, told him the dead body of a child had been found nearby.[110]

* * *

(2)   **Beilis**.   Immediately after his arrest on the morning of July 22, 1911, Beilis is marched off to the jail at the secret police headquarters. He writes: "On the street, we met many of the workers going toward our factory. I felt ashamed and asked the police to walk with me on the sidewalk instead of on the street, as was the custom when police escorted arrested persons. They refused to grant me that favor, however."[111]

Malamud.   Malamud describes Yakov Bok's post-arrest walk to secret police headquarters: "He had begged the colonel to let him walk on the sidewalk to lessen his embarrassment, but was forced into the wet center of the street, and people on their way to work had stopped to watch."[112]

* * *

(3)   **Beilis**. Beilis describes his first day in the secret police jail:

> Then tea was brought in. I was asked whether I should like something to eat, but I thanked them for their

courtesy. I could not touch the tea, though my tongue was dry as hot sand…. About four in the afternoon I heard the weeping of a child; it sounded like my own. I finally recognized the voice of one of my children. Out of sheer horror, I began to knock my head against the wall.[113]

Malamud. Malamud describes Bok's first day in the secret police jail: "When an orderly brought in tea and black bread, he could not eat though he had eaten nothing that day. As the day wore on he groaned often, tore his hair with both fists, and knocked his head repeatedly against the wall."[114]

* * *

(4) **Beilis.** In a session with the sympathetic Investigating Magistrate, Fenenko, Beilis asks, "Will I be sent to jail? Will I have to wear prison clothes?"[115]

Malamud. In a session with the sympathetic Investigating Magistrate Bibikov, Malamud's Yakov Bok asks, "Will I be sent to jail, your honor? . . . Will I have to wear prison clothes?"[116]

* * *

(5) **Beilis.** In the first interrogation, Beilis is questioned by the hostile District Attorney Karbovsky:

> The District Attorney, Karbovsky who had been leaning back on his chair, watching me intently, suddenly bent over the table and asked me:
> 'They say there are people among you Jews who are called 'tzadikim' (pious men). When one wishes to do harm to another man, you go to the 'Tzadik' and give him a 'pidion' (fee), and the 'tzadik' uses the power of his

_____
232

word which is sufficient to bring misfortune upon other men. . . .'

The Hebrew words that he was using, 'Tzadik', 'pidion' and the like were written down in his notebook and each time he wanted to use the word he would consult his notebook. I answered:

'I am sorry but I know nothing about 'tzadikim', 'pidionoth' or any other of these things. I am a man entirely devoted to my business, and I don't understand what you want of me.'[117]

Malamud. Malamud depicts Yakov Bok's interrogation by the hostile Prosecuting Attorney Grubeshov:

Grubeshov addressed Yakov, reading aloud certain words from his notebook and pronouncing them slowly.

'There are those among you – are there not? – Jews who are called 'tzadikim'? When a Jew wishes to harm a Christian, or as you call him 'goyim', he goes to the 'tzadik' and gives him a 'pidion,' which is a fee of some sort, and the 'tzadik' uses the power of the word, in magical incantations, to bring misfortune on the Christian. Isn't that a true fact? Answer me.'

'Please,' said Yakov, 'I don't understand what you want of me. What have I to do with such things?'[118]

* * *

(6)   **Beilis**.   The District Attorney also asks Beilis to which kind of Jewish sect he belongs: "Are you a 'chassid' or a 'misnagid'"?[119]

Malamud. The Prosecuting Attorney also asks Bok to which kind of Jewish sect he belongs: "Are you a 'Hasid' or 'Misnogid'"?[120]

* * *

(7) **Beilis**. As Beilis is on his way to prison, the owner of the house where the Cheberyaks live consoles him: "'Brother,' he said, 'don't lose spirit. I myself am a member of the Doubleheaded Eagle, but I tell you that the stones of the bridge may crumble, but the truth will out.'"[121]

Malamud. A fellow inmate consoles Bok: "'Little brother,' he said to Yakov, making the sign of the cross over him, 'don't lose hope. The stones of the bridge may crumble but the truth will come out.'"[122]

* * *

(8) **Beilis**. Beilis reports that when he first arrived at the Kiev prison one of the officials said to him: "Well, here we'll feed you Matzoth and blood to your heart's content . . ."[123]

Malamud. Malamud has the deputy warden of the prison say to Bok: "Here we'll feed you flour and blood till you shit matzos."[124]

* * *

(9) **Beilis**. Beilis describes his reactions when he first donned prison garb: "As I took off my boots, the blood rushed to my head, darkness swept over me, and I felt I was going to faint."[125]

Malamud. Malamud describes Bok's reaction as he first donned prison garb: "As he was pulling off his boots to change into a pair of stiff prison shoes, a wave of oppressive darkness swept over him. Though he felt like fainting he wouldn't give them the satisfaction."[126]

* * *

(10) **Beilis**. Beilis describes the common cell:

> About noon I was brought into my residence, where I found about forty prisoners . . . The appalling smell of dirt and unwashed humanity was nauseating. The crowd of prisoners was jumping around, dancing, cutting crazy pranks. One was singing a song, the other telling smutty stories, some were wrestling and sparring.[127]

Malamud. Malamud describes Bok's common cell:

> There were about twenty-five men in the room, their searing stench in the almost airless cell nauseating. Some sat on the floor playing cards, two men danced closely together, a few wrestled or sparred, fell over each other, got kicked and cursed at.[128]

* * *

(11) **Beilis**. Beilis describes his first meal in the common prison cell:

> While I was thus in deep thought, the door of the big cell was opened and a drunken voice shouted: 'Dinner.'
>
> When I had first come into the cell, I had noticed several pails on the floor, like those used in our bathhouses. When the call for dinner rang out, several prisoners rushed for the pails, of which there were four or five. There were about forty men in the room. There was no dispute about the pails, for ten people could easily eat from the same pail. But there were only three spoons. Who was to eat first? A free-for-all began at once. The fierce scuffle lasted for some time, and after some had been injured and most everybody was tired, the spoons fell into the hands of the strongest and quickest. Peace was declared and the men sat down on the floor to eat. Each had just so many spoonfuls and then passed the spoon to the next man. At times a man would cheat on the number of spoonfuls, and would take

235

one or two extra spoonfuls. Another scuffle would begin with its accompaniment of the choicest and finest language to be found in the felons' dictionary.[129]

Beilis goes on to describe further eating-related incidents in subsequent days:

> I was also informed that the pails from which we were eating were also used as wash-pails in the laundry.
>
> The first two days I was registered on the ration-list and received no bread. On the third day I was marked down as a regular boarder, and began getting my bread ration, which was the only thing I could bear to eat. I could not touch the soup because of the bath- pails. Once while we were having dinner, one of the men found a quarter of a mouse in the pail, which must have gotten there from the fine grits in the prison-stores. The man who found it exhibited it, not so much to protest against the prison administration, as to deprive the others of their appetite and get more for himself.[130]

Malamud. The foregoing incidents and descriptions appear in *The Fixer* as follows:

> A guard with a gun outside the grating shouted 'Supper!' and two other guards opened the cell door and delivered three steaming wooden pails of soup. The prisoners ran with a roar to the pails, crowding around each. Yakov, who had eaten nothing that day, got up slowly. A guard handed out a wooden spoon to one prisoner in each group around the three pails. Sitting on the floor before his pail, the prisoner was allowed to eat ten spoonfuls of the watery cabbage soup, thickened with a bit of barley, then had to pass the spoon to the next one in line. Those who tried to take extra spoonfuls were beaten by the others. After each prisoner had had his quota, the first began again.
>
> Yakov edged close to the nearest pail but the one eating the soup, a clubfoot with a scarred head, stopped spooning, reached into the pail, and with a shout of triumph plucked out half a dead mouse, its entrails hanging. The prisoner held the mouse by the tail, hastily spooning down the soup with his other hand. Two of the prisoners violently twisted

the spoon out of his hand and shoved him away from the pail.[131]

Malamud then describes Bok's next morning in prison:

> At breakfast he gulped down the weak tea that smelled like wood rotting but could not touch the watery gray gruel in the pails. He had heard the wooden pails were in use in the bathhouse when they were not filled with soup or gruel. He asked for bread but the guard said he was still not on the list.[132]

Additional Note: Students of folklore would be interested to observe how the piece of mouse grew as the story was retold. In the original Yiddish version, Beilis reports someone finding simply a "fisl" (leg) of a mouse.[133] The English translator upped it to "a quarter of a mouse" and Malamud raised it to "half a dead mouse, its entrails hanging."

* * *

(12) **Beilis**. Beilis receives a package of food from his family, which is immediately stolen and devoured by the other prisoners. To avoid a beating, Beilis has to "put on a happy face... and to say: 'Eat heartily, boys.'"[134]

Malamud. A well-connected prisoner receives packages of food and distributes food to the other prisoners, saying, "'Here, boys, eat hearty.'"[135]

* * *

(13) **Beilis**. When Beilis is in the common cell, the other prisoners test him by giving him a "preliminary beating" to see whether he will report it

to the guards. One of the prisoners hits him on the head so that blood flows. On being offered water to wash off the blood, Beilis initially refuses. Then one of the prisoners shouts, "Stab him! Do away with him. You can see – he is going to squeal."[136]

Malamud. When Bok is in the common cell, the other prisoners test him by giving him a preliminary beating to see whether he will report it to the guards. One of the prisoners hits him in the head so that blood flows. On being offered water to wash off the blood, Bok initially refuses. Then one of the prisoners says, "I told you he's a shitnose squealer… Finish him off."[137]

* * *

(14) **Beilis**. A spy pretends to befriend Beilis, and Beilis attempts to send a letter to his family through him. Because of this, Beilis receives a punishment of "strict confinement."[138]

Malamud. A spy pretends to befriend Bok, and Bok attempts to send letters through him. Because of this, Bok receives a punishment of "strict confinement."[139]

* * *

(15) **Beilis**. In an exceptionally poignant passage, Beilis describes seeking treatment for his swollen blistered and bleeding feet:

> I was in agony. The officials were merciful enough and sent me a 'feldscher' (surgeon's aide). The feldscher looked at the sores and said that I was to be transferred to the hospital. Later a guard came in and shouted – 'hurry

---

238

up, let us go', I could not move, however; my feet were so swollen that I could not stand up. He did not want to listen to any reasons and kept shouting, 'Move on.'

One of the prisoners who happened to be in the hall brought some rags and wrapped them around my knees. And in this manner, crawling on my knees over the snow and ice, I dragged myself to the hospital.[140]

Malamud. Malamud, following Beilis, gives Bok horrendously swollen feet which he describes in vivid color: "His pulpy feet, the soles covered with live scabs and red pussing sores, were like bags blown up about to burst."[141] Malamud recounts at length Bok's tormented crawling to the infirmary, and even incorporates Beilis's account of a fellow prisoner binding his knees with rags.[142]

Additional note: Ignorant of Malamud's plagiarism from Beilis's memoir, *Time*'s reviewer read Malamud's version of the foregoing incident as Malamud making a Christ symbol of Bok: "In a horrible re-enactment of the via dolorosa, he is made to crawl on bloody knees from one cell to another."[143]

* * *

(16) **Beilis**. At the hospital, Beilis is treated by an anti-Semitic doctor:

After the good rest I had... I was operated upon by the physician. When he commenced to open the sores, the pain made me wince and scream. The doctor smiled and observed, 'Well, Beilis, now you know for yourself how it feels to be cut up. You can imagine now how Andriusha had felt when you were stabbing him and drawing his blood – all for the sake of your religion.' You can imagine how cheerful I felt at this raillery of the doctor. He kept on cutting leisurely and I had to bite my lips not to let myself scream.[144]

239

Malamud. Malamud's Bok is treated by an anti-Semitic doctor:

> When he awoke, the surgeon, smoking a cigar, unwound the bandages and operated on his feet. He cut into the pussing sores with a scalpel, without anesthetic. The prisoner, biting his lips to be silent, cried out at each cut.
> 'This is good for you, Bok,' said the surgeon. 'Now you know how poor Zhenia felt when you were stabbing him and draining his blood, all for the sake of your Jewish religion.'[145]

* * *

(17) **Beilis**. During a meeting with one of his lawyers, Beilis asks whether it would be possible to appeal to the Czar. His lawyer disabuses Beilis of the hope of receiving mercy from the Czar, relating that when the lawyer was an assistant prosecutor, he witnessed a conversation between the Czar, who was then visiting Kiev, and prosecutor Chaplinsky:

> [Chaplinsky], upon being introduced to the Czar, said to the latter: 'Your Majesty, I am happy to inform you that the real culprit in Yustchinsky's murder has been discovered. That is, Beilis, a zhid.' Upon hearing that, the Czar bared his head and made the sign of the cross as an expression of his thanks to God.[146]

Malamud. The prosecutor Grubeshov [a character based on Chaplinsky] informs Beilis of his meeting with the Czar:

> I had the honor to inform [the Czar], 'Sire, I am happy to report that the guilty culprit in Zhenia Golov's murder has been apprehended and is now in prison. He is Yakov Bok, a member of one of the Jewish fanatic groups, the Hasidim.' I assure you His Majesty bared his head in the rain and made the sign of the cross to express his thanks to

---

240

the Lord for your apprehension.[147]

* * *

(18) **Beilis**. Beilis writes of a Polish cellmate, Pashlovski, who rejects the authorities' request to spy on Beilis, telling them:

> 'Look here, gentlemen, I grew up among Jews. At the age of six I lost my father and mother, became a total orphan. My relatives apprenticed me to a Jewish locksmith, and I learned the trade.... I daresay I know all the Jewish customs, and a good deal about their religious rites. I know it from A to Z. Small wonder since I grew up in a Jewish house as one of them. I know they would not eat an egg if there is a bloodclot in it. It is a "Tref" with them. I have seen it a hundred times if once. I have seen them salting their meat and have asked the mistress of the house why they do it. ''Because this drives all the blood out of the meat," she told me.'[148]

Malamud. Malamud has Bok respond to Grubeshov during an interrogation:

> 'I've forgotten most of what I knew about the sacred books, but I've lived among the people and know their customs. Many an egg my own wife would throw out to the goat if it had the smallest spot of blood on the yolk . . . She also soaked for hours the little meat or chicken we ate, to wash out every fleck of blood, and then sprinkled it with salt so as to be sure she had drained out every last drop."[149]

Additional note: In the foregoing passage, Malamud's plagiarism is awkwardly evident from Bok's phrase, "I've lived among the people and know their customs." Why should a shtetl-raised Jew such as Bok have to proffer an explanation for his familiarity with Jewish practices? This

241

explanation would be necessary for a Pole, but it is odd for a Jew of Bok's origins, even one who had abandoned religion.

* * *

(19) **Beilis**. Beilis recounts that "not infrequently during the frost I used to find my hand frozen to the ice on the wall."[150]

Malamud. Malamud writes: "In December, frost appeared on the four walls in the morning. Once he awoke with his hand stuck to the wall."[151]

* * *

(20) **Beilis**. Every time Beilis was searched, all the locks on his cell had to be opened, which unnerved him: "[E]ach time the door was to be opened, all thirteen locks had to be shot back. The sound of the rasping lock-springs used to set my nerves on edge. I was obsessed with the illusion that somebody behind me was hitting me repeatedly upon the head – it was one blow after another."[152]

Malamud. Bok has the same reaction to the unlocking of his cell: "Hearing the six bolts being snapped back one by one, four or five times a day, put the fixer on edge."[153] ... Six times a day [the] key grated in the lock, and one by one the twelve bolts were snapped back, each with a noise like a pistol shot. Yakov put his hands to his head, obsessed by the thought that someone was hitting him repeatedly."[154]

* * *

---

(21) **Beilis**. Beilis describes the searches he had to undergo six times a day:

> The searches were usually performed by a squad of five under the supervision of one of the deputy wardens. Every time they would come in the first order for me was to undress. Often they had to unbutton me for my fingers were awkward because of the cold. They were quite rude and usually tore off a number of buttons during the operation. Some exercised their rude sense of humor. 'You liked to stab the boy Andriusha, to draw his blood. We will do the same thing to you now' - that was the standing joke. They would also look into my mouth lest I might have something hidden there. They would pull my tongue out in order to see deeper and better. All these tortures and insults I had to undergo six times a day. It is hard to believe, but it is the truth. No protests were of any avail. Their intentions were to inflict the utmost inconvenience upon me. [155]

Malamud. Malamud largely follows Beilis's account, but adds his special artistic touch, a degrading anal search:

> And twice a day since he had been in this cell there were inspections of the fixer's body; 'searches' they were called. The bolts of the door were shot back, and Zhitnyak and the Deputy Warden, with his smelly boots, came into the cell and ordered the fixer to undress....
> Yakov had first to raise his arms and spread his legs. The Deputy Warden probed with his four fingers in Yakov's armpits and around his testicles. The fixer then had to open his mouth and raise his tongue; he stretched both cheeks with his fingers as Zhitnyak peered into his mouth. At the end he had to bend over and pull apart his buttocks.
> 'Use more newspapers on your ass,' said Zhitnyak.
> 'To use you have to have.'
> After his clothes were searched he was permitted to dress. It was the worst thing that happened to him and it happened twice a day. [156]

(22) **Beilis**. Beilis describes a draconian prison regulation:

> On one of the walls of my cell there hung a set of prison rules. One of its clauses was to the effect that a prisoner insulting a guard or being insubordinate could be murdered on the spot, and the guard was to receive a reward to the amount of three rubles.[157]

Malamud. The warden directs Bok's attention to a notice on the wall:

> *Obey all rules and regulations without question. If the prisoner is insubordinate or insulting to a guard or prison official, or he attempts in any way to breach the security of the prison, he will be executed on the spot.*
> 'Furthermore,' said the old warden, the guard receives a monetary commendation for defending the regulations.'[158]

* * *

(23) **Beilis**. After describing the "tortures and insults" attendant on being searched six times a day, Beilis states, "I believe they wanted to drive me to suicide." Beilis also recounts that the prison authorities more than once tried to provoke him into a quarrel so that they could have a pretext for shooting him. But Beilis resolves to stay alive because "the shameful charge of ritual murder must be wiped off the good name of the Jewish nation."[159]

Malamud. Bok at one point plans to commit suicide, in effect, by provoking a quarrel while he is being searched: "He would refuse to undress, and when they ordered him to, he would spit in the Deputy

Warden's eye."[160] However, Bok changes his mind and resolves to live: "[H]e must endure to the trial and let them confirm his innocence by their lies."[161]

* * *

(24) **Beilis**. Beilis is warned by his attorney that the anti-Semitic Black Hundreds might attempt to kill him by poisoning his individual portions of prison food and thus stave off a loss in an open trial. Beilis therefore petitions the court authorities to allow him to take food from the common kettle:

> My petition was at first refused. I was told, 'if you want to eat, eat what you are given – if not, you can starve. No special privileges for you. We shall not poison you – it is your Jews that you have to beware of. They are not satisfied with using our blood and are inventing additional lies to make us appear ridiculous.'
> I had reasons to be stubborn. I declared a hunger strike. Three days elapsed – whenever a prisoner doesn't eat for a few days the P. is summoned to investigate. The P. appeared. I told him I should like to get my food myself from the kettle – not to have it brought into my room.
> His reply was: 'It cannot be permitted; you must not leave your cell. You are supposed to be under strict confinement. The other prisoners and guards must not even look at you.'
> 'Well,' I answered, 'let them turn away when I draw my ration.'
> Somewhat to my surprise, after considerable bickering and argument I was allowed to get my food from the common kettle. I was again reduced to the half starvation diet. I was receiving no food from home and the prison broth was unfit to eat.[162]

Malamud. In *The Fixer*, Bok is actually poisoned by prison authorities, goes on a hunger strike, then demands to eat from the common pot. The almost verbatim borrowings from Beilis are italicized:

'I won't eat what you give me. You can shoot me but I won't eat.'

'If you expect to eat, eat what you get. If not you'll starve.'

For the next five days Yakov starved. He exchanged the sickness of poisoning for the sickness of starving. He lay on the mattress, sleeping fitfully. Zhitnyak threatened him with a whipping but nothing came of it. On the sixth day the warden returned to the cell, his cross-eye watering and face flushed. 'I command you to eat.'

'Only out of the common pot,' Yakov said weakly. 'What the other prisoners eat. I will eat. Let me go to the kitchen and take my gruel and soup out of the common pot.'

'It cannot be allowed,' said the warden. 'You mustn't leave your cell. You are under strict confinement. Other prisoners are not allowed to look at you. It's all in the regulations.'

'They can turn their heads while I draw my rations.'

'No,' said the warden. But after Yakov had fasted another day he consented. Twice a day the fixer, accompanied by Zhitnyak holding his drawn pistol, went to the prison kitchen in the west wing. Yakov drew his bread rations in the morning and filled his bowl from the common pot as the prisoners working in the kitchen momentarily faced the wall. He did not fill the bowl too full because if he did Zhitnyak poured some of it back.

He returned to half starvation.[163]

* * *

(25) **Beilis**. As he looks out from his coach on the way to the first day of his trial, Beilis sees that the streets are lined with people. Many wear Black Hundreds badges. He also sees Jewish onlookers: "During my progress I noticed Jewish faces, men and women, some wringing their hands, and wiping their tears with their handkerchiefs. I also did my share of the crying."[164]

Malamud. As Bok looks out from his coach on the way to the first day of his trial, he sees that the streets are lined with people.[165] Some wear Black Hundreds badges.[166] Bok also sees Jewish onlookers: "Among those in the street were Jews of the Plossky District. Some, as the carriage clattered by and they glimpsed the fixer, were openly weeping, wringing their hands."[167]

* * *

(26) **Beilis**. During the trial, Beilis describes that when the testimony begins to implicate Vera Cheberyak, friend and fence for a gang of thieves suspected of the murder, she "took [her] gay hat off and threw a shawl over her head so as to shield herself somewhat and to make herself less recognizable."[168]

Malamud. In *The Fixer*, when investigators begin to implicate Marfa Golov, friend and fence for a gang of thieves suspected of the murder, she removes her white hat decorated with bright cherries and covers her head with a coarse black shawl.[169]

* * *

(27) **Beilis**. Beilis recollects the trial testimony of an honest deacon who had taught the murdered boy:

> 'I had known Andriusha Yustchinsky as a dear little boy. I could almost say a saintly boy. He wanted to become a priest when grown up. I was preparing him for the seminary. When I asked him once why he wished to become a priest he told me he liked the vestments very

much . . .'[170]

Malamud. When Malamud's Bok is brought to the crime scene, the charlatan Father Anastasy speaks of the murdered boy:

> 'It was reported to me that he was being prepared for the seminary,' said the priest. 'One of the monks told me he was a dear boy, in some respects a saintly boy. I understand he had already had a mystical experience. I was also told he loved our priestly vestments and hoped some day to wear them . . ."[171]

* * *

(28) **Beilis**. Beilis reports the trial testimony of a monk: "'My dear brethren, if only the earth was to give up its dead, and you could see how many Christian children had been murdered by the Jews.'"[172]

Malamud. Malamud has Father Anastasy declaim at the crime scene:

> 'My dear children,' said the priest to the Russians, wringing his dry hands, 'if the bowels of the earth were to open to reveal the population of human dead since the beginning of the world, you would be astonished to see how many innocent Christian children among them have been tortured to death by Christ-hating Jews.'[173]

* * *

(29) **Beilis**. One of the witnesses at the trial, a priest, tells a story about a lady who was building a house. A Jew offered to loan her money, but the priest told her to refuse.[174]

Malamud. In Marfa Golov's letter to Bok, she states, "A Jew wanted to lend a friend of mine money to build a house, but she went to the priest for advice and he... advised her to take nothing from a cursed Jew."[175]

* * *

(30) **Beilis**.   Beilis describes a dialogue between prosecution and defense when the trial is brought to the brickyard where Beilis had been a supervisor:

> Standing near the kiln, Schmakov, the lawyer for the prosecution, turned to the jury. 'Look', said he, 'there is from here a straight road to the cave where Andriusha's body was found.' Mr. Karabchevsky immediately retorted: 'But permit me to draw your attention to the fact that the road from Tchebiriak's house to the cave is shorter and straighter.'[176]

Malamud.   Malamud presents a dialogue between the prosecuting attorney and investigating magistrate near the cave:

> 'There is from here an almost straight road from the brick factory where Zhenia was presumed to be killed,' Grubeshov said.
> 'But, permit me, Vladislav Grigorievitch, to draw your attention to the fact that the road from Marfa Golov's house is just as straight and a little shorter,' said Bibikov.[177]

* * *

(31) **Beilis**.   One day, as he travels in the prison coach on the way to trial, Beilis is alarmed by the explosion of a bomb. He later learns that one of the guard soldiers was so badly wounded by the explosion that his leg

had to be amputated.[178]

Malamud. As Bok travels in the prison coach on the way to trial, there is a bomb explosion. One of the guard soldiers loses his foot in the explosion.[179]

* * *

(32) **Beilis**. In his closing statement to the jury, Beilis's Jewish attorney, Oskar Gruzenberg, exhorts Beilis: "[I]f ever you are convicted, proclaim, 'Hear, O Israel, the Lord is Our God, and He is one God.'"[180]

Malamud. While Bok is in a trolley car on the way to receive his indictment, a Jew shouts at him, "If they convict you... cry, 'Shma Yisroel, the Lord our God, the Lord is one!'"[181]

* * *

(33) **Beilis**. On the last day of the trial, Beilis is picked up from the prison by his guard escort. When he is already in the custody of his escort, the deputy warden sends word to bring him back to be searched. The escort initially refuses to comply with the deputy warden's order. However, the deputy warden insists that a telegram has arrived from the Czar himself, ordering that Beilis be searched thoroughly.[182]

Malamud. On the first day of the trial, Bok is picked up from the prison by his guard escort. When he is already in the custody of his escort, the deputy warden sends word to bring him back to be searched. The escort initially refuses to comply with the deputy warden's order.

However, the deputy warden insists that a telegram has arrived from the Czar himself, ordering that Bok be searched thoroughly.[183]

* * *

(34) **Beilis**. During the last search, the deputy warden orders Beilis to remove his undershirt, which Beilis had never been required to do in previous searches. Losing his temper, Beilis tears the undershirt off and throws it in the face of the deputy warden. Beilis comes close to being shot as the deputy warden draws his revolver and points it at Beilis.[184]

Malamud. During the last search, the deputy warden orders Bok to remove his undershirt, which Bok had never been required to do in previous searches. Losing his temper, Bok tears the undershirt off and throws it in the face of the deputy warden. Bok comes close to being shot as the deputy warden draws his revolver and points it at Bok.[185]

* * *

The following, final illustration of Malamud's plagiarism is perhaps the most distressing, though it does not involve as much verbatim copying as many of the others.

(35) **Beilis**. After one year of imprisonment, Beilis reports being approached by a curious contingent led by a general:

> The general came closer to me and said: 'Beilis, you will soon be let free.' 'On what grounds?' I ask him. His answer was: 'The tercentary jubilee of the reign of the Romanoff dynasty is soon to be celebrated. There will be a manifesto pardoning all 'katorjniks' [convicts].

———

'That manifesto,' said I, 'will be for 'katorjniks,' not for me. I need no manifesto, I need a fair trial.'

'If you will be ordered to be released, you'll have to go.'

'No, - even if you open the doors of prison, and threaten me with shooting, I shall not leave. I shall not go without a trial. I am strong enough to suffer all until the trial.'[186]

Malamud. After years of imprisonment, Malamud's Yakov Bok is informed that in celebration of the three-hundredth anniversary of the rule of the House of Romanov he is "to be pardoned and permitted to return to his village."[187] Bok demurs, however, since he would be pardoned as a criminal and not released as innocent. "Yakov said he wanted a fair trial, not a pardon. If they ordered him to leave the prison without a trial they would have to shoot him first."[188]

Additional note: As detailed below in section G, critics have congratulated Malamud on his great inventiveness in making up the pardon incident, not realizing that the incident actually happened, and that Beilis's heroic refusal of a pardon was lifted by Malamud from Beilis's memoir.

* * *

All of the foregoing are unattributed takings. Malamud had many opportunities to acknowledge his debt to Beilis's memoir, but he never did so, either in *The Fixer* or in subsequent statements about the book.

B. *Other Sources?*

For most of the items we have listed, Malamud's only possible source was Beilis's memoir, in English or Yiddish. The frequent identity of language between *The Fixer* and *The Story of My Sufferings* suggests that Malamud used the English, not the Yiddish edition. Malamud spoke and understood Yiddish, but it is unclear if he read Yiddish. Whether Malamud copied from the English edition or from the Yiddish edition doesn't really matter, however, insofar as the ethics of Malamud's conduct is concerned.

For items that represent trial proceedings, it is conceivable that Malamud could have had some source other than Beilis's memoir, or some source in addition to Beilis's memoir. The transcript of the trial had not been translated into English when Malamud wrote *The Fixer*, and indeed most of it still has not been translated into English. However, Malamud doubtless consulted sources other than Beilis's memoir in researching *The Fixer*, such as newspaper reports, and one of his sources might have contained trial excerpts that paralleled items referenced by Beilis.

We would be remiss, in this connection, if we did not mention that Malamud makes use of one part of the trial that appears nowhere in Beilis's memoir. In *The Fixer*, the hostile prosecutor Grubeshov is attempting to hound Bok into confessing:

> 'You can deny it all you want, we know the truth,' Grubeshov shouted. 'The Jews dominate the world and we feel ourselves under their yoke. I personally consider myself under the power of the Jews; under the power of Jewish thought, under the power of the Jewish press. To speak against the crimes of the Jews means to evoke the charge that one is either a Black Hundred, an obscurantist, or a reactionary. I am none of these things. I am a Russian patriot! I love the Russian Tsar!'[189]

This speech is taken from the closing statement of State Prosecutor Vipper at the trial:

> I feel impelled to say openly that I find myself under Jewish domination, that I am weighted down by the power of Jewish thought and the power of the Jewish press....

[I]n criticizing them, one invites instant rebuke and disapproval. In doing so, you are either a reactionary, an obscurant, or a member of the Black Hundred.[190]

Beilis describes part of Vipper's closing statement,[191] but he does not include the above-quoted part, in either the English or the Yiddish edition of his memoir. Therefore, Malamud must have taken that passage from some other source.

Nevertheless, Malamud clearly copied, from Beilis alone, material on the trial that would not have been referenced in other accounts. Ezekiel Leikin's book *The Beilis Transcripts* and Maurice Samuel's book *Blood Accusation* both contain substantial excerpts from the trial transcript. Malamud did not have access to these books in writing *The Fixer*, but they give some indication of what even comprehensive accounts of the trial were likely to omit. As far as we can tell, none of the 35 copied items, listed in the previous section, appears either in Leikin or in Samuel. It is thus unlikely that Malamud had any source other than Beilis for copied items involving trial proceedings. And as noted, Malamud could have had *no* source other than Beilis for those copied items – the majority – that do not involve trial proceedings.

C. *Malamud's Plagiarism Went Unnoticed in the Literary World*

Remarkably, the issue of Malamud's plagiarism escaped notice in the literary world for forty years. Malamud's novel was widely known to be based on the Beilis case, and there were a small number of critics who, in reviews of *The Fixer*, noted the existence of Beilis's memoir. But none explored the possibility of out-and-out misappropriation.

The one initial reviewer who comes closest to grasping the true value of Beilis's memoir and its influence on the creation of *The Fixer* is Morris U. Schappes, editor of *Jewish Currents*.[192] In a 1967 review of *The*

Fixer, Schappes writes movingly of his father's purchase of Beilis's leather-bound Yiddish memoir, *Di Geshichte fun Meine Leiden*, in 1925, and how his mother would read it aloud in their kitchen. Schappes, while remarking that Malamud "transformed" some of Beilis's memoir in *The Fixer*,[193] does not realize that the book exists in English translation, a translation that Malamud clearly read and used. Schappes laments:

> Would only that Mendel Beiliss' own autobiography could be made available in English translation not only to add to its own documentary dimension but to make more readily possible a comparison of its first half with Malamud's imaginative recreation and transformation of the materials for his own moral and intellectual purpose.[194]

After Schappes, there appears to be an interval of more than thirty years before Beilis's influence on Malamud is again recognized. In an article published in 2000, Susan Mizruchi notes that Malamud's "faithfulness" to the details of the Beilis case "is exemplified most obviously by the parallels between *The Fixer* and *The Story of My Sufferings*, the autobiography Mendel Beilis wrote in 1926."[195] In a 2004 article, Michael Tritt discusses Malamud's "extensive debt to *The Story of My Sufferings*."[196] Neither Mizruchi nor Tritt explicitly raises the issue of plagiarism, however.[197]

The first explicit recognition that there is a serious issue as to Malamud's plagiarism probably came with the publication of Philip Davis's biography of Malamud in 2007.[198] Jay Beilis, the grandson of Mendel Beilis (and one of the editors of this volume), had sent to Professor Davis an earlier draft version of this essay. In his biography of Malamud, Davis notes that this earlier draft version makes "a case for plagiarism against Malamud, quite properly and carefully detailing some close verbal parallels."[199] Davis also offers a justification of Malamud's conduct, however; he argues that "[w]hen it mattered most, [Malamud's] sentences offered a different dimension and a deeper emotion."[200] We address and reject Davis's justification of Malamud in the next section.

D. *Is it Plagiarism*?

To plagiarize, according to the conventional definition, is to copy without attribution.[201] Under this definition, Malamud plagiarized extensively from Beilis's memoir in writing *The Fixer*. He copied a large amount of verbatim dialogue, verbatim descriptions, states of mind, and events. He failed to credit Beilis's memoir in any way.

Many believe, however, that a laxer standard of plagiarism should apply to writers of fiction than to writers of non-fiction. And when a fiction writer copies from a non-fiction source such as a memoir, many believe, that should be judged by a laxer standard than if the fiction writer had copied from another work of fiction. These are serious viewpoints, and they bring out complications in the definition of plagiarism. Although not often stated explicitly, such forgiving views of plagiarism would essentially define plagiarism as *wrongful* copying without attribution, it being understood that not all uncredited copying is wrongful.

Insofar as there is a consensus in the literary world on copying by a novelist from a memoirist, it seems to be that a small amount of copying is justifiable, perhaps even without attribution, but that extensive copying without attribution is unjustified plagiarism.[202] Even under this relatively lax approach, the conclusion that Malamud plagiarized from Beilis should be unassailable, in view of Malamud's extensive and often verbatim copying. If it is at all possible for a novelist to plagiarize from a memoirist, Malamud did so. And while anti-plagiarism standards are perhaps more strict today than when Malamud's *The Fixer* was published, even then Malamud's conduct was no doubt below what was expected of an author. It is unlikely that Malamud would have received the Pulitzer Prize and the National Book Award if his plagiarism had come to light immediately.

Our main concern in this essay is to demonstrate Malamud's extensive and uncredited copying. The reader can make up her own mind as to how plagiarism should be defined, and as to whether Malamud's conduct constitutes plagiarism. We do, however, wish to respond to Philip Davis's argument that "[w]hen it mattered most, [Malamud's] sentences offered a different dimension and a deeper emotion."[203] In his biography of Malamud, Davis does not explicitly deny that Malamud plagiarized, and it might seem that in the above-quoted passage, Davis is defending Malamud's art rather than Malamud's ethics. Nevertheless, in email correspondence to us., Davis has clarified that he means not only to assert that Malamud improved on Beilis, but also to assert that Malamud, as a result, was not guilty of plagiarism.

We cannot agree that it is ethically acceptable to copy another author's work without attribution if one improves on the source of the copied material, adding "a different dimension and a deeper emotion." Davis's argument harkens back to an older view of the relationship between artists and the world. According to this view, the lives of ordinary people are but clay in the hands of the great artist. Ordinary people should be grateful that the artist deigns to render their lives worthy through art; they certainly should not complain about anything the artist has done. The artist is not bound by the same ethical strictures as an ordinary mortal.

This view, we hope the reader will agree, is inappropriate to modern democratic society. We accept that some may think plagiarism standards should be laxer for fiction. We also accept that unattributed copying is worse if the alleged plagiarist adds nothing to his source and simply copies language verbatim. What we cannot accept is that an alleged plagiarist is exonerated if he transforms his source into something better, but not if he transforms his source into something worse or merely something different. The Pulitzer Prize cannot be a get-out-of-jail-free card for plagiarists.

We must also record our disagreement with Davis's relative valuation of Beilis's memoir and Malamud's novel. *The Fixer* is a good book, but we believe that Beilis's *The Story of My Sufferings* is a better book, and that Malamud actually did *not* improve on Beilis in his treatment of the material that he copied from Beilis. We will offer some examples to support our point of view (still using the 1926 English translation of Beilis's memoir).

Our first example involves the resolve of each protagonist not to commit suicide or to allow himself to be killed, but to survive so that he can prove his innocence at the trial. In Beilis, the relevant passages occur after he describes the daily search routine:

> They wanted me to die without resorting to actual murder. They would not poison me outright, for that would create trouble. I believe they wanted to drive me to suicide. Cases of suicide were quite frequent in the prison. Prisoners used to hang themselves to get rid of persecution and torture. The administration must have thought that I would succumb under their persecution. A weaker vessel in their opinion, would not be able to stand it and would take his own life. In such an eventuality, the charge of ritual murder would never be wiped off the Jewish nation....
> My life was thus hanging on a hair. I saw once how another prisoner was shot to death in the prison hall after some altercation with one of the guards. This murder was easily explained away.... On one of the walls of my cell there hung a set of prison rules. One of its clauses was to the effect that a prisoner insulting a guard or being insubordinate could be murdered on the spot....
> Nevertheless, in spite of all the inconveniences that were heaped upon me, and all the dangers, they only served to

strengthen my determination and to give me more courage to go through with this great trial…. *One thing I always had before me: the shameful charge of ritual murder must be wiped off the good name of the Jewish nation. It was my fate, it had to be done through me, and in order to be effected, I was to remain alive. I had to exercise every ounce of power, I had to suffer all without murmuring, but the enemies of my people were not to triumph.*[204]

Beilis's portrayal of his resolve is thrilling and genuine, the sort of thing that makes a reader sit bolt upright.

As previously indicated (copying instance #23), Malamud's character Yakov Bok initially plans to provoke the guards into shooting him. He then changes his mind, however, and resolves to live. Bok begins to acquire this resolve after awaking from a dream in which he sees his father-in-law Shmuel in a coffin, apparently shot through the head. Bok thinks to himself that Shmuel "may even die for my death if they work up a pogrom in celebration of it."[205]

The section of *The Fixer* in which Bok resolves to live is lengthy and, we believe, somewhat labored. The two paragraphs most comparable to the above-quoted passage from Beilis are as follows:

> Not that he is afraid to die because he is afraid of suicide, but because there is no way of keeping the consequences of his death to himself. To the goyim what one Jew is is what they all are. If the fixer stands accused of murdering one of their children, so does the rest of the tribe. Since the crucifixion the crime of the Christ-killer is the crime of all Jews. 'His blood be on us and our children.'
> He pities their fate in history. After a short time of sunlight you awake in a black and bloody world. Overnight a madman is born who thinks Jewish blood is water. Overnight life becomes worthless. The innocent are born without innocence. The human body is worth less than its substance. A person is shit. Those Jews who escape with their lives live in memory's eternal pain. So what can Yakov Bok do about it? All he can do is not

make things worse. He's half a Jew himself, yet enough of one to protect them. After all, he knows the people; and he believes in their right to be Jews and live in the world like men. He is against those who are against them. He will protect them to the extent that he can. This is his covenant with himself. If God's not a man he has to be. Therefore he must endure to the trial and let them confirm his innocence by their lies. He has no future but to hold on, wait it out.[206]

Malamud's version has its attractions, but it falls short of the original. Reading Malamud, it is a little hard even to get the gist of why Bok has decided not to kill himself. Bok's resolve is obscured by meandering philosophical observations that are not particularly profound ("A person is shit") and that are in any event distracting. A key sentence – "Not that he is afraid to die because he is afraid of suicide, but because there is no way of keeping the consequences of his death to himself" – is poorly crafted and momentarily confusing. Apparently, Malamud means, by this sentence, that there is no way for Bok to *limit* the consequences to himself; he does not mean that there is no way for Bok to keep the consequences to himself, in the sense of keeping them a secret. But the reader has to do extra work to penetrate this meaning.

Eventually the reader does get the gist of Bok's reasoning, but it has nowhere near the emotional impact of Beilis's direct and stirring presentation of his resolve to live. Here it is Beilis, not Malamud, who offers "deeper emotion." And this, we dare say, is one of the times "[w]hen it matter[s] most."

Our second example is the undershirt incident (copying instance #34). Before the last day of his trial, the day on which the verdict will be rendered, Beilis is subjected to a pointless additional search by the deputy warden, even though he has already been given over to the custody of the guard convoy for transportation to the trial. Beilis is ordered to remove his undershirt, though he has never been required to do so in previous searches. Despite his long-held resolve not to be provoked, as discussed in the previous example, Beilis loses his temper and is almost shot:

> I was told to undress, and complied with the order. I never removed the undershirt during these searches. This time the official ordered me to remove the undershirt as well. I became irritated, and in my excitement I tore the undershirt from my body, tore it into pieces and threw it into his face. He snatched his pistol and aimed it at me. He was so inflamed with anger that he looked more like a wild man than a human being. It was [fortunate] for me that the [guard] convoy, attracted by the noise, came on the run. Had not the convoy been responsible for my safety at the moment they would not have dared to protect me. But since they had already signed for me, they felt responsible. One of the escorts grabbed the revolver from the Deputy Warden's hand, and the alarm was sounded. The officials and guards came on the run. The Warden came in very excited, and turned to me.
>
> 'What are you doing? Is it not the last day of your trial, and you are starting new trouble?'
>
> I exclaimed, 'What do you want of me? Why does this man subject me to new insults? Was I not once searched? Why does he search me again in that most insulting manner?'
>
> The Deputy Warden left. A few minutes later he returned and put down my escorts as witnesses of the incident. He intended, apparently, to press charges against me.
>
> 'Don't you imagine, Beilis, you are free. I will square my account with you yet. You will not escape from our hands and we shall see you with chains on your hands.'
>
> I replied, 'You will never live to see it.'[207]

Malamud relates the same basic incident, except that it occurs before the first day of the trial, and it ends somewhat differently:

> 'Take off that stinking undershirt,' ordered the Deputy Warden.
>
> I must calm my anger, thought the fixer, seeing the world black. Instead, his anger grew.
>
> 'Why should I?' he shouted. 'I have never taken it off

before. Why should I take it off now? Why do you insult me?'

'Take it off before I tear it off.'

Yakov felt the cell tremble and dip. I should have eaten, he thought. It was a mistake not to. He saw a bald-headed thin naked man in a freezing prison cell ripping off his undershirt and to his horror watched him fling it into the face of the Deputy Warden.[208]

At this point in Malamud's *The Fixer*, the deputy warden draws his revolver and is about to shoot Yakov Bok. However, a guard, Kogin, intervenes and points his own revolver at the deputy warden. There is a commotion, another guard tries to draw his gun, Kogin shoots at the ceiling, and the escort convoy rushes in. At the end of the scene, we learn that the deputy warden has shot Kogin, who sinks to his knees.[209]

As to this incident, we once again prefer the original Beilis to Malamud's fictionalized version, though we realize some may disagree. Malamud's version has a number of problems. When one begins to read the key sentence, "He saw a bald-headed thin naked man... ripping off his undershirt...," one is yet again momentarily confused: what bald-headed thin naked man is Malamud talking about? That is because the sentence conjures up an image that is false to the story – Bok would not see his own bald head, no matter how psychologically detached he was from his actions. A second problem is that the guard Kogin's act of pointing his pistol at the deputy warden is not credible. In the story, there has been some friendliness between Bok and Kogin, but that does not provide sufficient motivation for Kogin's act.

We would like to make another, related comparison between Beilis and Malamud in connection with this example. In Malamud's retelling of the undershirt incident, a character is psychologically detached from his own action. Beilis also uses this device in his memoir; he uses it to describe the dramatic opening of his trial (for Beilis, it is not just a literary device, but also the truth). As far as we can tell, both authors use this device only once. Possibly Malamud picked up the idea from Beilis, though of course we cannot assert that with any confidence. In any event, here is Beilis describing the opening of his trial:

> Upon my entrance there had been considerable noise in the Court Room. Many people were holding conversation in loud tones. Some were walking back and forth. Various officials were coming in with their brief cases and reports. The confusion and din impressed one as though an orchestra was tuning up the instruments prior to starting the concert.
> There descended at once a complete silence. The Sergeant-at-arms shouted: 'Silence, the Court is entering.' The public rose from the benches as one man. More officials came in, and immediately it became very quiet and one could hear the least sound, as if all had suspended breathing.
> The Presiding Judge, Boldirev, interrupted the silence. He directed himself to me with a question.
> 'To what religion do you belong'?
> I did not recognize my own voice when I answered in something approaching a shout: 'I am a Jew'.[210]

This is of course a pivotal moment. Beilis's shout demonstrated his defiance and resolve and set a tone for the trial. Beilis's description of this moment, including the sense of psychological detachment, is once again thrilling and genuine. By contrast, as we have suggested, Malamud's use of the device of detachment, in the undershirt incident, is labored and poorly executed.

Why does Malamud's biographer Philip Davis think that "[w]hen it mattered most, [Malamud's] sentences offered a different dimension and a deeper emotion?"[211] To support this claim, Davis compares Beilis's description of the daily searches he had to undergo with Malamud's parallel description of the searches Bok had to undergo (copying instance #21). Here are the relevant passages:

(21) **Beilis**. Beilis describes the searches he had to undergo six times a
day:

> The searches were usually performed by a squad of five
> under the supervision of one of the deputy wardens. Every
> time they would come in the first order for me was to
> undress. Often they had to unbutton me for my fingers
> were awkward because of the cold. They were quite rude
> and usually tore off a number of buttons during the
> operation. Some exercised their rude sense of humor. 'You
> liked to stab the boy Andriusha, to draw his blood. We will
> do the same thing to you now' - that was the standing joke.
> They would also look into my mouth lest I might have
> something hidden there. They would pull my tongue out in
> order to see deeper and better. All these tortures and
> insults I had to undergo six times a day. It is hard to
> believe, but it is the truth. No protests were of any avail.
> Their intentions were to inflict the utmost inconvenience
> upon me.[212]

Malamud. Malamud largely follows Beilis's account, but adds
his special artistic touch, a degrading anal search:

> And twice a day since he had been in this cell there were
> inspections of the fixer's body; 'searches' they were
> called. The bolts of the door were shot back, and Zhitnyak
> and the Deputy Warden, with his smelly boots, came into
> the cell and ordered the fixer to undress....
> Yakov had first to raise his arms and spread his legs. The
> Deputy Warden probed with his four fingers in Yakov's
> armpits and around his testicles. The fixer then had to open
> his mouth and raise his tongue; he stretched both cheeks
> with his fingers as Zhitnyak peered into his mouth. At the
> end he had to bend over and pull apart his buttocks.
> 'Use more newspapers on your ass,' said Zhitnyak.
> 'To use you have to have.'
> After his clothes were searched he was permitted to

dress. It was the worst thing that happened to him and it happened twice a day.[213]

* * *

Comparing the two versions, Davis makes the following comments:

> It was precisely Beilis's sense that 'it is hard to believe, but it is the truth' which was in need of Malamud's transformation.... The search was the worst, [Malamud] wrote, and the worst was what happened twice a day, every day: this sort of sentence, together with the defiant Jewish wit of 'To use you have to have,' Beilis could never offer.[214]

In response, we hardly think that Malamud's sentence, "It was the worst thing that happened to him and it happened twice a day" demonstrates any special artistry, or that it even adds much to Beilis's "All these tortures and insults I had to undergo six times a day" And as to the idea that Malamud showed his greatness by putting some Yiddish brogue into the dialogue ("to use you have to have"), we must ask: From this Davis concludes that Malamud was no *goniff* [thief]?

Davis is also quite wrong to assert that Beilis could never offer "defiant Jewish wit" to equal that of Malamud. Beilis's memoir shows that he was easily Malamud's equal in this respect. We will mention a couple of examples.

When Investigating Magistrate Fenenko interrogates Beilis at the brick factory, he asks questions about Beilis's religious observance: Where does Beilis pray, is there a synagogue here, and so on. Reflecting on this interrogation, Beilis observes: "I simply could not understand the necessity of these questions about my piety and as to whether I went to synagogue. Had the authorities become so pious that they could not

―――

265

tolerate my praying without the official ten (minyan) required by the Jewish law?"[215]

In Chapter 19, Beilis describes the conclusion of his journey to the courthouse on the first day of his trial: "The gates of the courtyard swung open and our coach drove in. Alighting from it, I said to the driver with a smile: 'I shall pay you on my way back.' The Chief of Police and a police captain who were standing near by could not refrain from laughing."[216]

While Beilis's memoir is hardly a work of humor, there are several other such examples of irony and wit. They are best appreciated in the original Yiddish, of course, but some of them come through well enough in English.

We realize that many will disagree with us as to the relative merit of Beilis's memoir and Malamud's novel. We are admittedly somewhat biased in the matter, and the relative sales of *The Story of My Sufferings* and *The Fixer* seem to indicate that people are more interested in reading Malamud than Beilis. Still, we recur to the point we made at the beginning of this section: artistic merit should not be considered a license to plagiarize.

E. *Transforming Beilis into Bok*

We believe we have demonstrated that Malamud copied so extensively from Beilis that *The Fixer* could be considered a fictionalized version of *The Story of My Sufferings*. Nevertheless, there are also many differences between Malamud's novel and Beilis's memoir. For readers aware that *The Fixer* is based on the Beilis case, these differences may have caused some confusion over the years as to Beilis's character and the character of his wife.

The actual Mendel Beilis was a dignified, respectful, well-liked, fairly religious man with a faithful wife, Esther, and five children. When arrested, Beilis had been working as superintendent of the Zaitsev brickworks for about fifteen years,[217] and by all accounts he was good at his job. As noted in the Introduction, Beilis was extremely well-liked by his co-workers and neighbors. Lindemann states that Beilis "seems to have been one of the most respected, even beloved men in his neighborhood."[218] Similarly, Samuel writes:

> In two respects Beiliss was fortunate: the friendliness of his disposition and his good relations with his neighbors. They called him 'nash Mendel' – our Mendel – and at the trial they had nothing but good to say of him; the child witnesses smiled at him in court.[219]

Beilis's extraordinarily good reputation was a factor in his trial, these historians agree, because the government had difficulty fabricating evidence against him. One of the witnesses who had given a pre-trial statement against Beilis, a lamplighter, reportedly had a grudge against Beilis because Beilis had threatened to have him arrested for repeatedly stealing wood from the brickworks. Fortunately, the lamplighter repudiated the incriminating statement he had given; he testified at trial that the government had plied him with vodka to get him to incriminate Beilis.[220] Still, if even one other person had held a grudge against Beilis, if even one co-worker had disliked him, the result of the case might have been different.

Beilis was not a totally observant Jew. He worked on Saturday (fortunately for him, as he was signing shipping slips and dealing with co-workers during the time when he was alleged to have kidnapped Yushchinsky.) Nevertheless, Beilis was fairly observant. Here is how he describes his first Friday night in jail:

> As night came on, I remembered that this was the first

Friday night in all my life that the evening was spoiled. I thought of my usual Friday nights with the candles on the table, with the children dressed in their Sabbath best, and everybody so warm and friendly. And now? The house in disorder. My wife alone at the cheerless table. No light, no joy. And all of them weeping their eyes out. I almost forgot my own troubles, thinking of my unfortunate boy [briefly imprisoned at the secret police jail] and my mourning family.[221]

The *New York Times* story on Beilis's funeral, dated July 10, 1934, begins: "Orthodox Jewry paid tribute yesterday to one of its leaders when more than 4,000 attended funeral services for Mendel Beiliss."[222] This was inaccurate in that Beilis was not a leader of Orthodox Jewry; a more accurate statement would have been that "Orthodox Jewry paid tribute to one of its honored figures." Still, the *Times* story is an indication that Beilis was part of the world of traditional Judaism. Another indication is the letter of Rabbi Abraham Isaac Kook, Ashkenazi Chief Rabbi of Palestine under the British Mandate, which Beilis included in the 1931 Yiddish edition of his memoir (reproduced here as Appendix C).[223]

As drawn by Malamud, Yakov Bok has some of the heroism of Beilis, but he also has qualities foreign to Beilis. Yakov Bok is angry, foul-mouthed, cuckolded, and childless. Also, he is not at all religious; indeed, he is anti-religious.

A penniless shtetl Jew just arrived in Kiev, Bok has virtually no friends and virtually no family save his father-in-law Shmuel. His faithless wife Raisl has deserted him. Bok appears to bear much or most of the responsibility for the breakup of their marriage: he treated her poorly, blaming her for their failure to have children.

When his father-in-law implores him not to forget his God, Bok replies: "Who forgets who? . . What do I get from him but a bang on the head and a stream of piss in my face. So what's there to be worshipful about?"[224] On the way to Kiev, Bok admonishes his horse: "I'm a bitter man, you bastard horse. Come to your senses or you'll suffer."[225] And these events occur even before Bok is victimized by the blood libel!

While Bok is in prison, his wife Raisl visits him. She exclaims: "Oh, Yakov, what have they done to you? What did you do to yourself? How did such a terrible thing happen?"[226] He responds: "You stinking whore, what did you do to me? It wasn't enough we were poor as dirt and childless. On top of that you had to be a whore."[227] During this meeting, Yakov's wife informs him that she has had a child as a result of a relationship with another man, evidently one of several such relationships. He thinks: "There's no bottom to my bitterness."[228]

In many respects, then, Yakov Bok is clearly less admirable and less fortunate than was Beilis: Malamud debased Beilis by transforming him into Bok. As to the religious issue, opinions may diverge. Some may not see Malamud's transformation of Beilis from a fairly religious man into the anti-religious Bok as a debasement. Probably Malamud did not see it so; Malamud himself was not religious, and he may have remade Beilis in his own image when he transformed Beilis into Bok. In effect, Malamud may have appropriated Beilis's heroism for his own world-view.

Another difference between *The Fixer* and the actual Beilis case should be noted, as it may cause confusion to those who are interested both in the case and in the novel. In *The Fixer*, Zhenia is the name of the murdered boy. In actuality, Zhenya was the name of the playmate of the murdered boy.

F. *David Beilis Confronts Malamud*

1. *Plagiarism*

While Malamud's plagiarism escaped notice in the literary world for decades, it was immediately apparent to Beilis's surviving family.

David Beilis, one of Mendel Beilis's five children (and the father of Jay Beilis), complained to Malamud about Malamud's plagiarism soon after *The Fixer* was published. Though the copyright on Mendel Beilis's memoir had expired in 1954 and the work had entered the public domain, the ethical question of unattributed taking remained alive. Malamud responded to David Beilis, in a letter dated November 11, 1966, that he was trying to persuade his publisher, Roger Straus, Jr. of Farrar, Straus & Giroux, to reprint Beilis's memoir, with royalties going to David and his brother.[229] Malamud noted, however, that while initially seeming interested, Straus had cooled to the idea, thinking the book would not sell. Malamud closed the letter saying that he would continue to urge Straus to consider republication, as "I still think it a good book to republish."

David Beilis was not impressed with what seemed to him a dubious offer of assistance and responded to Malamud in a December 11, 1966 letter: "You wrote to me that you spoke to your publisher about reprinting my father's book, but from my point of view, they're not such a fool after all, they know that you took the principal points out of it."[230]

This letter was forwarded to Roger Straus, Jr. who replied to David Beilis on December 22, 1966 as follows:

> Mr. Malamud did suggest to us that we reprint your father's book. We did take the matter under serious consideration and, with the desire of doing a good job and presenting the historical background of your father's trial and vindication to present-day readers who needed this orientation, we asked several prominent non-fiction authors to do the introduction. They turned us down and that alone is why we did not go ahead with the reprint.[231]

While we give Malamud credit for his effort, we cannot help having a slight twinge of skepticism as to whether Mr. Straus, a man with considerable clout and connections in the world of publishing. could have failed so abjectly in finding a competent non-fiction author to write an introduction for Beilis's memoir. This, we, note, was the second of two rationales, expressed by or imputed to Straus, as to his decision not to republish; the first was that the book would not sell (admittedly, the two rationales are not completely independent).

2. *Debasement*

One reason, perhaps, why Malamud's plagiarism did not come to light sooner, as a result of David Beilis's protests, is that Malamud's plagiarism was actually not David Beilis's main objection to *The Fixer*. His greatest concern was the debasement of his father's memory and that of his mother, Esther Beilis. David Beilis was devoted to preserving his parents' memory, and was, therefore, greatly displeased that the filthy-mouthed Yakov Bok, a lukewarm Jew, and his faithless wife Raisl should be assumed to be his parents, and that the image of his father, a hero of the entire Jewish people, should be transformed and disfigured.

When David Beilis first contacted Malamud, he had apparently not read *The Fixer* very thoroughly. After reading Malamud's novel, David Beilis continued to complain about plagiarism, but he also complained, even more urgently, about Malamud's debasement of his father's memory. In his letter of December 11, 1966 to Malamud, David Beilis criticized *The Fixer* as "lousy" and as "an unkind view" of his father.[232] David Beilis felt that Malamud's portrayal of Bok as a God-despising Jew demeaned his father's crucial role as surrogate for the Jewish people and its holy texts, which were collectively accused of ritual murder by the Russian Black Hundreds. David Beilis wrote, "Everybody knows that in the defendant's dock at the trial with my father sat fifteen million Jews with the glorified book the Bible which we are proud of for centuries before, and to come." This complaint of David Beilis echoes the 1930 letter of Rabbi Kook:

> The man Beilis endured these severe tests in a spirit of truth and righteousness, fortified by the sanctity of

Judaism, and with an unwavering conviction that his hands were innocent and clean. He emerged with honor, crowned with the wreath of victory. And his honor was also that of our entire nation and the honor of the holy and pure Torah.[233]

David Beilis wrote another letter protesting *The Fixer* to Francis Brown, editor of The New York Times Book Review, who then forwarded the letter to Malamud. Malamud responded in a brief missive dated April 19, 1967: "Though *The Fixer* is based on an historical event it is a fiction and makes no attempt to portray Mendel Beilis or his wife. Yakov and Raisl Bok, I am sure you will agree, in no way resemble your parents."[234] The problem, of course, is that readers of *The Fixer*, knowing that the character Yakov Bok was based on Mendel Beilis, might well believe that Yakov and Raisl Bok did resemble Mendel Beilis and his wife Esther. In creating a character, Yakov Bok, so close to Mendel Beilis in historical details, in fortitude and courage, yet endowed with many unappealing personal traits, Malamud assaulted the reputation and dignity of Mendel Beilis, his wife, and his descendants.

G. *The Two Confusions*

It might be thought that by complaining both about plagiarism and debasement, David Beilis was making, and we are endorsing, two inconsistent accusations against Malamud. Are we saying both that Malamud's character Bok is too much like Beilis and not enough like him?[235]

In fact, the accusations are not inconsistent. In writing *The Fixer*, Malamud caused two kinds of confusion about Beilis. First, he created the perception that Beilis's work, which he copied without attribution, was in fact Malamud's own work. Second, he created the perception that the traits of his characters Yakov and Raisl Bok were the traits of Mendel and Esther Beilis. Both of these confusions can exist at the same time; indeed, they can coexist in the same reader.

We will illustrate what we have called the two confusions through the response of literary critics to *The Fixer*. We will demonstrate that David Beilis's complaints about *The Fixer* were not farfetched and speculative, but right on the mark.

The first kind of confusion (the perception that Malamud originated what in fact he copied from Beilis) is of course to be expected when there is plagiarism as extensive as Malamud's. This confusion is reflected in critical commentary on the rejected-pardon incident (copying instance #35). As previously described, Beilis was told he would be pardoned through a manifesto marking the 300th anniversary of the Romanov dynasty. His response was as follows:

> 'That manifesto,' said I, 'will be for 'katorjniks [convicts],' not for me. I need no manifesto, I need a fair trial.'
> 'If you will be ordered to be released, you'll have to go.'
> 'No, - even if you open the doors of prison, and threaten me with shooting, I shall not leave. I shall not go without a trial. I am strong enough to suffer all until the trial.'[236]

Malamud copies the basic details of this incident, patterning Yakov Bok's response after Beilis's: "Yakov said he wanted a fair trial, not a pardon. If they ordered him to leave the prison without a trial they would have to shoot him first."[237]

Several critics have called attention to this incident as the high point of the entire novel. Sheldon J. Hershinow, author of *Bernard Malamud*, writes:

> The tsar has agreed to grant certain classes of criminals, including Yakov, amnesty. But Yakov does the

273

unimaginable, he refuses – because he is to be pardoned as a criminal rather than freed as an innocent man. The gesture is absurd but magnificent, an affirmation of his personal dignity and moral integrity. This emotional high point of the novel inspires the reader at the same time that it defeats Yakov's enemies.[238]

In his essay "The Hero as Schnook", in *Bernard Malamud and the Critics*, Alan Friedman writes:

[L]ater he [Bok] is offered freedom *without* conditions – he need sign nothing, he need confess to no crime: 'He was to be pardoned and permitted to return to his village' . . . And Yakov Bok, long victimized by a horror and degradation that would make the strongest of men despair, and long after we who have identified with him – and to read the book *is* to identify with him – long after we have stopped hoping for a way out, have in fact asked ourselves again and again why the poor schnook doesn't simply give up this farce, this absurd parody of human life, then Yakov Bok is offered this way out – and he refuses, refuses because he is to be pardoned as a criminal rather than freed as the innocent man he is. And our shock at his absurdly magnificent refusal is intense, and it endures long after we have finished the book, and it remains with us as perhaps its supreme affirmation.[239]

With vast unintentional irony, Friedman then adds: "No one, we feel, no one… could have made such a grand refusal under such circumstances."[240]

At least implicit in these reactions to Bok's heroism is the belief that it is so magnificent in conception that it must have been the invention of Malamud; it is seen as a credit to Malamud's great inventiveness. In fact, however, this "absurdly magnificent refusal", this "emotional high point," was not the invention of Malamud at all, but rather the courageous act of Beilis himself, lifted by Malamud from Beilis's memoir.

The second kind of confusion (the perception that the traits of Malamud's characters Yakov and Raisl Bok were the traits of Mendel and Esther Beilis) is illustrated in the work of the famous literary critic Alfred

Kazin. In 1997, Kazin published an article on Malamud in *The New York Review of Books*, titled "A Single Jew." Shockingly, Kazin had this to say about Beilis:

> Beilis… could never forgive even the many Jews and non-Jews who backed him up against the hatred that had seeped into his prison cell.
>   As Dreyfus was personally not liked by many who fought for his release from Devil's Island, so Beilis was not a favorite with many who knew him best.[241]

These unsourced insults are demonstrably false. Kazin's statement that "Beilis was not a favorite with many who knew him best" is contradicted by the view of historians, based on the trial transcript, that Beilis was well-nigh universally liked, even loved, by his neighbors and co-workers in Russia, as discussed above in section E. Beilis's defense attorney, in his summation, referred to Beilis's co-workers who had testified at the trial: "You have seen these simple, earthy Christian workers, who worked alongside of Beilis day in and day out. Did they utter one derogatory word against Beilis?"[242] Beilis's reputation was so sterling that the prosecutor, Vipper, had to argue that a good man could commit ritual murder. Maurice Samuel describes Vipper's argument as follows:

> Apart from his participation in ritual murders, argued Vipper, Beilis might very well be an admirable character…. So many witnesses had testified in his favor, none in his disfavor. 'It is entirely possible,' said Vipper, 'that Mendel Beiliss is a fine family man, a virtuous and industrious worker like any other Jew living in modest circumstances, and a religious one. But does that prevent him from committing a crime?'
> …
> It might trouble the jury, said Vipper, that a man with such an excellent reputation should be capable of ritual murder, but they were not for that reason to suppose that the

reputation was undeserved. On the contrary, the more Beiliss deserved the good opinion of his neighbors, the more likely was it that as a Jew he practiced ritual murder.[243]

This overwhelming evidence of Beilis's good reputation relates to his life in Russia. It is, however, difficult to believe that his personality underwent so complete a change when he moved to Palestine, or to America, that he metamorphosed from a very likeable person into a very disagreeable one. Such a metamorphosis would also seem to be inconsistent with Beilis's daughter Rachel's recollection that in New York, "The Hunts Point apartment was full of visitors.... After a while my father would say, 'My dear Jewish people, you put such a big monument on top of me, I'll never get out of my grave!'"[244]

Kazin's statement that Beilis "could never forgive even the many Jews and non-Jews who backed him up against the hatred that had seeped into his prison cell" is also demonstrably false. Beilis's memoir is brimming with gratitude to the many Jews and non-Jews who aided him.[245] Beilis continued to express such gratitude until he died, as illustrated below in section H.[246]

We have probably spent too much space debunking Kazin. The important issue is how his false notions about Beilis relate to Malamud's character Yakov Bok. Let us quote Kazin again, this time in broader context:

> Beilis... could never forgive even the many Jews and non-Jews who backed him up against the hatred that had seeped into his prison cell.
> As Dreyfus was personally not liked by many who fought for his release from Devil's Island, so Beilis was not a favorite with many who knew him best. Malamud describes Bok's gruffness, his hatred of the deserting wife, and especially his refusal to ask God for help.[247]

Thus, in the very next sentence after asserting falsely that Beilis was generally disliked, in the very same paragraph, Kazin goes on to describe some qualities of Bok that made him disliked or unlikable. It is obvious, from this context, that Kazin thinks the less favorable character traits Malamud gave to Bok represent traits of the actual Mendel Beilis. This confusion, on the part of a leading literary critic, proves the worthlessness of Malamud's blithe reassurance to David Beilis that *The Fixer* "makes no attempt to portray Mendel Beilis or his wife."[248]

Granting that David Beilis was right to be concerned about the memory of his parents, it might be wondered whether he or anyone else can justly complain about the debasement of a real person in fiction. Authors of novels often base their characters on real people and portray those characters in an unflattering light. Countless parents and spouses of novelists have suffered heartache as a result. Sometimes novelists base their characters on historical figures, such as Beilis, or on people in the news. Was Malamud's transformation of Beilis any different from what novelists do as a matter of course?

We believe that false and unflattering portrayals of real persons in fiction do present a general issue of ethics. A more recent example involved the novel *Primary Colors*,[249] in which a presidential candidate, based on Bill Clinton, had a sexual liaison with a character who was a Harlem librarian. The actual Harlem librarian on which this character was apparently based sued for libel. She alleged that as a result of the novel, some of her co-workers came to believe, falsely, that she had had sex with Clinton.[250]

In the *Primary Colors* case, the plaintiff's suit was dismissed on the ground that the novel's statements about a fictional character, even one apparently based on the plaintiff, did not so clearly refer to the plaintiff as to be "of and concerning" her.[251] Assuming this legal resolution to be correct, the ethical question remains. Joe Klein, the author of *Primary Colors*, can be criticized for writing a sex scene between his Clinton-based character and a character based on a real person, one who (unlike Clinton) had not sought the limelight.

Even leaving aside the general ethical issue that might be raised as to many novelists, Malamud is particularly subject to rebuke. It is surely worse for a novelist to portray a real person in an unflattering light when that person has come into the public eye because he or she has suffered unjustly. Imagine if Joe Klein had written a sex scene between his Clinton-based character and a character who was a refugee from some ethnic conflict. If Klein's refugee character were based on an identifiable real person, Klein's decision to use that person in an unflattering way would presumably be subject to additional criticism.

But Malamud's conduct is worse still, because he plagiarized so extensively from Beilis's memoir. Having plagiarized so extensively, we contend, Malamud forfeited any artistic license to give his Beilis-based character, and that character's wife, unfavorable traits that would predictably be imputed to Beilis and his wife.

We have been asked: what should Malamud have done, ideally, to prevent confusion about the relationship between his work and Beilis's work and life? Is it possible to remove one kind of confusion without strengthening another kind? As to Malamud's plagiarism, the obvious remedy would have been a notice along the lines of the following: "Some of the language and many of the events in this novel were taken from *The Story of My Sufferings*, the memoir of Mendel Beilis." It may seem incredible that any novelist would openly admit to such extensive borrowing, but that should only cement the conclusion that Malamud was guilty of unjustifiable plagiarism. If Malamud would not have been comfortable borrowing so extensively *with* attribution, he should not have done so without attribution. As to the debasement of Mendel and Esther Beilis, Malamud could have added a second line: "However, the character of Yakov Bok has unfavorable qualities that were not possessed by Mendel Beilis, and the character of Bok's wife, Raisl, is a complete invention, bearing no relation to the wife of Mendel Beilis."

H. *Insult to Injury*

We now examine statements Malamud made about the origin of *The Fixer* after the novel was published. Malamud had many opportunities to acknowledge his debt to Beilis. So far as we can tell, he never did so, and some of his statements are misleading by reason of that omission.

Some time in 1966, Malamud wrote an explanation of how he came to write *The Fixer*. It is reprinted in *Talking Horse* as "Source of *The Fixer*",[252] and it is quoted in a book review in *The Saturday Review*, dated September 10, 1966.[253] Here is part of what Malamud wrote:

> In *The Fixer*... I use some of his [Beilis's] experiences, though not, basically, the man, partly because his life came to less than he had paid for by his suffering and endurance, and because I had to have room to invent. To his trials in prison I added something of Dreyfus's and Vanzetti's, shaping the whole to suggest the quality of the afflictions of the Jews under Hitler. These I dumped on the head of poor Yakov Bok.[254]

Malamud's statement that he used "some of his [Beilis's] experiences, though not, basically, the man" is not in itself very misleading, even though Malamud neglects to mention that he obtained Beilis's experiences by copying them from Beilis's memoir. However, one of the reasons Malamud gives for not using Beilis the man in addition to Beilis's experiences – the statement that "his life came to less than he had paid for by his suffering and endurance" – is odd. To a reader of *The*

Fixer, the life of Malamud's character Yakov Bok seems likely to amount to *less* than the life of the historical Mendel Beilis. Malamud does not tell us that Bok, like Beilis, will be found innocent; indeed, the *New York Times*'s reviewer opined that a reader of *The Fixer* is supposed to assume Bok will be found guilty.[255] Since Bok's life seems likely to come to less than Beilis's life, why is it a reason not to use Beilis "the man" that Beilis's life "came to less than he had paid for by his suffering and endurance?"

Beilis was acquitted, became a hero and celebrity, and published a memoir of his experience. By his actions, Malamud indicated that Beilis's memoir was very useful to him, as he plagiarized from it so extensively. So Malamud's somewhat belittling reference to how Beilis's life turned out seems misleading in the absence of any disclosure of Malamud's copying.

On May 6, 1967, the *New York Post* published an interview with Malamud in which he discussed the origin of *The Fixer*. Malamud said: "My attempt is to break away from history.... Almost to create a mythology. I don't want history to tell me what to do. I'd never even been to Russia until I had finished a draft and a half of my book."[256] Once again, this is misleading by omission. A reader would doubtless greet Malamud's statement differently if he knew that while Malamud produced a draft of his novel without visiting Russia, he did not produce a draft without copying extensively from Beilis's memoir.

Malamud's most misleading statement, we believe, was given in an interview published in *The Paris Review* in 1975, and republished in *Talking Horse*. In this interview, Malamud stated:

> My father told me the Mendel Beilis story when I was a kid. I carried it around almost forty years and decided to use it after I gave up the idea of a Sacco and Vanzetti novel. When I began to read for the Sacco and Vanzetti it had all the quality of a structured fiction, all the necessary elements of theme and narrative. I couldn't see any way of re-forming it. I was very much interested in the idea of

prison as a source of the self's freedom and thought of Dreyfus next, but he was a dullish man, and though he endured well he did not suffer well. Neither did Beilis, for that matter, but his drama was more interesting – his experiences; so I invented Yakov Bok, with perhaps the thought of him as a potential Vanzetti. Beilis, incidentally, died a bitter man, in New York – after leaving Palestine, because he thought he hadn't been adequately reimbursed for his suffering.[257]

It's unclear to us exactly what Malamud meant when he said that Beilis (and Dreyfus) did not suffer well.[258] We will charitably assume that Malamud was not referring to such qualities as courage and heroism, but that he was making a literary evaluation: Beilis did not suffer in such a way as a good literary character should suffer. Even so, the non-disclosure of plagiarism seems particularly misleading here, because Bok, as written by Malamud, often suffers in a manner *identical* to Beilis. Not only does Bok have the same experiences, but he also reacts and behaves the same, and his state of mind is often the same. Examples include copying instance #20 (when the bolts on the cell door are snapped back, each is obsessed by the thought that someone is hitting him repeatedly from behind); copying instance #34 (each loses his temper and flings his undershirt in the face of the deputy warden); copying instance #2 (each is ashamed at having to do the Czarist "perp walk," at being forced to walk on the street instead of the sidewalk); copying instance #3 (on the first day in jail, each refuses food and knocks his head against the wall); and many others. Since Malamud made his character, Bok, suffer in the same ways that Beilis had suffered, how could he deny that Beilis had suffered well?

Malamud did not want to reveal his debt to Beilis, and he never did so. Let us consider again, however, Malamud's reported interest in aiding in the republication of Beilis's memoir, stated in correspondence to David Beilis. We have expressed skepticism at the rationale offered by Roger Straus, Jr. for Straus's refusal to republish – that Straus could not find a non-fiction author to write an introduction. Still, we give Malamud the benefit of the doubt; we assume that he did make some effort to arrange for the republication of Beilis's memoir. If so, it is certainly to Malamud's credit. While Malamud did not want to reveal his debt to Beilis, that debt would more likely have come to light if Beilis's memoir had been republished so soon after Malamud's novel was published. In trying to arrange for republication of *The Story of My Sufferings*, Malamud may have acted against his own interest, perhaps motivated by a guilty conscience. In so doing, perhaps Malamud made an implicit recognition of his debt to Beilis.

As this book is about the memory of Mendel Beilis, we hope we will be forgiven for returning to and commenting upon Malamud's statement in *Talking Horse* that "Beilis, incidentally, died a bitter man, in New York – after leaving Palestine, because he thought he hadn't been adequately reimbursed for his suffering."[259] Unlike the patently false insults of Kazin, quoted previously, Malamud's statement has an element of truth. It is quite misleading, however – not misleading by omission of Malamud's plagiarism, like the other Malamud statements we have discussed in this section, but simply a misleading description of Beilis's life.

Let us consider first the assertion that Beilis "thought he hadn't been adequately reimbursed for his suffering." This is not actually an insult. It would be natural for someone in Beilis's situation to think that he hadn't been adequately reimbursed for his suffering.[260] But while this view would be natural, it wasn't exactly Beilis's view.

First, it is important to distinguish between a general sense of entitlement and a sense of entitlement to the fulfillment of specific promises. In his memoir, Beilis does complain repeatedly about the unfulfillment of specific promises, particularly the promise he received

———

from notables in Kiev, and later from others, to be given a farm in Palestine. By contrast, there is not much of a sense of a general entitlement to compensation. The only place in Beilis's memoir where he claims his ordeal entitles him to anything is where he attempts to discourage his eldest son from joining the Turkish army in World War I. Beilis's son tells him:

> I want to do something for the Jewish people.... If we should serve Turkey faithfully, the government will treat us more leniently after the War. Our possibilities for acquiring Palestine will be much increased.[261]

In an unsuccessful attempt to dissuade his son, Beilis responds: "But my service suffices for both of us.... I have suffered enough for the both of us."[262] This claim of entitlement is incongruous to the rest of the memoir, so much so that the reader may be taken aback. And even here, of course, Beilis is not saying that his son is obligated to him, but rather that he has already fulfilled whatever obligation his son might have.

In the interview that Beilis gave in December, 1933, six months before he died, Beilis continues to complain about the unfulfillment of specific promises. In this interview, however, he does also seem to express a more general sense that he should have been compensated:

> I did not ask to be chosen as a victim, a 'korban', to stand up for the entire Jewish race. I was happy where I was. I had my work, my family, my friends. Suddenly I was taken away from this and became a symbol for the entire Jewish people. But since fate had chosen me, I went through the ordeal. I suffered, and my family suffered.
> Then when it was all over, I was promised a life of ease. Through me Jewry had been vindicated, but they forgot about me very quickly. And the burden of reconstructing my life was thrust on my shoulders. Why? I was not asked whether I wanted to be a symbol for Jewish suffering. But I was chosen, and now I have been forgotten.[263]

Here, Beilis may display some sense of general entitlement by the statement "Through me Jewry had been vindicated, but they forgot about me very quickly." We note that Beilis's words are echoed by an editorial published in the Yiddish newspaper *Der Tog* on Beilis's death: "He suffered on behalf of everyone, and should be remembered by everyone. But we forgot about him."[264]

In any event, while Malamud's assertion that Beilis "thought he hadn't been adequately reimbursed for his suffering" has an element of truth, it is, as we have said, misleading in that it ignores the specific promises Beilis received, the unfulfillment of which was Beilis's main complaint. But a more important reason why Malamud's assertion is misleading is that it leaves out a far more central element of Beilis's self-view: his sense of obligation.

Beilis's chief reaction to his ordeal was not that it conferred an entitlement on him, but that it imposed an obligation on him – to continue to act as befitted a symbol of the Jewish people. That is why, when Beilis was released from prison, he chose a hard life in Palestine, where he certainly would not otherwise have gone; that is why he rejected all the offers that would have allowed him to capitalize on his fame. We cannot forbear to make the obvious comparison: Beilis, from a heightened sense of obligation, turned down a fortune that was rightfully his, while Malamud, from a heightened sense of entitlement, appropriated that which was not rightfully his.

What, then, of the first part of Malamud's statement, the assertion that Beilis died a bitter man? Once again, there may be an element of truth here. But however bitter Beilis was at the end of his life, he was probably less bitter than others would have been in his place. The last question Beilis was asked, in his 1933 interview with the *Jewish Daily Bulletin*, was "Could Mr. Beilis give one outstanding impression of the trial in Kiev?"

Beilis responded:

> Yes. The Russian Gentiles, who sacrificed themselves
> for me. There was real heroism, real sacrifice. They knew
> that by defending me their careers would be ruined, even
> their very lives would not be safe. But they persisted
> because they knew I was innocent.
> But I lived to see the rotten Czarist regime crumble. I
> lived to tell the whole story, and that is a miracle.[265]

Thus, Beilis's last public statements were (1) a final tribute to the Russian Gentiles who aided him, at risk to their careers and lives; and (2) a marvel that he survived to tell his own story. In these remarks, Beilis does not sound very bitter to us.

Approximately two months before his death, Beilis sent a letter to Oskar Gruzenberg, who had been the lead defense counsel at the trial in 1913. After Beilis's death, Gruzenberg made the letter public, and it was published in English translation by the Jewish Telegraphic Agency. As published, Beilis's April, 1934 letter to Gruzenberg begins:

> I can never forget you. In your works then you suffered
> just as I did, and your great pride and courage gave me
> much strength.
> I remember very well when you, my dear friend, came to
> me when I was in the prison at Lukianov. When I saw you
> for the first time I was immediately comforted. I am
> happy. God permitted me to live and I am able to write to
> you. I have not lived a single day without mentioning you.
> I read in an American newspaper what you wrote [on the
> twentieth anniversary of the trial]. At each word I shed
> tears, and I kissed each of your words, dear friend.[266]

In this letter – probably the last recorded utterance of Mendel Beilis, written while he was in failing health – we once again do not detect much bitterness.

We have criticized Bernard Malamud at length for his plagiarism,

---

285

his debasement of Beilis's memory, his refusal to acknowledge his debt to Beilis, and the gratuitously belittling statements he made about Beilis. We want to make it clear, however, that the term "blood libel," in the title of this book, does not refer to anything that Malamud did. The blood libel was visited on Beilis by the "wicked, bestial hands of [the] enemies" of the Jewish people, in Rabbi Kook's phrase,[267] not by a novelist. We do not believe that Beilis would have wanted mere literary misbehavior to be equated with the blood libel perpetrated by the anti-Semites in Czarist Russia.

Some may wonder if it is even worthwhile to expose Malamud's plagiarism at this late date. After all, Malamud is dead, as are Mendel Beilis and David Beilis (who of all Mendel Beilis's children was most upset at Malamud's treatment of his father). The confusions that Malamud created persist, however. People continue to read *The Fixer* and continue to believe, falsely, that Malamud invented those parts that he copied from Beilis. Not only does Beilis continue to be denied credit for his work and deeds, but people continue to be misled by *The Fixer* as to Beilis's true character. In order to do justice to the memory of Mendel Beilis, it is necessary to clear away the confusions created by Malamud.

In any event, the most valuable part of this book is not our criticism of Malamud, but Mendel Beilis's own memoir. It has been our privilege to present the story of this great hero to a new generation.

AFTERWORD

by Jay Beilis

My father, David Beilis, was never sure what day he was born. His actual birthday was sometime in the summer, but he celebrated it every year on October 28, which he told me was the date of the not-guilty verdict in the trial of my grandfather, Mendel Beilis.

I was thirteen years old when Bernard Malamud's *The Fixer* was published. My father was angry at Malamud's plagiarism, but far angrier that people could think that his mother, Esther Beilis, was running around with men while her husband was in prison.

I told him, "Dad, it's fiction, he can say whatever he wants."

He said, "You don't understand. Go out and play."

As I matured, I came to share my father's view of Malamud's plagiarism and of Malamud's insult to my grandparents' memories. I hope that some of the confusion created by Malamud will disappear with the publication of this book on the life and memory of Mendel Beilis.

Over the years, I've gotten some inkling of how big an event my grandfather's trial was. Starting in 1963, my family would spend every summer in a "borscht belt" bungalow colony near the Catskill mountains in New York. As per the norm, my father would work in the city during the week, then join us during the weekend. When word got around that my family was there, we would get visitors who would tell us, with great joy and appreciation, that their parents left Russia and many other countries in

287

Europe around the time of Mendel Beilis's trial, saving them from the Holocaust. Their parents left because they saw what happened to my grandfather as a warning to Jews to leave Europe, just like Kristallnacht was to German and Austrian Jews some twenty-five years later. I enjoyed the visits from these total strangers because they usually brought sweets and candies (my mother, who was diabetic, could have done without the attention).

In 1985, I attended the premiere in New York of Claude Lanzmann's movie *Shoah*. Before the movie started, several dozen people were waiting outside the theater for the doors to open. Among them was Claude Lanzmann himself. I noticed that at age 32, I seemed to be the youngest person in the audience by far. Many of the people were Holocaust survivors.

As I was going into the movie, one nice old lady asked me if I had lost family in the Holocaust. I told her I had lost some family on my mother's side, and I also mentioned that I was the grandson of Mendel Beilis. As the movie started, I saw her nudge her friend and point to me, and I heard whispering. When the lights came on for intermission, thirty sets of eyes were looking at me. Even after experiencing the worst tragedy in our history, they had not forgotten my grandfather.

In 2003, I was invited to a conference in Russia to mark the 90th anniversary of the trial of Mendel Beilis. Unfortunately, much of the focus then was on drawing parallels between my grandfather's case and the case of Mikhail Khodorkovsky, a Russian-Jewish tycoon who has been imprisoned and stripped of his wealth by the authorities in Russia. Whatever injustice Mr. Khodorkovsky has suffered, I do not see the two cases as very similar. I hope that in 2013, when people mark the 100th anniversary of my grandfather's trial, more of the focus will be on my grandfather.

Of all Mendel Beilis's children, my aunt Rachel lived the longest; at her passing in August, 2011, she was 102. She and I were pretty close. When my uncle Teddy died without children in 1972, my aunt Rachel received some benefits from the government. She tried to give the money to my father, but he was too proud to take it. So they decided that Rachel and I would visit Israel together. We went to Israel in February, 1973. This was a very emotional time for Rachel, because she was reuniting with friends she had not seen in more than fifty years. The bonus for me was that some of these people were now high-ranking officials in the government and military, and I was able to see places no ordinary tourist would be shown.

My aunt Rachel was only two and a half when her father Mendel Beilis was arrested in July, 1911. It made an enormous impression on her. After all, she didn't see her father again until she was almost five. She would often speak of it, especially after she started to become a little confused. She would say, "They came in the middle of the night and took him away. Why did they do this to my father? He never did anything, everybody liked him. Everybody knows that Jewish people don't do things like this."

Many people helped my grandfather to escape the evil blood libel: the neighbors and coworkers who testified on his behalf, the honest officials in Kiev who tried to prosecute the real murderers, the lawyers, Jewish and Gentile, who represented him so well. I thank them all once again.

I am happy that my grandfather's memoir is now back in print. It is an important part of Jewish history and a great, true story that still inspires after all these years.

Appendix A

Summary of Changes Made to the 1926 English Edition

As indicated in the Preface, the version of Beilis's memoir presented in this volume is based on Harrison Goldberg's elegant translation for the 1926 English edition. We have gone back to the original Yiddish in many places to correct errors made by Goldberg, or to achieve greater clarity. However, we have not undertaken a completely new translation.

Many of Goldberg's errors arise from his unfamiliarity with Russian legal procedure. We have already mentioned the most serious error: When Beilis relates that the jury pronounced him not guilty, Goldberg incorrectly adds that the verdict was unanimous.

In transliterating Russian and Ukrainian names, we have adopted the current conventions – "Cheberyak" rather than "Tchebiriak," for example.

Throughout most of his Yiddish-language memoir, Beilis refers to Palestine as "*Eretz Yisroel*." Goldberg translates this term as "Palestine," but we have opted for the more literal "Land of Israel." Beilis does sometimes use the word "Palestine" in the original Yiddish, as when he refers to the Anglo-Palestine Bank or when he makes a play on the word "Palestine" and the Russian word "*Pushtina*" (desert or wasteland). In such cases, we too use the word "Palestine."

In the original Yiddish, Beilis frequently refers to non-Jews as "Christian." Goldberg generally translates "Christian" as "Russian," but we have for the most part restored the term "Christian."

—

We have made some stylistic changes to the 1926 English edition. One change we frequently made was to split up the text into a greater number of paragraphs (which often led us to adopt the paragraphing in the Yiddish version).

We have tried not to change the meaning of Beilis's memoir. A rare exception that perhaps deserves note is that we have softened slightly Beilis's treatment of Yushchinsky's mother. Thus, for example, in Chapter 2 of the original Yiddish and English editions, when Beilis relates the rumor that Yushchinsky's father left him a trust fund, perhaps providing a motive for murder, Beilis relates this rumor as fact. As the rumor was disproved, we have added the word "supposedly." We do not believe that Beilis, if he were in full possession of the facts, would have wanted to cast suspicion on another innocent. Beilis does accurately relate, in Chapter 26, that when Yushchinsky's mother was called to the stand, she unexpectedly gave no help to the prosecution and did not at all attempt to incriminate Beilis or the Jewish people.

Appendix B

Note on the 1992 Edition, *Scapegoat On Trial*

A version of Beilis's memoir was published in 1992 by CIS Publishers under the title *Scapegoat On Trial: The Story Of Mendel Beilis*.[268] Now out of print, the 1992 edition includes a fine introduction and postscript by the editor, Shari Schwartz. It also includes an essay titled "The Jewish Response," by Sora F. Bulka, that provides unusual insight into the perspective of Hasidim on the Beilis case.

We commend the editor and publisher of *Scapegoat On Trial* for re-publishing Beilis's memoir. We disagree with a number of their decisions and statements, however. Probably the greatest problem with *Scapegoat On Trial* is that it omits Chapters 38, 39 and 40 of Beilis's memoir. Parts of Chapter 37 are also omitted, including the two passages in which Beilis refers to Rabbi Kook. As Beilis later included Rabbi Kook's letter in the 1931 Yiddish edition of his memoir, we would not want to omit those passages; indeed, we would not want to omit any part of Beilis's memoir.

The editor of *Scapegoat On Trial*, Schwartz, seems not to have consulted the original Yiddish version. Schwartz may not even have been aware that a Yiddish edition of Beilis's memoir was published; she states, in her postscript, that the memoir was "[o]riginally composed in Yiddish but published in English."[269] As there was no apparent reference to the Yiddish edition, many of the mistakes in the 1926 English edition are uncorrected, including the statement that the verdict of the Russian jury was unanimous.[270]

292

In *Scapegoat On Trial*, there are numerous stylistic changes to the text of the 1926 English edition. In general, we do not believe that these changes represent improvements. Schwartz writes well, but she lacks the elegance of Beilis's translator Harrison Goldberg. Take, for example, the dramatic opening of Beilis's trial. The presiding judge begins the proceedings by asking Beilis his religion. The 1926 English translation by Harrison Goldberg describes Beilis's response as follows: "I did not recognize my own voice when I answered in something approaching a shout: 'I am a Jew.'"[271]

Schwartz changes the English text slightly to read, "I did not recognize my own voice as I answered in a tone approaching a shout, 'I am a Jew.'"[272] We prefer the original translation.

In her introduction, Schwartz refers to Harrison Goldberg's elegant translation as "an awkwardly written English translation."[273] We believe, to the contrary, that Schwartz's version is more often awkward. Even if we thought that Schwartz improved on Goldberg (and on a few occasions, perhaps she does), Goldberg was the translator selected by Beilis. We would not so readily deviate from his translation. Admittedly, this difference between our approach and that of Schwartz is a matter of degree and of selection. We have ourselves made some stylistic changes to the language of the 1926 English edition.

Sometimes Schwartz's editorial decisions appear to reflect a religious bias. In Chapter 4 of Beilis's memoir, his son is released from the secret police headquarters on a Saturday, after being held briefly for questioning. The guard takes Beilis's son to a streetcar, but the boy refuses to board it, running home instead. In a footnote to this passage, Schwartz states: "To have used the streetcar would have constituted a violation of the Sabbath. Incidents such as this reveal that the Beilis family was accustomed to observing Jewish laws and customs."[274]

While it is certainly possible that Beilis's son refused to take the streetcar because it was Saturday, he may also have run home because he wanted nothing more to do with the authorities. In the original Yiddish, the guard tells Beilis:

"Hot er gezogt az er vet nit forn, nor loyfn tsu fus aheym.
Er hot zikh aponim geshrokn far mir." (He said he wouldn't ride, but run home instead. He was apparently afraid of me.)[275]

We do appreciate the sentiments expressed by Schwartz at the end of her postscript. Among other things, Schwartz expresses the hope that the republication of Beilis's memoir "will… correct certain misconceptions about Beilis that may have arisen after the publication of Bernard Malamud's *The Fixer*".[276]

Appendix C

Letter of Rabbi Kook, from the 1931 Yiddish Edition

(translated from the Hebrew and Yiddish by Jeremy Simcha Garber)

A Letter

From the Rabbi and Illustrious Scholar Avraham Yitzhak HaCohen Kook of the Land of Israel. With G-d's help - the 4th day of the month of Iyar, 5690 (1930)

Our dear brothers, inhabitants of America!

Behold, with this letter I have the honor to awaken your pure hearts regarding a holy duty that, though ancient, must always be new in our hearts; the obligation of "restitution". Every member of our People is obliged to contribute funds to the man who endured terrible suffering, and fell as a victim under the wicked, bestial hands of our eternal enemies, that is the precious but downtrodden, Mr. Menachem Mendel Beilis, may his light shine, whose trials and miseries are known to the entire House of Israel. He suffered and was tortured at the hands of the evil ones because of the false and revolting accusation of the blood libel, with which they sought to defame our entire people. The man Beilis endured these severe tests in a spirit of truth and righteousness, fortified by the sanctity of Judaism, and with an unwavering conviction that his hands were innocent and clean. He emerged with honor, crowned with the wreath of victory.

And his honor was also that of our entire nation and the honor of the holy and pure Torah. But now, my heart breaks to learn how this dear man, having reached a time of old age and illness, has none to give him succor and aid, has no one to soothe his pain. It is a terrible thing!

And behold, has he not printed this book to tell generations to come all that happened to him with abiding truth and unflagging faith; and is it not, therefore, a double obligation for every Jew to buy this very book from him? For it has become like the Book of Lamentations for our generation. And every Jew should pay a full and proper price to honor both the book and its author, and in doing so provide honorable support to our suffering and tortured brother.

Dear brothers of ours, may these, my words, find favor with you and cause you to turn your hearts to our dear unfortunate brother and to purchase the book, *Mendel Beilis*, and may it be kept in your homes as a memorial and may you regard him, one of our tormented martyrs, with the respect and admiration he deserves. And may G-d grant you His blessing from Zion and Holy Jerusalem, just as I, your brother, bless you with love from the holy mountain, from Jerusalem.

Avraham Yitzhak Ha Cohen Kook.

ABOUT THE EDITORS

MARK S. STEIN, J.D., Ph.D, is an attorney in Chicago. He is the author of the book *Distributive Justice and Disability* (Yale University Press, 2006). He has also published articles in scholarly journals.

JEREMY SIMCHA GARBER is an attorney in New York. His translations of Yiddish and Hebrew works have appeared in a number of books and periodicals.

JAY BEILIS is the grandson of Mendel Beilis.

The editors can be reached at BeilisBook@gmail.com.

MENDEL BEILIS

Beilis at the Trial

Beilis Leaves Street Car Under Guard

P. A. BOLDIREV, Presiding
Judge, Kiev Supreme Court

The Sessions of the Kiev Supreme Court

The Jury

BEILIS AND HIS COUNSELLORS

O. O. Gruzenberg   W. A. Maklakow   B. Karabchevsky

MENDEL BEILIS

A. S. Zarudny   Arnold D. Margolin   D. G. Grigorovich-Barsky

A. I. VIPPER
Assistant Prosecuting Attorney

CHAPLINSKY
Prosecuting Attorney

EXPERTS AND WITNESSES FOR THE DEFENSE

RABBI MAZE
Expert for the Defense

Prof W. M. BACHTEREV
Expert for the Defense

Prof. A. I. KARPINSKY
Expert for the Defense

Prof. O. O. KADIAN
Expert for the Defense

Prof. I. G. TROYITZKI
Expert for the Defense

PAVLOV, the Czar's Surgeon
Expert for the Defense

NAKONETCHNY
Witness for the Defense

PSICHIATOR SIKORSKY
Expert for the Prosecution

Prof. KOSTOROTOV
Expert for the Prosecution

Student GOLUBEV
Expert for the Prosecution

N. Z. ZAMISLOVSKY
Private Complainant

PRIEST PRANAITIS
Expert for the Prosecution

304

Beilis and His Family After the Trial

Beilis After His Acquittal

The gravesite of Mendel Beilis

(photo by "GB77," from
http://en.wikipedia.org/wiki/File:Mendel_Beilis_grave.jpg)

BIBLIOGRAPHY

American Library Association, "Librarian's Libel Suit Over Primary Colors Dismissed" (Oct. 20, 2003), available at http://www.ala.org/ala/alonline/currentnews/newsarchive/2003/aloct03/librarianslibel.cfm (last visited November 2, 2009).

Andrews, Lucilla, *No Time for Romance* (London: Chambers Harrap, 1977).

Beilis, Jay, Jeremy Simcha Garber, and Mark S. Stein, "Pulitzer Plagiarism: The Malamud-Beilis Connection," *Cardozo Law Review de novo* (2010): 225-241, available at http://www.cardozolawreview.com/content/denovo/BEILIS_2010_225.pdf

Beilis, Mendel, *Di Geshichte fun Meine Leiden* (New York: Mendel Beilis Publishing Co., 1925).

Beilis, Mendel, *Di Geshichte fun Meine Leiden*, Second Edition. (New York: Mendel Beilis Publishing Co., 1931).

Beilis, Mendel, *The Story of My Sufferings*, trans. Harrison Goldberg (New York: Mendel Beilis Publishing Co., 1926).

Beilis, Mendel, *Blood Libel: The Life and Memory of Mendel Beilis* (Chicago: Beilis Publishing, 2011).

Berkowitz, Joel, "The 'Mendel Beilis' Epidemic on the Yiddish Stage," *Jewish Social Studies* 8, no. 1 (Fall, 2001): 199.

Cheuse, Alan and Nicholas Delbanco, eds., *Talking Horse: Bernard Malamud on Life and Work* (New York: Columbia University Press, 1996).

Cowell, Alan, "Eyebrows Are Raised Over Passages in a Best Seller by Ian McEwan," *New York Times*, November 28, 2006.

Davis, Philip, *Bernard Malamud: A Writer's Life* (New York: Oxford University Press, 2007.

———

Dundes, Alan, ed., *The Blood Libel Legend: A Casebook in Anti-Semitic Folklore* (Madison, WI: University of Wisconsin Press, 1991).

Eckman, Fern Marja, "The Writing Teacher and His Prize," *New York Post*, May 6, 1967, 28.

Frankel, Haskel, "One Man to Stand for Six Million," *Saturday Review*, September 10, 1966, 37.

Fremont-Smith, Eliot, "Yakov's Choice," *New York Times*, August 29, 1966.

Friedman, Alan, "The Hero as Schnook," in *Bernard Malamud and the Critics*, ed. Leslie and Joyce Field, (New York: New York University Press, 1970).

Gruzenberg, Oskar O. *Yesterday: Memoirs of a Russian-Jewish Lawyer* (Berkeley: University of California Press, 1981).

Hershinow, Sheldon J., *Bernard Malamud* (NY: Frederick Ungar, 1980).

"Mendel Beilis Broods on Obscurity After Ritual Murder Fame," *Jewish Daily Bulletin*, December 24, 1933, 11.

"Beilis' Last Letter is Revealed by Attorney Who Defended Him," *JTA*, August 26, 1934, available at http://archive.jta.org/article/1934/08/26/2818650/beilis-last-letter-is-revealed-by-attorney-who-defended-him.

Kazin, Alfred, "A Single Jew," *The New York Review of Books*, October 9, 1997, 9.

Klein, Joe, *Primary Colors: A Novel of Politics* (1996).

Leikin, Ezekiel, *The Beilis Transcripts: The Anti-Semitic Trial that Shook the World* (Northvale, NJ: Jason Aronson Inc., 1993).

Levy, Richard S., ed., *Antisemitism: A Historical Encyclopedia of Prejudice and Persecution* Santa Barbara, CA: ABC-CLIO, 2005).

Lindemann, Albert S., *The Jew Accused: Three Anti-Semitic Affairs* (New York: Cambridge University Press, 1991).

309

Lindemann, Albert S., "Beilis Case," in *Antisemitism: A Historical Encyclopedia of Prejudice and Persecution*, ed. Richard S. Levy (Santa Barbara, CA: ABC-CLIO, 2005).

Malamud, Bernard, *The Fixer* (New York: Farrar, Straus and Giroux, 1966).

Malamud, Bernard, "Source of *The Fixer*," in Alan Cheuse and Nicholas Delbanco, eds., *Talking Horse: Bernard Malamud on Life and Work* (New York: Columbia University Press, 1996), 88-89.

Margolin, Arnold D., *The Jews of Eastern Europe* (New York: T. Seltzer, 1926).

Mark, Jonathan, "Redemption on East Tremont," *Jewish Week* (March 26, 1999), available at http://www.thejewishweek.com/viewArticle/c36_a11520/News/New_York.html, *reprinted in Best Contemporary Jewish Writing*, ed. Michael Lerner (San Francisco, CA: Jossey-Bass, 2001), 36.

McEwan, Ian, *Atonement* (London: Jonathan Cape, 2001).

Mizruchi, Susan L., "The Place of Ritual in Our Time," *American Literary History* 12, no. 3 (2000): 481, *reprinted in* Mizruchi, ed., *Religion and Cultural Studies* (Princeton: Princeton University Press, 2001).

"Beiliss Acquitted but Pogrom Feared," *New York Times*, November 11, 1913.

"Mendel Beilis Coming," *New York Times*, January 25, 1921.

"Beiliss Dies at 62; In 1913 Kieff Trial," *New York Times*, July 8, 1934.

"Beiliss Funeral Attended by 4,000," *New York Times*, July 10, 1934.

Patai, Raphael, *The Jews of Hungary: History, Culture, Psychology* (Detroit, MI: Wayne State University Press, 1996).

Pentateuch and Haftorahs, Second Edition., ed. J. H. Hertz (London: Soncino, 1969).

Polland, Annie and Bill Moyers, *Landmark of the Spirit: The Eldridge Street Synagogue* (New Haven: Yale University Press, 2008).

Pulley, Brett, "Librarian Speaks Out on 'Primary Colors' Suit", *New York Times*, February 19, 1997.

Samuel, Maurice, *Blood Accusation: The Strange History of the Beiliss Case* (New York: Knopf, 1966).

Schappes, Morris U., "Anti-Semitic Blood Libel in Fact and Fiction," *Jewish Currents* (February, 1967): 8.

Schwartz, Shari, ed., *Scapegoat On Trial: The Story Of Mendel Beilis* (Lakewood, NJ: CIS Publishers, 1992).

Stern, Daniel, "Bernard Malamud, The Art of Fiction No. 52," *The Paris Review* 61 (Spring, 1975), available at http://www.theparisreview.org/interviews/3869/the-art-of-fiction-no-52-bernard-malamud, *reprinted as* "The Writer at Work," in Alan Cheuse and Nicholas Delbanco, eds., *Talking Horse: Bernard Malamud on Life and Work* (New York: Columbia University Press, 1996), 18.

Tager, Alexander, *The Decay of Czarism: The Beiliss Trial* (Philadelphia: Jewish Publication Society, 1935).

"Books: The Outsider," *Time*, September 9, 1966, 106.

"Mendel Beilis" (editorial), *Der Tog*, July 10, 1934.

Tritt, Michael, "Mendel Beilis's *The Story of My Sufferings* and Malamud's *The Fixer*: A Study of Indebtedness and Innovation," *Modern Jewish Studies* 13, no. 4 (Summer, 2004): 70.

Wisse, Ruth R., *The Modern Jewish Canon: A Journey Through Language and Culture* 16 (New York: Free Press, 2000).

NOTES

[1] Mendel Beilis, *Di Geshichte fun Meine Leiden* (New York: Mendel Beilis Publishing Co, 1925). A second edition of the Yiddish version was published in 1931.

[2] Mendel Beilis, *The Story of My Sufferings*, trans. Harrison Goldberg (New York: Mendel Beilis Publishing Co., 1926).

[3] "Beiliss Funeral Attended by 4,000," *New York Times*, July 10, 1934.

[4] Ibid.

[5] Annie Polland and Bill Moyers, *Landmark of the Spirit: The Eldridge Street Synagogue* (New Haven: Yale University Press, 2008), 128.

[6] We include material from the 1925 and 1931 Yiddish editions that has not previously been published in English. A summary of the changes we have made to the 1926 English edition can be found in Appendix A.

[7] Bernard Malamud, *The Fixer* (New York: Farrar, Straus and Giroux, 1966).

[8] See, for example, Eliot Fremont-Smith, "Yakov's Choice," *New York Times*, August 29, 1966. Among book reviewers, the wide recognition that Malamud's book was based on Beilis's life was due in part to the fortuitous appearance of an excellent non-fiction account of the Beilis case only weeks before publication of *The Fixer*: Maurice Samuel, *Blood Accusation: The Strange History of the Beiliss Case* (New York: Knopf, 1966).

[9] Alan Dundes, ed., *The Blood Libel Legend: A Casebook in Anti-Semitic Folklore* (Madison, WI: University of Wisconsin Press, 1991), viii ("evil legend").

[10] Leviticus 17: 12 ("Therefore I said unto the children of Israel: No soul of you shall eat blood, neither shall any stranger that sojourneth among you eat blood."). *Pentateuch and Haftorahs*, 2nd Edition, ed. J. H. Hertz (London: Soncino, 1969), 487.

[11] Raphael Patai, *The Jews of Hungary: History, Culture, Psychology* (Detroit, MI: Wayne State University Press, 1996), 183-84.

[12] Maurice Samuel, *Blood Accusation: The Strange History of the Beiliss Case* (New York: Knopf, 1966), 4.

[13] Samuel, 135.

[14] Samuel, 135; "Beiliss Acquitted but Pogrom Feared," *New York Times*, November 11, 1913. The *New York Times* article appears to be erroneous in dating the liberal *Duma* proposal at one month after Yushchinsky's murder, rather than one month before.

[15] Albert S. Lindemann, *The Jew Accused: Three Anti-Semitic Affairs* (New York: Cambridge University Press, 1991), 180; Samuel, 123-24.

[16] Beilis, *The Story of My Sufferings* (1926), 69; Samuel, 28. Lindemann states that the Czar himself "was not directly involved." Lindemann, *The Jew Accused*, 180.

[17] Lindemann, 186.

[18] Beilis (1926), 41; Beilis (2011), chapter 4.

[19] Lindemann, 186; Samuel, 57.

[20] Samuel, 58.

[21] Beilis (1926), 24; Beilis (2011), chapter 1.

[22] All dates of events occurring in Czarist Russia are given under the old Russian calendar.

[23] Samuel, 16.

[24] Samuel, 15.

[25] Samuel, 16.

[26] Samuel, 152.

[27] Samuel, 17, 19.

[28] Samuel, 37.

[29] Samuel, 22.

[30] Samuel, 16.

[31] Samuel, 25, 194-95. The section of pillowcase found with Yushchinsky's body was bloody and also had small semen stains. Yushchinsky had not been sexually molested, but semen stains were apparently common in Cheberyak's apartment, including on the walls. Samuel, 194.

[32] Samuel, 196-97.

[33] Samuel, 51-52.

[34] Samuel, 36.

[35] Samuel, 151. The context of this confession, as described by Samuel, makes it highly credible.

[36] Samuel, 204-05

[37] Samuel, 32-33.

[38] Samuel, 32.

[39] Samuel, 36.

[40] Samuel, 25.

[41] Samuel, 24-25.

[42] Samuel, 22.

[43] Samuel, 49.

[44] Samuel, 29-31.

[45] Samuel, 46.

[46] Samuel, 142.

[47] Samuel, 52-53.

[48] Samuel, 54. Brandorf had her rearrested on July 29, but Chaplinsky had her released again on August 8. Samuel, 65.

[49] Samuel, 62.

[50] Samuel, 53-54.

[51] Samuel, 142.

[52] Samuel, 142.

[53] Samuel, 54.

[54] Samuel, 53.

[55] Samuel, 162.

[56] Samuel, 68-73.

[57] Samuel, 67-68.

[58] Samuel, 187.

[59] Samuel, 43-44.

[60] Samuel, 66.

[61] Samuel, 73-75.

[62] Samuel, 34.

[63] Samuel, 188; Ezekiel Leikin, *The Beilis Transcripts: The Anti-Semitic Trial that Shook the World* (Northvale, NJ: Jason Aronson Inc., 1993), 93.

[64] Samuel, 189-90

[65] Samuel, 188-91. Beilis states, in his memoir, that Zhenya had accused him of abducting Yushchinsky in an interview with Investigating Magistrate Fenenko. Beilis (1926), 139; Beilis (2011), chapter 22. This appears to be erroneous. Zhenya was evasive in all his interviews with officials. However, he may have divulged some information to Fenenko on June 17, 1911, when his mother was in prison. In his book *The Decay of Czarism*, Alexander Tager quotes Zhenya's statement in the June 17 interview as follows: "When you questioned me before, Magistrate, I was very much afraid to tell you that the late Andrei came to see me last time and asked me whether I had any gunpowder… I was afraid to tell you about the powder the first time you questioned me because I thought that you would beat me. Now, however, after you explained to me that the Investigating Magistrate does not beat anyone, I tell you the truth… I saw Andrei the last time… about ten days before the discovery of his corpse… On the same evening my father sent me to a saloon (for beer)… When I came to the saloon, there were many people there, and I saw Fedor Nejinsky… Fedor was very drunk and stood with difficulty on his feet. When he saw me, he stopped and told me in a whisper: 'Andrei does not exist any more, he was stabbed.' … When Andrei was found dead, I told my mother what Fedor had said to me, and she told me that I was lying and that Fedor, probably, had not said anything of the sort." Tager, 84. It is hard to know what to make of this statement of Zhenya Cheberyak; Samuel does not mention it in his own work on the Beilis case.

[66] Samuel, 190. Dunya's father, a shoemaker named Nakonechny, was instrumental in impeaching the initially-damaging statements offered by Shakhovsky the lamplighter; it was Nakonechny who informed the authorities that Shakhovsky had a grudge against Beilis because Beilis had threatened to have Shakhovsky arrested for stealing wood. Samuel, 67-68.

[67] Samuel, 57; Beilis (1926), 139; Beilis (2011), chapter 22.

[68] Samuel, 66; Beilis (1926), 139; Beilis (2011), chapter 22.

[69] Samuel, 221. This was Zamyslovsky, one of the two private prosecutors supposedly representing Yushchinsky's mother to obtain a civil recovery against Beilis. A description of this Czarist Russian procedure is given in Samuel, 158-59.

[70] Samuel, 59.

[71] Lindemann, 184-85.

[72] Samuel, 158-59.

[73] Samuel, 40.

[74] Samuel, 172.

[75] Ezekiel Leikin, *The Beilis Transcripts: The Anti-Semitic Trial that Shook the World* (Northvale, NJ: Jason Aronson Inc., 1993), 217; Samuel, 227-28.

[76] Leikin, 217. Samuel gives a slightly different rendering. Samuel, 229.

[77] Leikin, 217.

[78] Leikin, 217-18

[79] Leikin, 218.

[80] Samuel, 250.

[81] Oskar O. Gruzenberg, *Yesterday: Memoirs of a Russian-Jewish Lawyer* (Berkeley: University of California Press, 1981), 186.

[82] Of course, one can point to cases that might be considered analogous, such as the anti-Semitic "doctors' plot" trials in the Soviet Union.

[83] "Mendel Beilis Coming," *New York Times*, January 25, 1921.

[84] Beilis (1926), 226; Beilis (2011), chapter 37.

[85] Beilis arrived in 1921. "Mendel Beilis Coming," *New York Times*, January 25, 1921. He then sent for his family, which may have arrived in 1922.

[86] "Mendel Beilis Broods on Obscurity After Ritual Murder Fame," *Jewish Daily Bulletin*, December 24, 1933, 11.

[87] For example, the books by Leikin and Samuel.

[88] Thus, the date of Beilis's arrest is given above as July 22, 1911, even though it occurred on August 4, 1911 under the modern calendar.

[89] Mendel Beilis, *The Story of My Sufferings*, trans. Harrison Goldberg (New York: Mendel Beilis Publishing Co., 1926).

[90] Shari Schwartz, ed., *Scapegoat On Trial: The Story Of Mendel Beilis* (Lakewood, NJ: CIS Publishers, 1992).

[91] Joel Berkowitz, "The 'Mendel Beilis' Epidemic on the Yiddish Stage," *Jewish Social Studies* 8, no. 1 (Fall, 2001): 199.

[92] Beilis (1926), 226; Beilis (2011), chapter 37.

[93] Jonathan Mark, "Redemption on East Tremont," *Jewish Week* (March 26, 1999), available at http://www.thejewishweek.com/viewArticle/c36_a11520/News/New_York.html. This article was included in an anthology of the best contemporary Jewish writing. Jonathan Mark, "Redemption on East Tremont," in *Best Contemporary Jewish Writing*, ed. Michael Lerner (San Francisco, CA: Jossey-Bass, 2001), p. 36.

[94] Mendel Beilis, *Di Geshichte fun Meine Leiden* (New York: Mendel Beilis Publishing Co, 1925).

[95] Mendel Beilis, *Di Geshichte fun Meine Leiden*, Second Edition (New York: Mendel Beilis, 1931).

[96] Beilis (1926), 260-64.

[97] Abraham Isaac Kook, "A Letter," in Beilis, (1931), 5-6.

[98] Ibid.

[99] "Mendel Beilis Broods on Obscurity After Ritual Murder Fame," *Jewish Daily Bulletin*, December 24, 1933, 11.

[100] "Beiliss Dies at 62; In 1913 Kieff Trial," *New York Times*, July 8, 1934, 20.

[101] "Beiliss Funeral Attended by 4,000," *New York Times*, July 10, 1934; Annie Polland and Bill Moyers, *Landmark of the Spirit: The Eldridge Street Synagogue* (New Haven: Yale University Press, 2008), 128.

[102] Jonathan Mark, "Redemption on East Tremont," *Jewish Week* (March 26, 1999), available at http://www.thejewishweek.com/viewArticle/c36_a11520/News/New_York.html.

[103] This essay includes material from a much shorter article: Jay Beilis, Jeremy Simcha Garber, and Mark S. Stein, "Pulitzer Plagiarism: The Malamud-Beilis Connection," *Cardozo Law Review de novo* (2010): 225-241, available at http://www.cardozolawreview.com/content/denovo/BEILIS_2010_225.pdf . We thank Cardozo Law Review for permission to reprint that article here.

[104] Mendel Beilis, *The Story of My Sufferings*, trans. Harrison Goldberg (New York: Mendel Beilis Publishing Co., 1926), cited here as "Beilis (1926)"

[105] Bernard Malamud, *The Fixer* (New York: Farrar, Straus and Giroux, 1966), cited here as "Malamud."

[106] Philip Davis, *Bernard Malamud: A Writer's Life* (New York: Oxford University Press, 2007), 241-43. Of other authors, Michael Tritt and Susan Mizruchi came closest to raising the issue of Malamud's plagiarism, as discussed below in section C.

[107] Davis, *Bernard Malamud*, 241-42.

[108] Albert S. Lindemann, "Beilis Case," in *Antisemitism: A Historical Encyclopedia of Prejudice and Persecution*, ed. Richard S. Levy (Santa Barbara, CA: ABC-CLIO, 2005), p. 63.

[109] Beilis (1926), 26; Beilis (2011), chapter 2.

[110] Malamud, 3.

[111] Beilis (1926), 38; Beilis (2011), chapter 3.

[112] Malamud, 71.

[113] Beilis (1926), 39-40; Beilis (2011), chapter 4.

[114] Malamud, 73.

[115] Beilis (1926), 47; Beilis (2011), chapter 5.

[116] Malamud, 95.

[117] Beilis (1926), 45; Beilis (2011), chapter 5.

[118] Malamud, 100.

[119] Beilis (1926), 45; Beilis (2011), chapter 5.

[120] Malamud, 99.

[121] Beilis (1926), 49; Beilis (2011), chapter 6.

[122] Malamud, 153.

[123] Beilis (1926), 50; Beilis (2011), chapter 6.

[124] Malamud, 144.

125 Beilis (1926), 50; Beilis (2011), chapter 6.

126 Malamud, 145.

127 Beilis (1926), 50; Beilis (2011), chapter 6.

128 Malamud, 146.

129 Beilis (1926), 51; Beilis (2011), chapter 6.

130 Beilis (1926), 52; Beilis (2011), chapter 6.

131 Malamud, 146-47.

132 Malamud, 147.

133 Beilis (1925), 45; Beilis (1931), 61.

134 Beilis (1926), 53; Beilis (2011), chapter 6.

135 Malamud, 156.

136 Beilis (1926), 56-57; Beilis (2011), chapter 7.

137 Malamud, 150-51.

138 Beilis (1926), 59-61; Beilis (2011), chapter 8.

139 Malamud, 162-63.

140 Beilis (1926), 64; Beilis (2011), chapter 9.

141 Malamud, 183.

142 Malamud, 185-86.

143 "Books: The Outsider," *Time*, September 9, 1966, 106. We do not say it is ridiculous to interpret these passages from *The Fixer* as an allusion to the *Via Dolorosa*. As the literary scholar Ruth Wisse notes, the the Jew as Christ-figure is a theme in Malamud's fiction. Ruth R. Wisse, *The Modern Jewish Canon: A Journey Through Language and Culture* 16 (New York: Free Press, 2000). Nevertheless, any such interpretation of these passages from *The Fixer* should be made in awareness of Malamud's plagiarism.

144 Beilis (1926), 64; Beilis (2011), chapter 9.

145 Malamud, 186.

146 Beilis (1926), 69; Beilis (2011), chapter 10.

147 Malamud, 222.

148 Beilis (1926), 72-73; Beilis (2011), chapter 11.

149 Malamud, 134.

150 Beilis (1926), 79; Beilis (2011), chapter 12.

151 Malamud, 195.

152 Beilis (1926), 79-80; Beilis (2011), chapter 12.

153 Malamud, 192.

154 Malamud, 263-64.

155 Beilis (1926), 80; Beilis (2011), chapter 12.

[156] Malamud, 194-95. The foregoing passage is not atypical of Malamud's lurid, sensational, coarse and scatological details and language, which he intermixes liberally into Beilis's generally restrained and dignified narration. Of course, we cannot exclude the possibility that an anal search really was part of the routine, and that Beilis chose not to mention it in his memoir.
[157] Beilis (1926), 81; Beilis (2011), chapter 12.
[158] Malamud, 187-88.
[159] Beilis (1926), 80-82; Beilis (2011), chapter 12.
[160] Malamud, 268.
[161] Malamud, 274.
[162] Beilis (1926), 99-100; Beilis (2011), chapter 16.
[163] Malamud, 200-01.
[164] Beilis (1926), 125; Beilis (2011), chapter 19.
[165] Malamud, 328.
[166] Malamud, 329.
[167] Malamud, 335.
[168] Beilis (1926), 145; Beilis (2011), chapter 22.
[169] Malamud, 128-29.
[170] Beilis (1926), 150; Beilis (2011), chapter 23.
[171] Malamud, 118.
[172] Beilis (1926), 151; Beilis (2011), chapter 23.
[173] Malamud, 130.
[174] Beilis (1926), 155; Beilis (2011), chapter 24.
[175] Malamud, 245.
[176] Beilis (1926), 173; Beilis (2011), chapter 27.
[177] Malamud, 130.
[178] Beilis (1926), 174; Beilis (2011), chapter 27.
[179] Malamud, 330-31.
[180] Beilis (1926), 181; Beilis (2011), chapter 28.
[181] Malamud, 218.
[182] Beilis (1926), 182; Beilis (2011), chapter 29.
[183] Malamud, 322-24.
[184] Beilis (1926), 183; Beilis (2011), chapter 29.
[185] Malamud, 325-26.

[186] Beilis (1926), 77-78; Beilis (2011), chapter 12. Notwithstanding Beilis's heroic refusal of a pardon, if the government had wanted to free Beilis without trial, it could presumably have done so whether or not Beilis approved. On some level, Beilis may have suspected that the offer of a pardon was a ploy to get him to implicate himself or other Jews. And in fact it probably was such a ploy, for immediately after Beilis stated that he was not interested in a pardon, the general told him: "You were a poor man and you did what you were told. If you tell us the truth you would be making a very fortunate move. You would be sent abroad and would be provided for the rest of your life…. However, you are persisting in hiding the truth – with your silence you think to protect the Jewish nation, and you are only ruining yourself." Beilis (1926), 78; Beilis (2011), chapter 12. As to this speech of the general, Beilis notes: "I could hardly keep my self-control while the man was talking. Every word of his was disgusting to me."

[187] Malamud, 294.

[188] Ibid.

[189] Malamud, 226.

[190] Ezekiel Leikin, *The Beilis Transcripts: The Anti-Semitic Trial that Shook the World* (Northvale, NJ: Jason Aronson Inc., 1993), 164.

[191] Beilis (1926), 177-79; Beilis (2011), chapter 28.

[192] Morris U. Schappes, "Anti-Semitic Blood Libel in Fact and Fiction," *Jewish Currents* (February, 1967): 8.

[193] Ibid.

[194] Ibid.

[195] Susan L. Mizruchi, "The Place of Ritual in Our Time," American Literary History 12, no. 3 (2000): 481. This article is reprinted in Mizruchi, ed., *Religion and Cultural Studies* (Princeton: Princeton University Press, 2001) We note that we do not agree with various conclusions Mizruchi draws.

[196] Michael Tritt, "Mendel Beilis's *The Story of My Sufferings* and Malamud's *The Fixer*: A Study of Indebtedness and Innovation," *Modern Jewish Studies* 13, no. 4 (Summer, 2004): 70.

[197] Tritt discusses Malamud's indebtedness at far greater length than Mizruchi, referring to some of the same passages we quote above in section A. We note that the manuscript on which this essay is based predates the publication of both Tritt's article and Mizruchi's article.

[198] Davis, *Bernard Malamud: A Writer's Life.*

[199] Davis, 241-42.

[200] Davis, 242.

[201] For example, *Merriam Webster's Collegiate Dictionary*, 10th ed. (1996) defines "plagiarize" as follows: "to steal and pass off (the ideas or words of another) as one's own... use (a created production) without crediting the source... to commit literary theft... present as new and original an idea or product derived from an existing source."

[202] We draw this conclusion from the reaction to Ian McEwan's borrowing of passages from Lucilla Andrews's memoir *No Time for Romance* (London: Chambers Harrap, 1977) for McEwan's novel *Atonement* (London: Jonathan Cape, 2001). See Alan Cowell, "Eyebrows Are Raised Over Passages in a Best Seller by Ian McEwan," *New York Times*, November 28, 2006. Many defended McEwan, but his borrowings were far less extensive than Malamud's, they related to technical matters such as the description of medical procedures, and McEwan, unlike Malamud, actually acknowledged his indebtedness in a note at the end of his novel.

[203] Davis, 242.

[204] Beilis (1926), 80-82 (emphasis added) ; Beilis (2011), chapter 12.

[205] Malamud, 273.

[206] Malamud, 273-74.

[207] Beilis (1926), 183; Beilis (2011), chapter 29.

[208] Malamud, 325-26.

[209] Malamud, 325-26.

[210] Beilis (1926), 135-36; Beilis (2011), chapter 21.

[211] Davis, 242.

[212] Beilis (1926), 80; Beilis (2011), chapter 12.

[213] Malamud, 194-95.

[214] Davis, 243.

[215] Beilis (1926), 34; Beilis (2011), chapter 3.

[216] Beilis (1926), 125-26; Beilis (2011), chapter 19.

[217] Beilis (1926), 25; Beilis (2011), chapter 1.

[218] Lindemann, 184.

[219] Samuel, 59.

[220] Samuel, 187.

[221] Beilis (1926), 41; Beilis (2011), chapter 4.

[222] "Beiliss Funeral Attended by 4,000," *New York Times*, July 10, 1934.

[223] Abraham Isaac Kook, "A Letter," in Beilis (1931), 5-6.

[224] Malamud, 17.

[225] Malamud, 24.

[226] Malamud, 285.

[227] Ibid.

[228] Malamud, 289. However, in a moving scene, Yakov does agree to sign a paper stating (falsely) that the child is his. Malamud, 291-92.

[229] Bernard Malamud, letter to David Beilis, November 11, 1966.

[230] David Beilis, letter to Bernard Malamud, December 11, 1966.

[231] Roger Straus, Jr., letter to David Beilis, December 22, 1966.

[232] David Beilis, letter to Bernard Malamud, December 11, 1966.

[233] Kook, "A Letter," in Beilis (1931), 5 (reproduced as Appendix B).

[234] Bernard Malamud, letter to David Beilis, April 19, 1967.

[235] Davis appears to suggest this criticism: "Malamud could not win against the continuing family pain: if he admitted indebtedness, he was accused of traducing the Beilis family by his portrayal of his protagonist; if he denied it, he was guilty of unacknowledged copying." Davis, 242.

[236] Beilis (1926), 77-78; Beilis (2011), chapter 12.

[237] Malamud, 294.

[238] Sheldon J. Hershinow, *Bernard Malamud* (NY: Frederick Ungar, 1980), 68-69.

[239] Alan Friedman, "The Hero as Schnook," in *Bernard Malamud and the Critics*, ed. Leslie and Joyce Field, (New York: New York University Press, 1970), 298.

[240] Ibid.

[241] Alfred Kazin, "A Single Jew," *The New York Review of Books*, October 9, 1997, 9. The ellipsized part of the first sentence is: "Beilis, who eventually settled in America, remained an extremely bitter man who could never forgive..." Kazin's reference Beilis as "extremely bitter" may be an embellishment of Malamud's reference to Beilis as "bitter" in *Talking Horse*. We address Malamud's statement below in section H.

[242] Leikin, 191.

[243] Samuel, 201-02.

[244] Jonathan Mark, "Redemption on East Tremont," *Jewish Week* (March 26, 1999), available at http://www.thejewishweek.com/viewArticle/c36_a11520/News/New_York.html.

[245] See, for example, Beilis (1926), 168; Beilis (2011), chapter 26.

[246] Beilis did believe that he had received specific promises that were unfulfilled, but that is a separate issue, also discussed below in section H.

[247] Kazin, 9.

[248] Bernard Malamud, letter to David Beilis, April 19, 1967.

[249] Joe Klein, *Primary Colors: A Novel of Politics* (1996).

[250] Brett Pulley, "Librarian Speaks Out on 'Primary Colors' Suit", *New York Times*, February 19, 1997.

[251] Carter-Clark v. Random House, 793 N.Y.S.2d 394 (N.Y. App. Div. 2005) (affirming dismissal). See also American Library Association, Librarian's Libel Suit Over Primary Colors Dismissed (Oct. 20, 2003), available at http://www.ala.org/ala/alonline/currentnews/newsarchive/2003/aloct03/librarianslibel.cfm (last visited November 2, 2009).

---

[252] Bernard Malamud, "Source of *The Fixer*," in Alan Cheuse and Nicholas Delbanco, eds., *Talking Horse: Bernard Malamud on Life and Work* (New York: Columbia University Press, 1996), 88-89.

[253] Haskel Frankel, "One Man to Stand for Six Million," *Saturday Review*, September 10, 1966, 37.

[254] Malamud, "Source of *The Fixer*," in *Talking Horse*, 89.

[255] Eliot Fremont-Smith, "Yakov's Choice," *New York Times*, August 29, 1966.

[256] Fern Marja Eckman, "The Writing Teacher and His Prize," *New York Post*, May 6, 1967, 28.

[257] "The Writer at Work," in *Talking Horse*, 18.

[258] Tritt expresses a similar perplexity. Michael Tritt, "Mendel Beilis's *The Story of My Sufferings* and Malamud's *The Fixer*: A Study of Indebtedness and Innovation," *Modern Jewish Studies* 13, no. 4 (Summer, 2004): 70.

[259] "The Writer at Work," in *Talking Horse*, 18.

[260] Indeed, Malamud's 1966 statement that Beilis's "life came to less than he had paid for by his suffering and endurance" suggests that Malamud himself believed that Beilis hadn't been adequately reimbursed; perhaps Malamud, in his later statement, was imputing to Beilis Malamud's own view of the matter.

[261] Beilis (1926), 230; Beilis (2011), chapter 38.

[262] Beilis (1926), 231; Beilis (2011), chapter 38.

[263] "Mendel Beilis Broods on Obscurity After Ritual Murder Fame," *Jewish Daily Bulletin*, December 24, 1933, 11.

[264] "Mendel Beilis" (editorial), *Der Tog*, July 10, 1934, quoted in Annie Polland and Bill Moyers, *Landmark of the Spirit: The Eldridge Street Synagogue* (New Haven: Yale University Press, 2008), 129.

[265] "Mendel Beilis Broods on Obscurity After Ritual Murder Fame," *Jewish Daily Bulletin*, December 24, 1933, 11.

[266] "Beilis' Last Letter is Revealed by Attorney Who Defended Him," *JTA*, August 26, 1934, available at http://archive.jta.org/article/1934/08/26/2818650/beilis-last-letter-is-revealed-by-attorney-who-defended-him.

[267] Kook, "A Letter," in Beilis (1931), 5 (reproduced as Appendix B).

[268] Shari Schwartz, ed., *Scapegoat On Trial: The Story Of Mendel Beilis* (Lakewood, NJ: CIS Publishers, 1992).

[269] *Scapegoat On Trial*, 249.

[270] *Scapegoat On Trial*, 208.

[271] Beilis (1926), 136; Beilis (2011), chapter 21. We have ourselves made a small correction to Harrison Goldberg's punctuation here, placing the period inside the quotes.

A more literal translation from the Yiddish would be "It was as if a voice other than my own shouted: 'I am a Jew!'"

272 *Scapegoat On Trial*, 148.

273 *Scapegoat On Trial*, 7.

274 *Scapegoat On Trial*, 47.

275 Beilis (1925), 32.

276 *Scapegoat On Trial*, 251.